# What You Need to Know to Go Global

## A Guide to International Trade Transactions

Stephen Creskoff

Archway Publishing books may be ordered through booksellers or by contacting:
Archway Publishing

1663 Liberty Drive
Bloomington, IN 47403
www.archwaypublishing.com
1 (888) 242-5904

ISBN: 978-1-4808-2991-6 (sc)
ISBN: 978-1-4808-2992-3 (e)

Library of Congress Control Number: 2016905911

Print information available on the last page.

Archway Publishing rev. date: 04/29/2016

# Contents

## Praise for *What You Need to Know to Go Global*

*What You Need to Know to Go Global* is a terrific book! Any SME wanting to compete in world markets should read *What You Need to Know to Go Global* written by an extremely knowledgeable expert with a lifetime of hands-on experience.

—William Krist, senior scholar, Wilson Center, and author of *Globalization and America's Trade Agreements*

I thoroughly enjoyed every part of *What You Need to Know to Go Global*. Rarely does a writing of this nature touch on all the pertinent aspects of a subject. I was reeducated on the topic of the history of international trade and transportation and I was entertained by the author's many observations of working in so many different environs. This should become the Trading 101 book for anyone entering the international arena and it should also be a handy reference to anyone who is currently engaged in international trade and transportation.

— Robert Kielbas, vice president, Global Development, Roanoke Group Inc.

As a practitioner of international trade law for 30 years, I am often asked for help with this very question—how do I go international with my business? Until now, I've never had a good answer.

Steve Creskoff's book fills a big gap in the available books on this subject. It is very practical and the stories based on his work and experience place the issues in context and allow the reader to understand the how and why not just the what. Chapter 9 alone is worth the price of the entire book.

The value provided in this book is worth hundreds or even thousands of dollars in consulting fees. The reader gets the benefit of the author's years of global experience for the price of the book, a real bargain.

I especially like chapters 2 and 3, just the sort of practical advice that many with international ambitions need.

—Jeff Snyder, general editor, Global Trade & Custom Journal, partner and chair, international trade group, Crowell & Moring LLP, Washington, DC

The Internet has made going global easier than it has ever been. But it still isn't child's play. You'll need a guide, and Stephen Creskoff's *What You Need to Know to Go Global* is just the one. Spiced with lively commentary from the author's lifetime of trade experience, Creskoff's book covers it all. It reviews the history of trade from the Silk Road to Skype and has a solid focus on the fundamentals, things like getting paid and staying out of jail. Old pros too will want to keep a copy nearby, though they may often find themselves muttering, I wish I'd had this when ...

—R. K. Morris, president, the Global Business Dialogue

Global book—global thinking. I was privileged to work with the author of *What You Need to Know to Go Global* Stephen Creskoff side by side in Kazakhstan and Russia, and this opportunity to hold his book in my hands is truly exciting. The book features Steve's invaluable experience in international consulting and trade. Numerous real-life examples together with conceptualizing summaries and conclusions are both striking and persuasive. They provide you with hands-on, practical tips, yet a global perspective.

The book is so well structured and easy to navigate that you can start reading almost from any page to locate answers to your particular questions without losing overall comprehension. The summing up 'takeaway' sections at the end of each chapter are a great tool to keep you on track.

Chapter 9 The Author's Journal deserves very special attention. I couldn't help reading and recalling recognizable situations and characters.

Overall, it's a great guide that very few live consultants could compete with. Surely, it will become my bible and 'first aid' in my work as a lawyer of an international retailer.

—Tatyana Alexandrova, corporate lawyer, Moscow, Russia

*What You Need to Know to Go Global* is a comprehensive nuts-and-bolts overview of a subject that has received too little attention. Steve Creskoff has been around this track, both in the private sector and in government service, and he really knows his stuff.

—Richard O. Cunningham, sr. international trade partner,
Steptoe & Johnson LLP

*What You Need to Know to Go Global* is an invaluable tool for anyone trying to understand and overcome the challenges of international trade. It is highly readable and full of insights and practical advice.

—Lynn Reaser, PhD, chief economist, Fermanian Business &
Economic Institute, Point Loma Nazarene University

I have benefitted immensely from Steve's wealth of uncommon professional experiences in trade law, trade policy and trade facilitation spanning more than four decades. I worked closely with Steve in finalizing the Nigerian Customs Act, evolving globally consistent Trade Policy Process and Trade Defense Process for Nigeria among other trade issues. I can safely attest to his exceptional academic and professional prowess on trade and related issues. The rub-off from interacting with him has inspired a new thinking in trade policy process in me and my country. I have had a great mentor in Steve in the physical. For those who do not have the privilege of physical contact with him, this book is an opportunity to tap from him. I see the book as a gift out of rare deposit of experiences to scholars, policymakers and trade practitioners.

—Olumuyiwa B. Alaba, PhD, professor of economics,
University of Ibadan

Globalization Meets a Local Developing Economy:
Empty Shipping Containers at the Port of Yangon,
Myanmar (Burma), December 2015 (photo by author)

Border Procedures May Delay International Shipments:
A Truck Customs Inspection at the Macedonia,
Kosovo Border, December 2012 (photo by author)

# Introduction

*What You Need to Know to Go Global: A Guide to International Trade Transactions* is intended as an overview of the opportunities and pitfalls of international trade transactions in the second decade of the twenty-first century. The book is designed like a travel guidebook. As such, it is not necessary to read the chapters or subsections in sequence. The reader can jump to topics that are of particular interest and ignore topics that are not. Each chapter summarizes the advice given in a concluding section. Also like travel guides, *What You Need to Know to Go Global* does not treat any topic in minute detail. The objective is to provide a comprehensive, up-to-date overview, not in-depth knowledge about a particular trade topic.

This guide is specifically designed for small- and medium-sized enterprises (SMEs) engaged in trade transactions. However, I hope that it will also be useful for large-firm executives, lawyers, and other professionals who would like an overview of trade transaction issues as well as for university students studying international business and international trade topics.

The book is a *personal* guide with illustrative case histories drawn from my personal international trade transaction experiences as well as the experiences of some of my clients and colleagues. These case histories are recounted in order to illustrate the various points in the guide. Most of my relevant personal experiences are included in chapter 9, "The Author's Journal." I hope my stories are interesting and instructive, but if not, feel free to skip them. In order to protect the privacy of the people and businesses involved, in most cases, I have not used the actual names of people and organizations. I have also altered some of the details for this same reason.

Multinational enterprises like Apple, Exxon Mobile, Google, and General Electric do not need a guidebook to international trade transactions. Those firms and other major multinationals are already doing business on a regular basis in many countries around the world, and they employ a legion of experts to help them to successfully conduct international trade transactions. SMEs, on the other hand, do not have these big-firm resources. They may be aware that important markets and/or suppliers for their goods and services exist throughout the world, but they usually do not have the in-house know-how or other resources to explore these potential markets and develop international customers and suppliers. This guide is intended to help meet this need by describing the rapidly changing landscape of international trade transactions in an understandable, accurate, and hopefully entertaining manner.

So why me? What qualifies me to tell you, Mr. and Ms. SME, how to navigate the choppy waters of international trade and bring your ship to a safe and profitable harbor? The short answer is that as a lawyer and consultant, I have represented clients involved with a wide variety of international trade transactions for more than forty years and in more than fifty countries. A summary of my professional background is in the "About the Author" appendix.

Let's be clear about some basic terms. This book is specifically written as a guide primarily for SMEs. So what are they? I use the terms "SMEs" and "small businesses" synonymously. Small businesses are privately owned, for-profit enterprises that are considered to be "small" based on their number of employees, assets, and annual sales as well as the fact that they are not dominant in their field. Examples include family farms; small retail stores; accounting, legal, consulting, software, and other service firms; Internet marketers; small manufacturers of goods; and so forth. However, the exact definition of "small business" varies. For instance, in the United States, the Small Business Administration has differing standards defining a small business depending upon whether the business is involved in agriculture, wholesaling, retailing, manufacturing, or services. "Small" businesses may have as many as five hundred employees. In other countries, the definition may primarily depend on the number of employees. However, by any measure, it is clear that the large majority of businesses around the world are small. This, of course, includes businesses in the "informal sector"; that is, businesses in many developing countries that are unreported for tax purposes. By some estimates, small businesses globally amount to about 50 percent of all value added and 77 percent of all business employment.[1]

International trade means the exchange of goods and/or services for value across international boundaries. If you, as a small business, purchase clothing manufactured in China or sell a software program to a customer in Japan, you are engaged in international trade. Similarly, if you travel to Thailand for hip-replacement surgery or provide hotel, sightseeing, and other hospitality services in the United States for international guests, you are also engaged in international trade. And if you grow

---

[1] "Small business: a global agenda." *Association of Chartered Certified Accountants*, September 2010, p. 6 and appendix 1.

wheat, corn, or soybeans in North America, your customers may be foreign, and the market price for your product may be determined by international supply and demand. In fact, current international trade transactions are so pervasive, so much a part of normal business activities, that probably no day goes by without your business being involved directly or indirectly in some aspect of international trade, whether you realize it or not.

Transaction costs are those additional costs that you, as a business, face when engaged in international trade transactions. These include communications costs (for example, using translators, courier services, and dealing with cultural differences); travel costs; additional insurance, shipping, and freight-forwarder expenses; broker and other service costs related to shipping goods internationally; the various costs related to entering a foreign market, such as customs duties and other taxes and fees; requirements relating to product standards and health as well as other national requirements; the cost of a local representative, when required; and costs relating to intellectual property protection and dispute resolution in foreign markets. Much of this book is about the additional transaction costs that small businesses face when involved in international trade transactions and how these costs can be minimized.

Definitions of other terms used in this book can be found within the text and the glossary of terms in the appendix.

Now let's look at the organization of the book. It is arranged to answer seven key questions you must answer if you are to successfully engage in international trade transactions. So let's take a first look at these questions.

## The Basic Questions

The first question is, why is international trade important to the future of your business? The importance of trade may not be immediately obvious if you are a US-based small business. Chapter 1 is a brief explanation of its importance. For those interested, chapter 1 includes a brief review the history of international trade transactions and the dramatic reduction of transaction costs in many economies. After reading this chapter, you should have a better appreciation for the environment in which international trade in goods and services takes place today and its future increased importance for most small businesses.

The second basic question is, how do you find and maintain international customers and/or suppliers? In other words, do you have a product or service that is attractive to international customers and/or that relies on international suppliers? If so, how do you make the initial contact and then grow the relationship? To answer this, I review the critical importance of tailoring your products to meet the requirements of international customers and suppliers. For your international customers, this means understanding your competitive advantage when selling internationally, fostering good customer relationships, meeting international standards for your products and/or services, and delivering high-quality products and services in a timely manner. For your international suppliers, this means developing reliable business relationships that take into account cultural differences, communications issues, quality control concerns, and contractual compliance. I use a number of case histories to help answer this question.

The third basic question is, how do you get paid? After all, there is no point in your business becoming involved with international trade transactions if you have serious problems with being paid for goods or services provided. Payment issues can be magnified by distance and unfamiliarity with customers. In addition, you can encounter all sorts of problems ranging from exchange-rate fluctuations, the details of letter of credit, and other bank financing mechanisms to dispute resolution provisions. I attempt to answer this basic question by discussing the importance of maintaining business relationships, how contracts should be structured, financing methods that allow small businesses to have confidence in being paid, and pitfalls to avoid. I use case histories to help answer this question.

Of course, the flip side to getting paid promptly is how you treat your suppliers. The same principles that will result in prompt payment for your products and services should be applied to your relationships with your international suppliers.

The fourth basic question is, how do you protect your intellectual property? No matter what your international trade transaction is, it is likely that intellectual property rights are involved. You almost certainly have a name and logo identified with your business that you want to protect. You may also have a unique design or packaging for your products or services. Trademarks, service marks, and trade dress rights protect this intellectual property. You also almost certainly have trade secrets that relate to your business. Trade secrets can include customer lists, financial data, manufacturing processes, methodologies for delivering services, and similar business materials. Trade secrets are protected intellectual property rights. If you are in the business of creating and publishing written materials, music, photographs, or movies your original work is protected by copyright laws. Lastly, you may have developed an invention or process that is the basis for your business. This can be protected under patent laws.

Protecting your intellectual property rights can present additional challenges when you engage in international trade transactions because your rights must be recognized in foreign jurisdictions. Chapter 4 discusses the steps you must take to do this.

The fifth basic question is, how can you minimize trade-transaction costs? For those businesses that are involved in international transactions regarding the purchase or sale of goods, logistics arrangements can make or break a transaction. Chapter 5 discusses the importance of trade facilitation, logistics, and value chains to international trade in goods and offers suggestions as to how logistics traps can be avoided and performance can be improved.

The sixth basic question is, how do you navigate government regulations? Chapter 6 discusses this question. It is critical to be aware of international and national requirements that may affect your business transactions. For example, if you plan to export products, when calculating your prices, it is essential to know the customs duties, taxes, and other charges that will be imposed when your products are imported by your international customer into their home market. Even if you are not legally responsible for paying these assessments because the contract terms makes your customer responsible for them, the prices you quote must be competitive with other suppliers that may also have to pay these assessments. Exports of high technology and so-called dual-use items may be subject to export restrictions. Exports of services may also face restrictions. For example, if you are a consultant retained to provide services in a foreign country and you are not a national or otherwise allowed to work in that foreign country, you must obtain an appropriate visa or work permit from the nation in which the services will be performed.

Regulations are also of concern when importing goods. For imports, you must know the duties, taxes, and fees that will be assessed on your imports in order to understand your total cost for the products. Goods must be properly labeled. Food and pharmaceutical imports must meet government safety and quality standards.

Special procedures may apply to goods that are subject to antidumping, countervailing duty, and safeguard measures. These trade remedies, which are authorized by the World Trade Organization (WTO) and applied by WTO members and other countries as well, may result in additional duties and, in some cases, quotas and other import restrictions. In addition, if you are a business being injured by low-priced imports, you may be able to use these trade remedies to protect your market position.

The seventh basic question is, why is social responsibility important to your "bottom line"? Chapter 7 discusses business social responsibility and how exercising this can add value to products and services and improve a business's bottom line.

Chapter 8, "The Future of International Trade Transactions: Five Predictions," makes predictions about the development of international trade in the "near future."

Chapter 9, "The Author's Journal," includes many of my personal experiences relating to the topics in chapters 1–8. Hopefully, these stories help illustrate the principles discussed in the previous chapters.

Navigating international trade transactions can be compared to driving west through the state of Colorado. Eastern Colorado is flat farmland with few obstacles. The roads are straight and well maintained, there are only a few towns to slow a driver's speed, and visibility is unobstructed. Routine trade transactions between businesses located in developed economies, such as the United States, Canada, and Germany, can be compared to this sort of driving. There are few obstacles, and the ones that exist are well known, transparent, and relatively easy to anticipate. However, after reaching Denver, the terrain in Colorado changes and becomes hilly, then mountainous. Secondary roads have substantial upgrades and downgrades, twists and turns, and sometimes potholes. The weather can turn quickly, even in summer, obscuring roads with heavy rain, ice, and snow. High winds can push vehicles off the road. Conducting trade transactions with businesses in many developing countries compares to driving in Colorado's mountains. There are many obstacles and dangers, so advance information about roads and weather is essential.

I hope that this book will be a useful map, guiding your business safely through both easy and challenging international trade transactions.

# Chapter 1

# Why Is International Trade Important to the Future of Your Business?

Every man lives by exchanging.

—Adam Smith

Many of you already know why international trade is important to the future of your business. The short answer is that international markets potentially provide many new customers for your products or services, allowing you to increase sales and profitability. At the same time, you may have to compete with international competitors in your existing domestic markets.

If you limit your horizons to your domestic markets, at best you will likely ignore potential customers, and at worst you may be put out of business by foreign competition. This sad story has played out many times in recent years. The previously successful small local retailer cannot compete with multinational retailers, such as Wal-Mart, that source many goods from overseas suppliers. A small manufacturer of automotive aftermarket accessories cannot compete with imports from China. A small local accounting firm cannot compete with an accounting firm that uses backroom services from India to reduce costs. Communities that have invested in infrastructure to attract call centers lose their call-center business to India and the Philippines.

### *Opportunities for Small Businesses*

On the bright side, many small businesses based in the United States have participated in the international market with great success. The following examples are drawn from my personal experience. Crowe & Co., a South Carolina–based firm that manufactures and sells explosive detection kits (EDKs), markets its product and services all over the world. Weld-Aid, a Michigan-based firm that manufactures and sells products to increase welding efficiency, offers its products in many countries around the world. Bergandi Machinery, based in California, produces and sells machines for the fencing industry in more than fifty countries. Small consulting firms, such as Nathan Associates, based in Virginia, sell their services to clients in many foreign markets.

### *Are You Already Convinced?*

If you are already convinced that international trade is important to the future of your business, after you read about Cheung's proposed business in the next section, you may want to skip the remainder of this chapter and read chapters 2 through 7—the how-to chapters. But for those of you who are not yet convinced that international trade is important to the future of your business or who (like me) enjoy history, this chapter provides the long answer to the question.

### *Cheung Was Convinced but Didn't Know about Trade-Transaction Costs*

When I was writing this book, a young Chinese man, Cheung, a recent green card arrival in the United States, asked my advice concerning shipping consumer goods from the United States to China. He had noticed that many consumer products are less expensive in America than in China and hoped to make some money, first by selling goods purchased here to his friends and acquaintances in China. If successful, he wanted to expand his business to commercial distributors in China. I said this might be a good idea. Significant price differences between national markets for goods or services are the basis for most international trade transactions, and he already had friends in China who would be his initial customers. But first he had to do some checking. Compared to a domestic sale of goods or services, there are many additional transaction costs involved in international trade transactions; therefore, the price differences between the US market and China that he noticed might be illusory.

For example, unlike China and most other foreign economies, the United States has no national sales tax, or VAT. In many economies, the VAT can be quite high; for example, Mexico has a 16 percent VAT, China has a 17 percent VAT, and Denmark a 25 percent VAT. This alone frequently makes goods sold at retail in the United States less expensive than the same goods sold in many foreign markets. And if Cheung shipped consumer goods to China, they would likely be subject to significant import duties and fees that might eliminate much of any perceived price difference.

Other transaction costs for international sales normally include compliance with various national health, safety, and product standards; product-marking requirements; packing for international shipping; the cost of international shipping by air; surface or sea freight; insurance against damage or loss during shipment; freight forwarding and customs clearance fees; and demurrage and warehousing (resulting from port/ airport delays, delays in customs clearance, and delays in delivery to customers). And if he started with small sales for relatively heavy products shipped by airmail, the transport costs could be particularly high.

The currency used for the sales transaction also involves significant risks. Although the US dollar is widely used throughout the world, the foreign buyer or seller may stipulate that the transaction be conducted in their nation's currency. This could result in a substantial loss to the buyer if that currency significantly appreciates between the time of the contract and the time of payment. As an example, China's currency, the yuan or renminbi (RMB), has been appreciating since 2006, when the rate was fixed at around 8.2 RMB to one dollar, but was then devalued in August 2015. If a contract is entered into in RMB when the exchange rate is 6.58 RMB to 1 US dollar (the exchange rate in January 2016), and the exchange rate has changed to 5.5 RMB to 1 dollar at the time payment pursuant to when the contract is due, a party that must exchange dollars for RMB will bear the loss. A party that must exchange RMB for dollars will have a windfall gain.

Even when the US dollar is used as the currency for the transaction, as is frequently the case, currency fluctuations may change the economic bargain, resulting in one of the parties being disadvantaged. For example, when I worked as a consultant in Astana, Kazakhstan, in 2014, the local currency (tenge) was devalued about 15 percent without warning; this made my contract more expensive for my client because my payments were, by contract, stipulated to be made in US dollars. On the other hand, since I was living in Astana, my local living costs were suddenly reduced by 15 percent.

Small value international sales of consumer products can be handled by credit card with additional international transaction fees assessed by the credit card company. However, assuring prompt payment for higher-value goods or services delivered may involve significant additional transaction costs for international sales. The safest option, of course, is for a seller to require payment in full prior to delivering the goods or services, but this is frequently not acceptable for international buyers. International customers understandably want to be assured of the quality and quantity of goods or services and that goods will be delivered on time before paying for them. These concerns are usually resolved by using trade finance and by inspections of the quality and quantity of goods by a certified third-party expert. Banks and other financial institutions offer trade finance to qualified traders. These are letters of credit and other documentary instruments that are used to assure payment when the seller of goods or services has complied with the terms of the contract. Other third parties, international inspection companies, may also be used to assure that the goods or services meet contract specifications. Needless to say, these trade services are not inexpensive, and they can add significant additional costs to international trade transactions.

Finally, even though my young friend planned to sell to his friends in China initially, the likelihood of disputes is higher in international trade transactions, and the means for resolving disputes that do occur is more problematic. Cultural differences, communication problems, and the sheer distance and time disparities between the seller and buyer make disputes more likely. Resolving a problem that does arise can be much more complex than is the case with a domestic business dispute. If the contract for the international sale of goods or services does not specifically provide for the applicable law and procedures for dispute settlement, the aggrieved party may have to resort to the laws and procedures of the home country of the breaching party to pursue a claim. This is like a visiting basketball team playing a game on the home team's court in front of hostile fans and biased referees.

But despite the additional transaction costs involved with international trade transactions, my young Chinese friend's business idea may nonetheless be successful. The economic, cultural, and political differences as well as the geographic separation between countries provide great opportunities for trading goods and services. I have seen these opportunities throughout my professional career. If you are interested, you can read about some of my experiences in chapter 9, "The Author's Journal."

### *International Trade and Trade-Transaction Costs through Human History: The Inverse Relationship*

International trade transactions have been part of human history since the earliest times, and so have the transaction costs associated with trade. These include

- communications costs (including communicating with someone of a different culture and speaking a foreign language);

- costs of transporting and storing goods or providing services over long distances;

- costs of assuring the safety of the goods from theft and accident, including insurance;

- costs of customs duties and other taxes and fees assessed by local governments during transport and at the destination;

- costs associated with the barter or sale of goods and services, including trade finance; and

- potential injury or death of traders (for the merchants conducting international trade in earlier eras, the cost of trading sometimes involved injury and death from shipwreck; pirates and robbers; accidents and illness; and local tyrants).

Throughout history, a general rule applies for trade-transaction costs when parties have a reason to trade: Lower trade-transaction costs result in increased trade. Conversely, increased trade-transaction costs reduce trade. And if the trade-transaction costs are so high that they eliminate the possibility of profit, trade ends.

Since the end of WWII, transaction costs have rapidly fallen, and international trade has grown exponentially. The following chart illustrates the trend for trade in goods.

Volume index (1950 = 100)

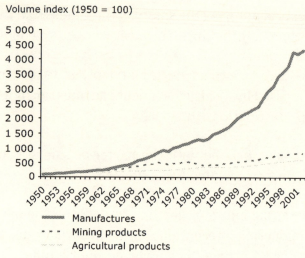

Source: European Environment Agency

I will now take you on a journey in time to show you how we arrived at the modern era of business globalization and generally low trade-transaction costs.

## Ancient Times: High Trade-Transaction Costs and Low Trade Volume

Although today we think of international trade as taking place between nations or economies (for example, the European Union), "nations" or "economies" as we know them today did not exist in ancient times. As the last ice age ended twelve thousand years ago and agrarian civilizations emerged in China, Mesopotamia, Egypt, Greece, and India, trade routes between these civilizations developed for the exchange of products of value that were not available locally. Early trade was exclusively barter, the exchange of one commodity for another. However, by around 1100 BC the Chinese had developed a form of currency, and by 600 BC, coins were introduced in Asia Minor.

The transaction costs for long-distance trade during ancient times were, of course, very high. Traveling merchants were subject to robbery and could lose their merchandise (and lives) to pirates and brigands. Overland travelers and travelers by river were frequently subject to "tolls" exacted by local rulers. Overland trade was mostly limited to light, high-value goods, such as silk, spices, gold, silver, gems, and jewelry because of the difficulty of overland transport. Salt, a very valuable and necessary commodity in regions without salt deposits, was an exception.

Trade by water greatly reduced transport costs and allowed heavier, bulkier goods to be transported long distances. Trade conducted by sea routes also eliminated most fees assessed by local rulers in transit and reduced the possibility of theft. The Phoenicians and then Greeks pioneered maritime trade in the Mediterranean, Aegean, and Black seas. Ships carried heavier commodities, such as jars of olive oil (essential for lamps), wine, timber, wheat, and pottery. In the East, Indian merchants traded by ships from Calcutta to Hong Kong.

Overland-trade-transaction costs lessened somewhat after Alexander the Great's conquests of Egypt, Turkey, Persia, and Northern India. Under the rulers that followed Alexander, exactions by local officials and the risk of banditry abated, and trade significantly increased in the Hellenistic world. Alexandria, Egypt's harbor with its enormous lighthouse, one of the seven wonders of the ancient world, was a center of this increased trade.

Many trade-transaction costs were again reduced during the Roman Empire, and trade correspondingly increased. The Romans built an extensive network of paved roads in the lands they ruled that significantly lowered the cost and increased the speed of overland transport, and their military provided greater protection against robberies. Latin was established as the common language, improving communications throughout the empire. Roman merchant vessels traded with merchants as far away as the Ceylon and brought back goods from the Far East to Rome.

Not all trade-transaction costs were reduced during the Roman Empire. A tax, called the "portorium," was assessed on trade transactions. This included a customs duty collected at the frontiers of provinces for the account of the state, the "octroy," collected at the time of entry or departure from a city for the account of the city, and the "toll," a passage tax to take a road or cross a bridge.[2]

With the fall of the Roman Empire in the fifth century, trade-transaction costs in Western Europe greatly increased and trade almost ended. The Roman system of roads decayed and lawlessness increased. During the Middle Ages, the trade that did exist was mostly confined to river routes, but merchants traveling these routes were subject to the exaction of tolls by local feudal lords. "In the thirteenth century, on one side of the Rhone there were four tollhouses on a stretch of little more than 30 km. In the fourteenth century, there were 74 tolls on the Loire, from Roane to Nantes ... There were 13 tollhouses on the Rhine between Mainz and Cologne."[3] Many of the tollhouses and castles along the river built to extract money from traveling merchants still exist now as tourist destinations.

---

[2] See Hironori Asakura, *World History of the Customs and Tariffs.* (WCO 2003), p. 55.
[3] Ibid., p. 123.

Bright spots in Western Europe during this time period were maritime trading centers in Italy, such as Genoa, Pisa, and Venice. Venice, then an Italian city of seagoing merchant-entrepreneurs, is located on the north Adriatic. Early forms of business organization evolved: Merchants who didn't have capital accompanied goods in transit and earned a share of profits if the trip was successful. Thanks to trade and a relatively inclusive political system, Venice became one of the largest and wealthiest cities in the world. Marco Polo, a Venetian merchant-traveler, kept a written account of his trip to China along the Silk Road and returned to Venice in 1295, after twenty-four years of travel. His book, *The Travels of Marco Polo*, introduced Western Europe to the Far East. It is still read today and is now even the subject of a popular Netflix TV series.

During the Middle Ages, the international trade situation in the Eastern Roman Empire (Byzantine Empire), based in Constantinople, was generally better than in the West. Constantinople, now Istanbul, is located on a narrow isthmus that divides the Black Sea from an outlet to the Mediterranean, an ideal trade route location. River trade routes from Russia via the Black Sea transported furs, grain, and other commodities to Constantinople.

Other land-sea trade routes linked Byzantium with India, Malaysia, and Ceylon, and the overland Silk Road linked Byzantium with China via central Asia. However, the Turkish Ottomans eventually conquered Byzantium, and Constantinople was occupied in 1453. The Ottoman Empire was highly absolutist, inward looking, and reactionary. It banned modern innovations such as the printing press, fearing change.[4] International trade did not flourish in such a restrictive environment.

During this period, China was much more advanced than Europe economically and technologically. China developed innovations such as gunpowder, the compass, papermaking, and printing. Industries grew up producing paper, silk, porcelain, and other commodities. However, the state monopolized trade, and private merchants were not permitted to trade with foreigners.[5] For a brief period, these restrictions were partially relaxed, and Admiral Zheng conducted six large trade missions to southeast Asia, Arabia, and Africa, using ships much larger and more advanced than those used in Europe at the time. But after 1433, overseas trade was again banned because of concern that trade could lead to political change, and the construction of seagoing ships was made illegal.

### Mercantilism and Colonialism: Trade-Transaction Costs Fall and Trade Increases for Colonial Powers

The discovery voyages of Portuguese, Spanish, Dutch, French, and English explorers in the fifteenth, sixteenth, and seventeenth centuries opened up trade between Europe and Africa, India and the Far East, and the Americas. The Ottoman Empire and the Russian Empire also colonized neighboring regions during this time. However, the trade that ensued was generally dominated by the rulers and elites of the colonial countries and was highly exploitive. The Portuguese specialized in slave trade from Africa and spice trade from India. The Spanish plundered Mexico and Peru of gold, silver, and other valuable commodities and then forced native workers in their

---

[4] See Acemoglu, Daron and James Robinson. *Why Nations Fail* (Crown Business 2012), p. 215.
[5] See ibid., pp. 232–233.

colonies, under slave-like conditions, to extract additional gold and silver and to produce valuable agricultural goods for export. The Dutch developed spice and other trades with the Far East. Later, the Dutch, French, and English colonized Caribbean islands and eastern North America. Manufactured goods were traded from the mother countries to colonies in exchange for slaves and commodities, such as rum, sugar, cotton, tobacco, beaver pelts, and cod.

The economist Dani Rodrik, in his book *The Globalization Paradox*, recounts the story of the development of beaver pelt trade by the English during this period.[6] In the late seventeenth century, beaver pelts were in high demand throughout Europe for hat making and other clothes. However, most pelts came from Russia, and merchants located in Baltic and Black Sea ports dominated trade. Moreover, overhunting resulted in high prices. The French in North America (then New France and now Quebec Province in Canada) also had developed a thriving trade in beaver pelts, but the English were excluded from this. In England, beaver pelts available through intermediaries were expensive and of inferior quality.

Two adventurers familiar with beaver trade in New France, Radisson, and des Groseilliers convinced Prince Rupert, the nephew of English King Charles II, to open up a new source of beaver pelts bypassing the French by sailing north into Hudson's Bay and trading directly with local Indian tribes. The King granted Prince Rupert and his partners a charter establishing the Hudson's Bay Company. Hudson's Bay Company was given exclusive rights to trade in the Hudson's Bay region, and they were also given exclusive rights to govern the region. The enterprise was highly successful, and its territorial control

---

[6] See Rodrik, Dani. *The Globalization Paradox*. W. W. Norton & Co. 2011.

continued until 1870, when the company sold "Rupert's Land" to Canada. The company continues today as HBC, Canada's largest retailer.

Hudson's Bay Company and similar trading regimes, such as the English East India Company and the Dutch East India Company, dominated international trade at the time. These enterprises lowered many trade-transaction costs, such as costs associated with communications, transport, protection against theft, trade finance, and dispute resolution, but resulted in monopoly prices for consumers. Moreover, the indigenous peoples of America, Africa, India, and Asia supplying the traded goods received low value for them since trade was monopolized and competition from other merchants was prohibited.

These trading schemes were a product of mercantilism and colonialism. Mercantilism was an economic policy to accumulate monetary reserves (usually gold) by running a favorable balance of trade. Manufactured goods were sold by nations following this policy to their colonies and others at high prices, and raw materials were imported from colonies and other sources at low prices. High tariffs and other restrictions were imposed on manufactured imports. The objective of mercantilism was to strengthen the state and undermine nation-state competitors. France at the time of King Louis XIV and his finance minister, Colbert, was a leading exponent of this policy.

A byproduct of mercantilism and colonialism was constant warfare between nation-states competing for colonies and trading rights. These conflicts included the Dutch-Portuguese War (1588–1654), the English-Spanish War (1585–1604), the Thirty Years' War (1618–1648), the Anglo-Dutch War (1652–1674), the Seven Years' War (1754–1763), and the American

Revolution (1775–1783). These wars, of course, increased trade-transaction costs during the times of conflict. Seagoing opportunists, called "privateers" in their country of origin and "pirates" or "buccaneers" in the countries of their victims, seized foreign trading vessels and stole their merchandise. This practice still exists today in the East Indian Ocean off the coast of Somalia.

### The Nineteenth Century: Technological Innovation, Industrial Revolution, and Liberalization: Trade-Transaction Costs Are Reduced and Trade Expands

At around the beginning of the nineteenth century, something remarkable happened. Throughout human history, the productivity of workers had remained relatively static, with slow increases over time as many new technologies were introduced. But starting a little over two hundred years ago, this changed, first in England, then later in Western European countries and in North America. The richest modern economies are now at least ten to twenty times wealthier than in 1800.[7]

Late eighteenth-century growth in productivity resulted primarily from rapid increases in land, capital, and population in England and its North America colonies as well as other European nations expanding their colonial holdings. However, by the first part of the nineteenth century, the introduction of the steam engine—used in railroads and steamships, canals, and improved roads—led to much more rapid transport, and the telegraph—resulting in almost instant communications over long distances—significantly lowered trade-transaction costs and expanded trade. By midcentury, mechanization of textile production and other manufactured goods in England,

---

[7] Clark, Gregory. *A Farewell to Alms: A Brief Economic History of the World.* Princeton University Press 2007.

and somewhat later in the American North, Germany, and other Western European countries, again resulted in increased trade between major agricultural producing areas, such as the American South, Argentina, and Australia, and the manufacturing centers.

In addition, government trade policies began to change with the publication of Adam Smith's book, *Wealth of Nations*, an intellectual repudiation of mercantilist policy, and the rebellion of most of England's North American colonies against mercantilist policies and absentee rule. In England, after a long debate the infamous "corn laws," imposing high tariffs on imported grains were repealed, and a generally free trade policy was adopted. By the 1870s, the international adoption of the gold standard—currency based on a set amount of gold— largely eliminated concern about fluctuations in the value of a national currency. The colonialist-imperialist political regimes of the time also reduced trade-transaction costs by using their military to protect national trade arrangements against encroachment from foreign interests. Lastly, immigration from the countries of Europe to North and South America was largely unrestricted, and great waves of European immigrants traveled to the Americas to seek a better life.

In the later part of the nineteenth century and early twentieth century, productivity in all sectors of the economy rapidly increased in the United States, the United Kingdom, and many Western European countries. This period saw the introduction of key inventions, such as the telephone, the internal combustion engine, electric lighting and power, steel production technologies, industrial chemistry (artificial fertilizers, explosives, and pharmaceuticals), high-speed printing and inexpensive paper produced mechanically from wood pulp, mechanized farm equipment, photography, improvements in sanitation and medical technologies, and finally, radio and the invention of the airplane. These new technologies led to much lower trade-transaction costs and greatly expanded trade. But the reduction of trade-transaction costs and the expansion of trade came to an abrupt end in 1914.

Many believe that these advances, which greatly lowered trade-transaction costs, ushered in the first modern globalization. The famous British economist John Maynard Keynes' comments reflect this view:

> What an extraordinary episode in the economic progress of men that age was which came to an end in August, 1914 ... The inhabitant of London could order by telephone, sipping his morning tea in bed, the various products of the whole earth, in such quantity as he might see fit, and reasonably expect their early delivery upon his doorstep ... He could secure forthwith, if he wished it, cheap and comfortable means of transit to any country or climate without passport or other formality ... [and] most important of all, he regarded this state of affairs as normal, certain and permanent, except in the direction of further improvement.[8]

But despite the acceptance of free trade policies by England and a few other nations, imperialist, mercantilist, and colonialist regimes imposing high tariffs and other trade restrictions continued in altered form well into the twentieth century. The United States historically followed a high tariff policy until the

---

[8] Keynes, John Maynard. "The Economic Consequences of Peace," (London: MacMillan 1919), pp. 10–11.

trade agreements legislation of 1934. In fact, the high tariffs advocated by the North in the nineteenth century to protect its infant manufacturing industries from English and other European competition were a major cause of conflict with the South, leading to the American Civil War.

Although slavery had been banned in most countries by the end of the nineteenth century, colonial powers continued to exploit local workers under near slave-like conditions. Large plantation systems produced tropical crops, such as coffee, tea, cocoa, rubber, and bananas as well as gold and other valuable metals and minerals. These products were exported to the colonial countries in return for manufactured goods. The remains of this pernicious system can still be seen today in the former Portuguese colony of Sao Tome Principe. Under Portuguese rule, large plantations were established to produce coffee and chocolate. Absentee landlords derived great wealth from these plantations, but the workers existed under slave-like conditions.[9] After the islands achieved independence in the mid-1970s, the Portuguese colonists fled, trade mostly ended, and the islands descended into subsistence poverty, alleviated almost solely by foreign aid.

### 1914–1945: Trade-Transaction Costs Increase and Trade Shrinks

The two world wars (1914–1918; 1939–1945) and the interwar Great Depression drastically increased trade-transaction costs and reduced international trade. All-out military conflict, of course, greatly reduced trade, as did the high tariff levels imposed to protect domestic producers during the Depression. Productivity, however, at least in the United States, continued to increase with

---

[9] See Tavares, Miguel Sousa. *Equator* (Bloomsbury 2008) for a fictional account of this era.

the development of new technologies and investments in infrastructure. In the 1920s, industrial-sector productivity in the United States grew at about 5 percent on average.[10] Electrification and mass production of automobiles led to a suburban housing boom. Despite the long depression, starting in 1929 and not ending until the advent of WWII, productivity continued to grow rapidly. Productivity continued to improve in the United States during the war years, fueled, in part, by innovations relating to the war effort. However, by the end of WWII, large parts of Europe and Asia were in ruins and, compared to the early years of the twentieth century, trade-transaction costs were high and trade had collapsed.

> ### Comparative Advantage, Free Trade, and Business and Labor Dislocation
>
> "Comparative advantage" is a well-accepted economic theory that holds that because of different factor endowments (for example, different costs of labor or materials or difference in technologies) *all* parties benefit from international trade transactions. This is true even if a business in country A is less efficient in every respect than its trading partner in country B. Comparative advantage is often cited as the reason for the reduction of tariffs and nontariff barriers to trade. However, as is also true of technological progress, freer trade inevitably results in some industrial and labor dislocations. This had led to strong opposition to freer trade from industry and labor groups that may be injured.

## Modern Times: Trade-Transaction Costs Rapidly Fall and Trade Greatly Expands

As WWII was drawing to a close, representatives of forty-four nations met in Bretton Woods, New Hampshire, to develop new rules for international trade and monetary regimes after the war. Led by the United States, represented by US Treasury official Harry Dexter White, and the United Kingdom, represented

---

[10] Shackleton, Robert. "Total Factor Productivity Growth in Historical Perspective" Congressional Budget Office March 2013.

by economist John Maynard Keynes, they created three new organizations to manage international financial, monetary and trade matters—the World Bank, the International Trade Organization, and the International Monetary Fund. However, the International Trade Organization died before it was born because the US Congress failed to approve it, expressing concern that it would infringe on Congress' power to set tariffs and oversee trade. Instead, the General Agreement on Tariffs and Trade (GATT), originally part of the International Trade Organization, became the primary international vehicle for expanding and regulating international trade relations.

The GATT, which was administered by a small professional staff based in Geneva, Switzerland, coordinated successive rounds of multilateral trade negotiations, initially designed to reduce tariffs and then broadened to also reduce and regulate nontariff barriers to trade. Originally, the GATT included only twenty-three founding contracting parties, but after several successful trade-round negotiations by the mid-1970s GATT, contracting members had expanded to over one hundred.

By the 1960s, the economies of Western Europe and Japan had recovered from the war and their rebuilt industries based on modern technologies fueled an export boom. This created trade tensions with the United States, as televisions and other consumer electronic goods made in Japan as well as automobiles and industrial equipment made in West Germany began to take significant market share away from US producers.

The Tokyo Round GATT trade negotiations from 1973 to 1979 included an effort to regulate, reduce, and simplify behind-the-border trade-transaction costs, such as government export related subsidies, product standards, dumping, and differing approaches to customs valuation.

Much more important to the advancement of international trade during this period than new trade agreements was the continual stream of innovations, which lowered transaction costs and increased productivity—particularly high-speed computers and other information technologies as well as other new technologies developed in connection with defense spending. Important transport innovations lowering transaction costs were the development of multimodal transport and intermodal freight containers. Jet aviation and larger cargo ships and tankers also increased the speed and reduced international trade transport costs. Improved air travel and telecommunications increased the speed and reduced the cost of international trade in services as well.

A negative effect on economic development and trade in North America and Western Europe during this period was the rapid increase in petroleum prices starting in 1974. The price of crude in constant 2013 dollars had fluctuated around $17 per barrel from 1907 to 1972.[11] But by 1974, the price had increased to $55 per barrel and by 1980, prices had reached $104 per barrel. North America, Western Europe, Japan, and China had become heavily reliant on petroleum imports from Saudi Arabia and other Middle Eastern countries and were now forced to pay much higher prices. But rather than benefiting the economies and people of oil-exporting countries, much of the wealth transfer related to trade in oil ended up in the bank accounts of rulers and oligarchs controlling the oil trade, funding lavish lifestyles. However, longer-term high prices stimulated oil exploration and the development of fracking technologies and alternative energy sources, such as solar and wind power as well as biofuels. By early 2016, oil prices had fallen to below $30 per barrel.

---

[11] Historical Crude Oil Prices, 1861 to Present, www.chartsbin.com

> ### *Free Zones*
>
> Free zones are territories that are, for customs and some tax purposes, outside the jurisdiction of the nation where they are located. They were developed to encourage international trade in so-called "free cities." Early examples include Gibraltar in 1704 and Singapore in 1819. In the United States, free zones are called "foreign trade zones." Over the last forty years, the US foreign trade zone program has grown exponentially from a handful of zones used mainly for the duty-free storage of goods to 177 zones, employing more than 390,000 people and processing more than $835 billion per year in goods.

Free zones and variants of free zones, export processing zones, and special economic zones have become an important trade and investment promoting mechanism around the world, and they have been the centerpiece of economic development for economies as diverse as Ireland, Dubai, Jordan, Panama, the Dominican Republic, and China. The story of China's use of special economic zones for economic and trade development over the last thirty years is particularly noteworthy.

## The Rise of China in International Trade

Prior to 1979, under the Communist regime established by Mao Tse Tung, the Chinese economy was relatively stagnant and inefficient, and trade was limited mainly to other "socialist" countries. However, after Mao's death, China's leadership decided to gradually reform the economy according to free-market principles and open up to trade and investment from the United States and other free-market economies. China's leader at the time, Deng Xiaoping, explained the change in policy in terms his largely agrarian nation could understand: "Black cat, white cat, what color does it matter the cat is, as long as it catches mice."

Economic control of enterprises was transferred to local governments, and these enterprises were permitted to operate on free-market principles. Trade barriers were reduced. Special economic zones (SEZs) were created in China's major port cities to pioneer new policies and attract foreign direct investment. Investments were encouraged as long as foreign investors partnered with Chinese in joint ventures and agreed to transfer their technology. These reforms led to large-scale investment and rapid productivity growth. GDP growth averaged about 10 percent per year. International trade also exploded. China's merchandise exports grew from $14 billion in 1979 to $1.9 trillion in 2013.[12] By 2009, China had become the world's largest exporter of goods, dominating sectors such as textiles and garments as well as consumer electronics.

As had been the case earlier with imports from Japan and Germany, the rapid increase in imports of goods from China resulted in trade tensions with the United States and the European Union. Trade remedy measures, such as antidumping, countervailing duty and safeguard procedures, and bilateral and multilateral agreements were used to provide some import relief for producers in developed economies losing market share to imports.

### Century's End: The "Asian Tigers," Peaceful Revolutions in the Soviet Union, and Eastern Europe and "the Washington Consensus"

In the Far East, Japan had rapidly rebuilt after WWII following an export-oriented economic policy. Japan's export oriented approach was subsequently emulated successfully by

---

[12] Morrison, Wayne. "China's Economic Rise: History, Trends, Challenges, and Implications for the United States." Congressional Research Service, October 2014.

South Korea, Taiwan, Hong Kong, and Singapore; these four economies became known as "the Asian Tigers." By the twenty-first century, all four had developed advanced economies. South Korea and Taiwan focused primarily on manufacturing exports. Hong Kong and Singapore, essentially city-states, specialized in finance and trade logistics.

Throughout the post-WWII era until the early 1990s, the economic world was frequently described as being divided into three parts: the "First World," consisting of the United States, Western Europe and Japan; the "Second World," consisting of the Soviet Union, China, Eastern European countries, such as Czechoslovakia and Hungary, and Vietnam, Cuba, and other economies organized along "socialist" (i.e., communist) principles; and the "Third World," consisting of developing economies, such as South Africa, India, Pakistan, and Thailand, many of which had only recently gained independence from their colonial masters. Trade between the First- and Second-World economies was very limited. Trade between the Third World and the First and Second World generally continued to follow the colonialist pattern established over the previous centuries: Third-World Countries, particularly least developed countries (LDCs), provided raw materials to First- and Second-World economies and received manufactured goods in return. However, with the economic reforms that began in China in 1979 and the breakup of the Soviet Union in 1991, these historic trading patterns began to break down, and vast new markets opened up for enterprises in economies around the world.

Communism in Eastern Europe and the Soviet Union had been sustained in the post-war period by political and military repression. But in the 1980s, communist "command" economies began to fail, and their political leadership was unwilling to use military force to maintain control. In November 1989, the most visible symbol of political and economic division in Europe, the Berlin Wall, was dismantled. By the summer of 1990, all the former communist governments of Eastern Europe had been replaced by democratically elected governments, and by the end of 1991, the Soviet Union itself dissolved into its constituent states.

Political and economic change in Eastern Europe and the former Soviet Union led to a change in trade patterns: Trade between the former communist bloc countries declined, and trade with Western Europe, East Asia, and North America expanded. State-trading firms were dissolved, and many state-owned enterprises were privatized, frequently enriching the former senior managers and communist party "nomenclatura" (senior officials). Consultants funded by national and international aid agencies, such as the US Agency for International Development and the World Bank, descended to advise these countries on how to restructure their governments and economies.

At the time, there was much self-congratulation in the developed economies of the West. An eminent scholar wrote a book titled *The End of History and the Last Man*,[13] arguing that liberal democracy and free-market organization represented the end point of human social evolution. The World Bank, International Monetary Fund, and US Treasury developed and espoused so-called "Washington Consensus" policies, advocating the removal of government regulations and other restrictions to promote free markets and the unrestricted movement of capital. As it later turned out, this self-congratulation was premature and "Washington Consensus" policies frequently did not work.

---

[13] Fukayama, Francis. *The End of History and the Last Man.* Avon 1992.

### *The North–South Divide: The Haves and Have-Nots*

By the early twenty-first century, the global economic narrative had changed from "First World, Second World, Third World" to the "North-South Divide." The "North" consisted of the United States, Western Europe, Japan, and other developed economies. The "South" consisted of Africa, Latin America, and developing countries in Asia and the Middle East. The "North" controlled most industry and trade. The "South" economies were generally poor and undeveloped, importing manufactured goods from the "North" and exporting metals, minerals, and agricultural commodities. This was essentially the old colonialist trading pattern relabeled.

Most South American economies continued to experience slow growth, political instability, and poverty primarily due to entrenched political regimes favoring a few wealthy business owners. In Argentina, immigration from Europe and vast amounts of fertile land stimulated agricultural production during the latter part of the nineteenth century and first part of the twentieth century. By the beginning of the first World War, Argentina was one of the richer countries in the world, thriving on agricultural exports. But a collapse of prices for agricultural goods combined with poor governance reversed its economic development. In recent years, political and economic instability and erratic monetary policies have continued to retard Argentina's development and increase trade-transaction costs.

Brazil is a different story. Brazil was a Portuguese colony until the first part of the nineteenth century. Its economy, even after independence, was typical for an overseas colony— sugar, cotton, tobacco, coffee, and later rubber were produced by slave labor and exported to Portugal. Manufacturing and trading with countries other than Portugal were prohibited. After independence, slavery was eventually abolished. With the 1930s came the beginning of industrialization. A military government gave way to a democratic regime. Today, Brazil is the largest economy in South America with well-developed agriculture, mining, manufacturing and service sectors, and an export-oriented economy. However, its exports are still mainly commodity dependent.

Chile also has had recent economic success after political liberalization and a free-trade agreement with the United States has been a particular benefit for trade. However, Chile's trade profile is still reminiscent of colonial times. Principle exports are copper, wine, and other agricultural products as well as wood pulp. Imports are manufactured goods.

Colombia has recently experienced rapid economic growth and surpassed Argentina as the second largest economy in South America after Brazil. However, most exports are commodities, such as petroleum, palm oil, and cut flowers, and large infusions of capital through money laundering are attributed to illegal cocaine trade. A drug cartel related insurgency continues in parts of the country.

The economic and trade situation has been far worse in sub-Saharan Africa than in South America. The largest economy, Nigeria, has been plagued with frequent ethnic and religious conflicts since its independence from the United Kingdom in 1960. Its economy is heavily dependent on oil exports. Unfortunately, much of the revenue from its considerable petroleum resources has ended up in the pockets of the elite, without improving national infrastructure or otherwise benefiting the population as a whole. Corruption is rampant. On the positive side, there are many highly trained and motivated academics and professionals who will be available as an important resource for economic development in the future.

South Africa, the second largest economy in the region and also a former British colony, is less reliant on commodity exports than other economies in the region and has a vibrant tourist and other-services sector. It is the only large economy in sub-Saharan Africa that is ranked as upper middle income on a per-capita basis. However, it is still plagued by high unemployment and crime.

The United Nations listed forty-eight least developed countries (LDCs) in 2014; most of these are in sub-Saharan Africa. Per-capita income in these countries is, on average, less than $900 per year. Liberia is a typical example. Liberia emerged from a devastating civil war in 2004 and, more recently, was an epicenter of an Ebola outbreak. Basic government services, such as roads, sanitation, and electric service, are undependable. Trade opportunities are generally limited to a few agricultural commodities as well as oil and other minerals. Personal safety and accommodations for international travelers are concerns.

Most Middle Eastern countries also fall into the "South" category. Many, such as Libya, Egypt, Syria, the Palestinian territories, Iraq, and Yemen, are or have recently been in political turmoil and military conflict. This, of course, impedes trade and increases transaction costs. In Egypt, as an example, tourism revenue declined 95 percent recently as a result of political unrest and security concerns. The Gulf economies (Saudi Arabia, United Arab Emirates, and Kuwait), Jordan, and Israel are exceptions. The Gulf economies are today among the wealthiest in the world as a result of oil revenue. In addition, they generally have low trade-transaction costs, partly as a result of employing free zones to stimulate trade in goods and facilitate the employment of foreign technical specialists. Trade in services, such as business consulting and tourism, has also thrived. The shopping malls of Dubai attract visitors from as far away as Kazakhstan and Russia.

Jordan is a stable Middle Eastern economy that has reached upper middle-level income status without petroleum resources, with the help of a strong cadre of experienced professionals, good governance, and international assistance from donors, such as the European Union and the United States. As an example, Petra Engineering Industries, a manufacturer of air conditioning equipment, was founded in Jordan in 1987 and in a little more than twenty-five years, it has grown to a large business with several thousand employees. Petra sells their HVAC products in more than forty-five countries around the world, including the United States, Spain, South Africa, and Russia.

### 2000–2016: New Technologies and International Agreements Accelerate the Decline in Trade-Transaction Costs

Trade expanded and transaction costs continued to decline for most economies during the first sixteen years of the twenty-first century. This progress was driven both by new technologies and by international agreements that removed tariff and nontariff barriers to trade.

New and improved technologies driving down trade-transaction costs include the development of high-speed Internet connections using fiber-optic cables and satellites; advances in Internet and Web surfing, including mobile Internet technologies; improvements in cell phone technologies (culminating in smartphones); rapid increases in computer processing speed; advances in Web-related analytical software; the adoption of electronic systems and single-window technologies by border agencies; and advances in cargo tracking, scanning, and other enhanced supply-chain and logistics management technologies.

A major boost for the growth of international trade in goods was the development of containerization and multimodal transport. Starting in the 1960s, shipping containers in standard dimensions, twenty feet and forty feet in length (container standards are now specified by the International Standards Organization, the ISO) came into use. These containers could be seamlessly transferred from trucks to flatbed rail cars to oceangoing container ships. Containerization also eliminated dockworkers involved with handling break-bulk cargos, the manual sorting of goods, some warehousing, and reduced shipping time and losses from theft and casualty. By 2009, 90 percent of all nonbulk cargo was being moved internationally by container ships.

Many new multilateral and regional trade agreements were also responsible for reducing trade-transaction costs. The World Trade Organization (WTO), located in Geneva, came into existence in 1995 as the culmination of GATT Uruguay Round trade negotiations. Over the last twenty years, major economies, such as China, Russia, Ukraine, Saudi Arabia, and Vietnam, have become WTO members. As of November 2015, the WTO had 162 members accounting for a high percentage of all world trade. More than twenty additional nations are seeking membership.

The WTO administers agreements relating to three main areas: multilateral agreements on trade in goods that "bind" (i.e., fix) tariff rates (the GATT) and also govern nontariff barriers to trade; an agreement on trade in services; and an agreement on trade-related intellectual property rights. The WTO is also the focal point for continuing multilateral and plurilateral negotiations relating to trade in goods and service and adjudicates trade disputes between members. It also conducts a variety of administrative, analytical and statistical services. A service particularly helpful to businesses planning to embark on trade transactions in an unfamiliar WTO member country are the periodic trade policy review reports published by the WTO Secretariat. These reports provide useful overviews regarding the economy and tariff levels, nontariff barriers to trade, and trade-related institutional arrangements of WTO members.

The "globalization" of international trade through WTO agreements involves the ceding of some national sovereignty over trade and accelerated "offshoring" (relocation of manufacturing and service firms from developed economies to lower cost developing economies). This, at times, has been controversial. At a WTO ministerial conference hosted in Seattle in 1999, activists concerned about labor and environmental rights staged large-scale violent protests. New WTO agreements proposed as part of the current WTO Doha Development Round negotiations initiated in 2001 have continued to be controversial, and progress has, for the time being, been mostly blocked. Agricultural trade issues in particular have been contentious. The US food industry has embraced biotechnology, whereas European Union farmers, consumers, and their governments remain skeptics. The EU has banned imports of hormone-treated meat from the US. The high subsidies of agricultural products, such as cotton by the US and a range of products by the EU, are of concern to major agricultural producers in other regions of the world, such as Brazil and Australia. Some WTO members, such as India, seek to provide for their "food security" by retaining the option of imposing import barriers on agricultural imports.

In December 2013, the WTO concluded the negotiation of a new Trade Facilitation Agreement (TFA) that will enter into force once two-thirds of the members have completed their domestic ratification process. The new agreement consists of various provisions designed to expedite the movement of goods in international trade. It also provides for trade facilitation technical assistance and capacity building for developing country members. Global businesses lobbied hard for adoption and implementation of the TFA in the hope that the adoption of its measures will further reduce trade-transaction costs.

Work in the WTO also has proceeded on plurilateral agreements, including government procurement, information technology, environmental goods, and trade in services.

Although progress on new multilateral trade agreements under the auspices of the WTO has mostly stalled, new regional trade agreements have proliferated, and these appear to be supplanting multilateral trade agreements. Regional trade agreements (RTAs) are reciprocal trade agreements between two or more economies where preferential treatment is given to the goods and/or services of the contracting members. RTAs may be bilateral or include three or more parties. They involve varying degrees of economic integration, ranging from simple preferential trade agreements, such as the friendship, commerce, and navigation treaties of the nineteenth century; to a free trade agreement, where tariffs and possibly nontariff barriers are eliminated; to a customs union, where in addition to the elimination of tariff and nontariff barriers a common external tariff (CET) is established; to a common market, where all internal restrictions to the movement of goods and services are eliminated; to finally an economic union, where the members also adopt common macroeconomic policies and possibly a common currency.

## *Progress Toward Greater Economic Integration by Trade Agreement*

| preferential trade agreements | free trade agreements | customs unions | common markets | economic unions |

According to WTO data, as of mid-2014, there were 379 active RTAs, mostly free-trade agreements. Examples of free-trade agreements entered into by the United States include the North American Free Trade Agreement (NAFTA) with Canada and Mexico; the Central America Free Trade Agreement (CAFTA-DR), and bilateral agreements with Chile, Columbia, Korea, Singapore, Israel, Jordan, and other countries. The European Union has entered into bilateral free-trade agreements with a number of countries around the world, including Norway, Switzerland, Egypt, Israel, Jordan, Mexico, South Africa, and Korea.

In addition to reducing or eliminating tariffs, some modern RTAs aim to reduce or eliminate various other trade-transaction costs. For example, the bilateral agreement between the United States and South Korea includes detailed provisions regarding customs administration and trade facilitation, sanitary, and phytosanitary standards and technical barriers to trade.

Customs Unions include the European Union plus Turkey; the Southern African Customs Union (SACU), including South Africa and five adjacent states; and the Eurasian Customs Union, currently including Russia, Kazakhstan, Belarus, and Armenia. Other proposed customs unions in varying stages of adoption include ASEAN (Indonesia, Thailand, Singapore, Malaysia, the Philippines, Vietnam, and several other Southeast Asian economies), ECOWAS (Nigeria and fourteen other West African states), Mercosur (Brazil, Argentina, Paraguay, Uruguay, and Venezuela), the GCC (Saudi Arabia and several Gulf states), the East Africa Community Customs Union (Kenya, Tanzania, and Uganda), and several others.

Currently, the European Union, now consisting of twenty-eight member states, is the only true common market and economic union. However, Russia and the other states that are members of the Eurasian Customs Union are proceeding with plans for the development of an economic union. From an economic perspective, an union for these economies makes sense because they share a common language, borders and legal traditions, and have historically had strong trade relations.

### Global Value Chains

As transaction costs declined, trade in goods and services became increasingly organized around global value chains (GVCs). GVCs are the full range of activities that businesses utilize to bring goods and services to consumers. These activities include R&D, design, production, logistics, distribution, and related services to support use by the ultimate consumer. One integrated firm may perform all of the activities or, more commonly, many of the activities may be shared with independent business organizations including small businesses. GVC participants are, by definition, located in multiple countries.

The degree of complexity of a GVC is related to the characteristics of the products or services involved and the additional costs incurred when production is sourced from varying international locations. By locating the production of constituent components of goods or services in economies where production costs are lower, businesses may decrease the overall cost of production and increase their competitiveness. However, when pursuing this strategy, production savings must be balanced against additional transaction costs resulting from a more complex supply chain. In recent years, supply chain management has become a subject that has been much studied in academic and business circles.

Some relatively simple GVCs have developed around large retailers of consumer goods, such as "big box" stores like Wal-Mart, and supermarkets, such as Kroger. The products sold are usually not complex—typically clothing and textiles in the case of Wal-Mart and groceries in the case of Kroger. The retailers focus primarily on marketing and sales and source products from a large network of independent suppliers around the world, many of them small businesses.

More complex GVCs typically exist in high-technology sectors. Because firms producing pharmaceuticals, sophisticated electronic products, automobiles, or smartphones depend heavily on R&D, design services, and multiple sophisticated components, they must closely manage all aspects of the GVC and safeguard their intellectual property rights. This, however, does not exclude participation by small-business suppliers.

Service providers, such as banks and other financial institutions, medical services and tourism providers, business consultancies, and law and accounting firms also employ GVCs. As an example, major consulting firms, such as Accenture,

Deloitte, McKinsey & Co., and Booz Allen Hamilton, have established offices around the world, transfer personnel regularly between these offices, and have specialists in an office in one country carry out some or all of a consulting project for a client in another country.

What all this means is that international trade in goods and services has become much more complex. Products, such as automobiles or smartphones, that we consider to be "goods" in fact contain important services components (for example, R&D, design, logistics management, and warranty service). Products that we consider to be services, such as banking, include some "goods" components (for example, ATM equipment and debit cards, checkbooks, and physical infrastructure for bank offices). Moreover, for both goods and services, intermediate inputs account for the majority of international transactions.[14] These intermediate inputs frequently end up in the final goods or services product that is exported. For instance, in China, Korea and Mexico around three quarters of all intermediate imports of electronics end up in exports.[15]

The details of supply chains for some high-tech and pharmaceutical products can be closely held secrets. However, Tom Friedman, in his 2005 book *The World is Flat: A Brief History of the Twenty-First Century*, describes in detail the GVCs developed by Dell for the manufacture and assembly of computer notebooks.[16] Teams of engineers in the United States and Taiwan design the notebooks, and the designs are frequently upgraded. Dell factories send e-mails to various

---

[14] OECD, "Interconnected Economies: Benefiting from Global Value Chains." OECD 2013. p.14.

[15] Ibid.

[16] Friedman, Thomas L. *The World is Flat: A Brief History of the Twenty-First Century*, pp. 414–19.

supply logistics centers telling them what parts must be delivered within the next ninety minutes. As soon as parts arrive, they are entered into the Dell system and are prepared for assembly. Dell uses multiple suppliers around the world for the various components included in a notebook. The suppliers and the assembly sites continually change depending on changing costs and other production and market considerations.

GVCs are also widely employed for agricultural products. A few years ago, I personally observed the GVC for cut flowers in Zambia, where flowers were grown, and in Amsterdam, where they are sold and distributed. Fresh flowers for Northern Hemisphere markets are frequently grown by large agricultural concerns in countries such as Kenya, Zambia, and Columbia, taking advantage of the difference in seasons. When mature, they are cut, cleaned and processed, and packed for air transport to Schiphol Airport in Amsterdam. Immediately after they arrive, early in the morning, the flowers are auctioned off at the Aalsmeer auction house near the airport. Aalsmeer is the largest commercial building in the world. About two-thirds of all cut flowers produced commercially are sold here. It is organized into auction theaters where the bidders sit on an incline in front of a stage displaying trolleys with lots of flowers. Data regarding the type of flowers as well as quantity and quality reports are provided. The bidding process is electronic. The price starts high and drops until an electronic bid is received; the first bid wins. The flowers purchased are then immediately shipped by air to the destination specified by the purchaser. After they reach their destination, they are distributed through wholesalers to retail outlets.

This is a good illustration of how services of various types contribute a significant percentage in value to a product like cut flowers. The GVC for cut flowers includes service components, such as inspection, transport, and logistics management, to the point of auction, auction services, logistics, and transport management to the country of distribution, storage, and overhead services, including advertising and marketing by retail establishments.

## A Snapshot of International Trade Today

More than one hundred years after John Maynard Keynes' ode to globalization circa 1914, world trade is many times more connected, faster, and efficient. To paraphrase Keynes, a businesswoman today can sip tea in bed in the morning while ordering all sorts of goods and services on her smartphone with a reasonable expectation that the services will be delivered immediately by Internet to her computer and that goods from anywhere in the world will be delivered within two to five days to her doorstep. Newspapers and books will be delivered to her instantly, electronically. She can also arrange for air travel using her smartphone or computer, receive an electronic ticket, and expect to arrive at her international destination in twenty-four hours or less. She will be able to communicate with people by voice and video anywhere frequently without cost. And like Keynes' London resident, she will have every expectation that this state of affairs will continue in the future and even improve. Economic and trade trends support her confidence.

Today, world trade in goods and services is rapidly increasing, growing much faster than world GDP. World merchandise trade and trade in services both grew about 8 percent per year from 2005 to 2012, whereas world GDP grew only about 2 percent per year.[17] For merchandise trade, the leading exporters in 2012 were China ($2 trillion), the United States ($1.5 trillion), Germany ($1.4 trillion), Japan ($800 billion), and the Netherlands ($660 billion). The

---

[17] See WTO International Trade Statistics 2013.

leading importers for merchandise trade in 2012 were the United States ($2.3 trillion), China ($1.8 trillion), Germany ($1.2 trillion), Japan ($890 billion), and the United Kingdom ($690 billion). The 2012 data shows a substantial merchandise trade deficit for the United States. However, by early 2016, US economic growth had accelerated, China's growth had slowed, the economies of most EU countries were static, US domestic production of petroleum products had increased, the world price for petroleum was in a steep decline, and the US dollar was strengthening against most currencies. These developments may result in more favorable terms of trade for exports and imports of goods for the United States in the foreseeable future.

Advanced economies today are primarily service economies. For example, services comprise about 79 percent of US GDP, 78 percent of France's, 79 percent of the United Kingdom's, and 93 percent of Hong Kong's.[18] Developing economies, such as China and India, are less reliant on services.[19] In 2012, the United States was by far the leading exporter of services ($620 billion), followed by the United Kingdom ($280), Germany ($250 billion), France ($210 billion), and China ($190 billion). The leading importers of services were the United States ($410 billion), Germany ($290 billion), China ($280 billion), Japan ($175 billion), and the United Kingdom ($175 billion).

A graphic depiction of the exponential increase in trade in goods and services from 1960 to 2010 for the United States follows:

---

[18] See data.worldbank.org/
[19] Ibid.

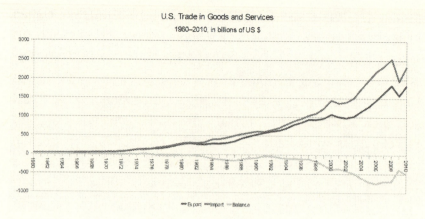

source: wikimedia.org

But despite rapidly increasing trade in goods and services, significant tariff and nontariff trade barriers still exist, and they impede trade transactions. According to WTO data, simple average applied tariff rates range from 1.5 percent for the Republic of Georgia, 3.4 percent for the United States, 4.9 percent for Japan, and 5.5 percent for the European Union to 9.9 percent for China and 13.5 percent for both Brazil and India. However, these average applied tariff rates conceal high tariffs, known as "tariff peaks," on some so-called "sensitive imports." The United States applies high tariffs on agricultural, textile, garment, and certain other manufactured imports, as does the European Union and Japan. Some of these tariffs are 100 percent of import value or even higher.

For trade in goods, nontariff barriers (NTBs) can be more restrictive and less transparent than tariff barriers to trade. NTBs include outright import prohibitions; quotas; rules of origin, product standards, sanitary and phytosanitary, labeling requirements applied in a discriminatory manner; burdensome border procedures, a particularly onerous NTB; and many other national regulations and procedures that may restrict trade. For trade in services, barriers include prohibitions on establishing a physical presence in a foreign country and then provide services through that physical presence, restrictions on the movement of business personnel (visa limitations), and government regulations that give preferential treatment to national service providers (for example, regulations that require citizenship as a condition to working as an accountant, lawyer, or doctor).

We will discuss these tariff and nontariff barriers and restrictions on trade in services in more detail in chapter 6: How Do You Navigate Government Regulations.

At the time this book was written, trade negotiations were underway to reduce further both tariffs and nontariff barriers. Some of these negotiations were taking place as part of the WTO's multilateral Doha Development Round initiative. Others involved proposed major regional trade agreements between the United States and ten other Pacific Rim countries (the Trans-Pacific Partnership, or TPP) and the United States and the European Union (the Transatlantic Trade and Investment Partnership, or T-TIP). Negotiations for the TPP concluded in early October 2015. It must now be approved by the US Congress and legislatures in the other TPP countries.

If successful, TPP and T-TIP will cover about two-thirds of the world's economy and further liberalize trade and investment in those economies. China is not currently part of TPP negotiations, but if the agreement is successful, China may join later. However, elements of TPP and T-TIP are very controversial with labor, agricultural, environmental, and other interest groups in the United States, Europe, and some Pacific Rim countries, so the political approval of these proposed agreements is not certain.

## *So Are You Convinced Yet?*

What lessons can you draw from the long historical progression, resulting in lower trade-transaction costs, corresponding increases in trade, and, in recent years, the globalization of many businesses? There are three important ones.

First, a "big picture" lesson: Trade-transaction costs have fallen rapidly and trade has increased exponentially in recent years. This has been driven by technological changes and the reduction of tariff and nontariff barriers by trade agreements.

Second, a "close-up look" lesson: The "map" of trade-transaction costs is uneven, with large flat and smooth areas but many "rough spots and peaks." Before engaging in trade transactions, you need to be aware of these rough spots and peaks. As examples, transaction costs are still high for trade in agricultural products, textiles and garments, footwear, and other "import sensitive" goods. Transaction costs can also be high for certain types of services, particularly services that involve the establishment of offices in foreign countries and the transfer of corporate personnel to those offices. Developing economies, such as Brazil and Russia, frequently impose higher trade-transaction costs on all goods and services than is the case for developed economies, such as the United States and the European Union.

Third, a "be prepared" lesson: To navigate around rough spots and peaks when conducting trade transactions, careful planning is required. The following chapters provide guidance for successfully completing international trade transactions. I hope you find the information useful and profitable as you develop international customers and suppliers for your business.

## *Takeaways from Chapter 1*

- The economic and cultural differences between nations and economies provide unlimited opportunities to profit from international trade transactions. The opportunities are all around if you look carefully.

- Trade-transaction costs have fallen rapidly over the last seventy years, and international trade in goods and services have rapidly expanded.

- Accelerating globalization is resulting in much greater market access to international markets for businesses.

- Your business will likely be involved with international trade in the future, and you need to be aware of the specific trade-transaction costs applicable to properly plan your trade transactions.

# Chapter 2

## How Does Your Business Find and Maintain International Customers and Suppliers?

Success is walking from failure to failure
with no loss of enthusiasm.

—Winston Churchill

So now that you are convinced that international trade will be important to your business in the future, how do you go about finding and maintaining international customers and/or suppliers? There are ten important tools for a small business to master. I discuss these tools in this chapter.

International marketing, or global marketing, is studied in business schools today, and academics write textbooks on the topic, discussing in depth issues such as the legal and institutional framework for international trade, the role of culture, differences in economic, political and legal environments, international market research, global branding, pricing strategies, marketing organizations, global distribution and logistics, the use of social media, and corporate social responsibility. However, these texts are usually researched and written from the perspective of large, multinational business operations. The information in this chapter and following chapters is intended to cover much of the same information as academic texts but with a focus on small businesses. I use case histories drawn from my experience and the experience of others as illustrations (most of these are included in chapter 9, "The Author's Journal").

## Tool 1: Evaluate Your Product or Service for Going International

As a small business, you are either selling or planning to sell a product, a service, or both. You may be looking for international customers for your product or service. Or you may be looking for international suppliers of goods or services to sell domestically or to incorporate into your product or service that you sell domestically. In all these cases, how can you predict if the product or service is appropriate for export or domestic markets? Ultimately, consumers will answer that question by either buying—or not buying—your product or service. However, there are two important predictors of success: product characteristics and price. I discuss these two predictors in this section.

### Identical or Similar Products, Lower Price

First, let's look at international trade transactions that are based primarily on the price of identical or similar goods or services. As a trade lawyer, I have had many small business clients who imported goods that competed solely on the basis of price. One example of this is a business that purchased trademarked consumer products, such as batteries or cameras, in overseas markets and then resold them in North American markets. I will call this small business Global Endeavors Inc. or GEI.

Multinationals producing and selling trademarked consumer products frequently intentionally sell the identical product at different price levels in different international markets. The reason for this has primarily to do with the characteristics of particular national markets. For example, trademarked consumer goods, such as batteries or cameras, may have originally been developed and produced in North America, Japan, or Western Europe and have a dominant market position in their original market. As a result of consumer recognition and acceptance, the multinational producer of these consumer goods may be able to charge a relatively high price. Other reasons for higher prices in principal markets may have to do with higher marketing and administrative costs allocated to that market, exchange rate fluctuations, or corporate decisions to allocate R&D costs to the principal market.

When a multinational introduces a consumer product developed and sold in North America, Japan, or Europe into a developing country foreign market, such as Brazil, China, or India, the product may be priced significantly lower in order to introduce it in the new market and because of market demographics (for example, consumers typically are poorer and younger in developing countries). The products, however, are identical in all respects to those sold in the company's principle markets; they are usually sold in identical packaging with identical trade dress and trademarks.

GEI was able to take advantage of these price differences between national markets, sometimes called arbitrage in goods, by buying genuine trademarked products in markets where they were sold at lower prices, shipping them to North

America, and reselling them to distributors and large retailers. GEI's profit was the difference between the selling price to wholesalers in the foreign market and the North American market, less international shipping costs and overhead. However, this is not always an easy business plan to execute because multinationals are frequently able to track leakage in their distribution system (for example, a local manufacturer or distributor selling to a customer like GEI to boost sales totals) and take steps to stop the sales.

Arbitrage may also occasionally work for services such as air travel. Some years ago, I traveled by air to Manila business class. I had to extend my business trip, and I had to purchase a new return flight. Much to my surprise and

---

### Arbitrage in Genuine Trademarked Goods

Price to North American wholesaler...........$150,000

Cost in developing country
market.................................................................$120,000

Shipping and Administrative costs..............$ 20,000

Profit...............................................................$ 10,000

---

delight, when I checked the price of tickets in Manila, it turned out that a one-way, business-class fare ticket between Manila and Los Angeles purchased in Manila was considerably less than a one-way, economy-class fare from Los Angeles to Manila purchased in the US on the same airline! Recently, when working in Pristina, Kosovo, I found that air travel to cities in Europe from Kosovo was priced significantly lower when the travel was booked from Kosovo rather than from a North American or Western European city.

This arbitrage model does not work with all consumer products sold internationally, even when there are significant price

differences between markets. Low-value, high-weight prod-
ucts, like Coca-Cola in bottles or cans, that are manufactured locally and sold at lower prices in developing countries than in North America or Europe, are too costly to transport. Others, like pharmaceutical products, are tightly regulated by government agencies that may prohibit the importation of identical pharmaceutical products sold at lower prices in foreign markets.

> **Buying Prescription Drugs in Canada**
>
> Prescription drugs are substantially less expensive in Canada. However, under US law, it is illegal for anyone other than the original manufacturer to bring pharmaceutical products into the United States. The US government is not enforcing this law for small quantities of prescription drugs purchased by US residents who travel to Canada or order from online Canadian pharmacies.

The most typical international trade transaction driven by price is when goods are available in international markets at lower prices. For example, some of my clients have been importers of various basic steel products. These businesses are usually already distributing and selling the same product purchased from domestic producers. They realize that they can increase market share and profit by sourcing less expensive foreign products of the same specifications and quality and underselling their competitors in the United States.

A client of mine that manufactured and distributed hand tools followed a variation of this approach. I will call them American Hand Tools (AHT). AHT manufactured tool forgings in Taiwan and China, where the steel and labor were much less expensive, and then did the final finishing and processing in the United States. The processing in the United States was sufficient to make it a product of the United States under US law, which added value because of a strong consumer preference for domestically produced hand tools. AHT's competitors soon copied this business model in order to remain competitive.

The same principle of offshoring to reduce cost and increase profit applies to trade in services. Some US accounting firms are offshoring the backroom work necessary to prepare tax returns and corporate financial statements to subcontractors in India and other foreign countries. The same quality services are performed at a lower cost. An additional advantage is that the workday is extended to close to twenty-four hours because India's daytime is North America's night (a 9.5-hour time difference between New York and New Delhi). Another example of offshoring is the relocation of many "call centers" to India and the Philippines. A call center is a centralized office used for processing inquiries about a firm's products or services by telephone. With modern Internet communications, call centers can be operated at lower cost in a low-wage economy, such as India or the Philippines.

Similarly, a number of the US-based consulting firms that I have worked with employ many foreign nationals to carry out consulting assignments. The quality of work is the same as US nationals, and the foreign nationals are paid much less than comparable US nationals. This practice also has the advantages of using consultants who speak the local language and fit in better with the local culture. In the tourism industry, cruise liners operating from US ports and carrying mainly North American customers use foreign vessels and foreign crews. Crewmembers from developing countries, like Georgia and Croatia, are paid much less than North American nationals.

But sometimes US-based businesses are the low-cost producers. They can then turn the tables and exploit export markets based on low cost. For example, the United States is a low-cost producer and by far the world's largest exporter of corn, soybeans, and sorghum. The United States, with abundant farmland and state of the art agricultural technologies, is also a low-cost producer and significant exporter of many other agriculture products. Grains and other agricultural products are commodities, and the world market determines their price. Therefore, low-cost producers, such as the United States, Canada, Australia, and Brazil, are incentivized to increase production for export sales. Unfortunately, as we will discuss in chapter 6, for political reasons, there are many more tariff and nontariff barriers to trade in agricultural products than is the case for trade in nonagricultural goods.

The costs of producing goods changes over time, and this can change decisions about where goods are produced. This is happening now in the trade relationship between the United States and China. Costs of producing goods in China have been increasing rapidly as labor, infrastructure, and environmental costs increase and the Chinese currency changes in value in relation to the US dollar. In the United States, by contrast, the recent boom in natural gas and oil production as a result of new fracking technologies and a decline in global oil prices have resulted in lower energy costs. This, in combination with political stability, better intellectual property protection, a low inflation rate and wage stability, and proximity to R&D and engineering personnel makes production in the United States more attractive. The trend is called "onshoring," when "offshored" production is returned to the United States. Small businesses can take advantage of this onshoring trend as multinationals constantly reevaluate their supply chain partners.

In the services sector, "similar product lower cost" can also work for US-based small businesses. Recently, I was lead expert for a consultancy assignment carried out in Kazakhstan by a small US-based consulting firm. The contract was with the Government of Kazakhstan. Approximately six bidders qualified, all bidding on the same work. The bidders were from large and small consulting firms located in Kazakhstan and around the world. We were awarded the project. Our bid was second lowest, and our technical proposal was judged the best.

The services sector in the United States is very competitive internationally. The United States had a services trade surplus of $232 billion in 2013. In some cases, this is because, as in the example above, services are price competitive. However, more frequently it is because US-based service providers offer high-quality or unique services. (Trade in services include royalty and licensing payments.)

Unique Products

Sometimes the product that you want to sell in an export market or import, or the service you want to export or import, may be of much better quality or even truly unique. This situation is the opposite of trade in identical products or services based upon price.

There are numerous high-quality or unique products and services that are sold mainly based on product quality and not price. Proprietary trademarks, special packaging, and unique design usually distinguish products of this type. The international market for luxury goods, such as watches, jewelry, high-end clothing and footwear, yachts, and high-performance automobiles, continues to grow. Small businesses can participate in this market, usually as suppliers to or distributors of the producers of these goods.

The work of artists and artisans can fall into the unique product category, and the work of renowned artists and artisans is sold worldwide. Some years ago, I represented a small family business selling high quality, unique Persian carpets. The business

> ### Luxury Goods in the United States
>
> The market for luxury goods in the United States is more than twice that of any other country. In addition to local consumers, luxury-goods consumers from around the world come to the United States on buying trips. Leading US-based luxury goods producers include Estee Lauder, Ralph Lauren, Coach, Tiffany, and Coty.

had sales outlets in Tehran, Paris, New York, and Los Angeles. The younger generation of the family wanted to sell the business and dispose of the inventory. However, because of sanctions imposed by the United States on trade with Iran, in order to transfer inventory from Paris to New York for sale, we had to prove that the Paris inventory had been transferred from Iran prior to 1979. Through business records, we were able to establish that many of the carpets had been transferred to Paris prior to 1979 and obtain a license permitting the importation of these carpets.

The Importance of Product Standards

Product standards relate to an agreed way of doing something; they specify the characteristics of goods and services regarding quality, safety, and fitness for a particular purpose. About 80 percent of world trade is affected by standards. Standards may be either mandatory or voluntary. Mandatory standards must be met as a matter of national law and are enforced by national agencies responsible for food and drug safety, consumer protection, and other national priorities. An example of a mandatory standard in the United States is the limit of one part per million of methyl mercury in fish marketed for human consumption established by the US Food and Drug Administration (FDA). Most product standards are voluntary. Voluntary standards are developed to improve the compatibility, interoperability, safety, and quality of products. An example is BS 5867, a standard regarding flame-retardant fabrics issued by the British Standards Institution (BSI).

In the United States, a variety of voluntary professional organizations develop industry-specific standards, and the American National Standards Institute (ANSI) serves as a clearinghouse and coordinator for the development of all voluntary standards. In the European Union, the European Committee for Standardization (CEN) is one of three EU organizations responsible for developing voluntary standards. Internationally, the International Organization for Standardization (ISO), which is comprised of national standards setting bodies, has issued more than 19,500 standards covering almost every industry. Another example of international standards making is the Codex Alimentarius Commission, devoted to the promulgation of international food standards and codes of practice.

In order to sell your product or service in international markets, you will have to meet the applicable standards established in those markets. In some cases, the standard applicable will be identical, perhaps because of adoption of the ISO standard in both markets.

### ISO 9001 certification

The ISO 9001 standard relates to a business's quality management systems. The standard specifies that an organization must maintain six documented procedures: control of documents, control of records, internal audits, control of nonconforming products, corrective action, and preventive action. ISO 9001 has received global recognition; many major purchasers now require their suppliers to be ISO 9001 certified.

In other cases, there may be mutual recognition of standards (a country accords equal treatment to goods produced in another country, even though the standards may be different because of different social policies). Another form of mutual recognition is by conformity assessment. This allows an importing country to recognize the testing and certification procedures conducted in an exporting country, even though there is no harmonization or mutual recognition of the underlying standard itself. In any event, your customer will specify the standard or standards that must be met in order to make the sale. In some cases, this may involve testing and certification for safety by the importing country's standards agency.

Is Your Product or Service Ready to Go International?

To sum up, your small business product or service is ready to go international if it can compete internationally based upon price, or it has unique characteristics and because of that it is in demand internationally irrespective of price. It is not always easy to evaluate uniqueness correctly, as I know from personal experience.

Shortly after Hungary and Bulgaria threw out their communist rulers and opened up to international business from the West, I participated with several other investors who were interested in introducing Hungarian and Bulgarian wines to the North American market. We thought we had a good business plan. Good wines are produced in Hungary and Bulgaria; one of our partners was well connected with North American wine distributors, and another was a Hungarian émigré. We were able to sign exclusive distribution agreements with some of the Hungarian and Bulgarian wineries, but as it turned out, we were never able to interest wine distributers in North America in their products. Unfortunately, Bulgarian and Hungarian wines had no significant price advantage, as there was a glut, at the time, of low-priced, reasonably good-quality wines from countries such as Spain, Argentina, Chile, South Africa, and Australia that, along with inexpensive wine produced by the major California wineries, already dominated the market. As far as North American wine distributors were concerned, there was nothing sufficiently distinctive about the Hungarian and Bulgarian wines that warranted an investment in distributing them.

### Tool 2: E-commerce Levels the International Playing Field for Small Business

Now that you have decided on your products or services suitable for international trade, how do you let potential customers or clients know about them? How do you market your product or services? Tool 2, and the following tools in this chapter, discuss market research—finding out about market opportunities for your products and services, marketing (getting information about your products and services to potential customers), and making sales.

E-commerce involves the production, adverting, sale, and distribution of products and services using the Internet. Cross-border electronic commerce (CBEC) refers to international business transactions using the Internet. CBEC can be business to consumer, abbreviated as B2C, business-to-business, or B2B, or even consumer-to-consumer, abbreviated as C2C. CBEC is rapidly growing. Although accurate statistics for CBEC are hard to obtain, a survey of China, a major user of CBEC, estimated approximately $500 billion in CBEC trade in goods in 2013, mostly B2B transactions.[20]

In recent years B2B and B2C e-commerce has developed rapidly. For example, In the United States Amazon sells a wide

---

[20] 2014 China Cross-Border e-Commerce Report, www.iresearchchina.com

variety of products on its website and arranges for rapid delivery through express courier services. Amazon's sales revenue increased from $24.5 billion in 2009 to $74.5 billion in 2013; over the same time period, its gross income increased from $5.3 billion to $19.8 billion. E Bay and Google have also developed successful B2C Internet platforms. Amazon is now trying to develop what it calls "Amazon Prime Air" delivery of packages within 30 minutes by drones. Clearly the handwriting is on the wall for many "brick and mortar" stores—soon B2C e-commerce may dominate retail sales.

Alibaba, a Chinese company, is reportedly the largest of all the e-commerce businesses. Transactions on its online sites totaled $248 billion in 2014, more than Amazon and eBay combined. In addition to B2C sales, Alibaba also specializes in business-to-business, or B2B, sales. In September 2014, Alibaba raised $25 billion in an initial public offering in the United States, the largest IPO in the United States to that date, and it is now traded on the New York Stock Exchange.

> Claire Mitchell, founder of The Girls Mean Business, saw the conversion of her Facebook "likes" into a business venture as an opportunity she couldn't let pass her by. Having done some business coaching already, she decided to use The Girls Mean Business brand to offer coaching programmes, webinars and e-books for women entrepreneurs. Using Facebook has expanded her reach on a global scale. Her page now has nearly 14,000 "likes", from countries as far and wide as Canada, Australia, the US and South Africa as well as the UK and the rest of Europe.
>
> —Emily Wight, Guardian Small Business Network (June 23, 2014)

Today, B2B systems range from single-firm legacy systems that involve the use of electronic data interface (EDI), to industry-sponsored marketplaces based on low-cost Internet platforms, to collaborative platforms, such as Alibaba, that aggregate supply-and-demand services. However, implementation of

B2B systems is much more complex than for B2C. Marketing requires the dissemination of more information because business customers usually require details regarding how products work and interact with other systems. Prices are variable. Volumes are much higher. Logistics issues are more complicated. The tax and regulatory issues involved with sales are also much more complex. Nonetheless, some predict that worldwide B2B e-commerce sales will amount to $6.7 trillion by 2020, more than twice the B2C market.[21]

If the predictions of the rapid development of B2B global markets are correct, this will mean that international markets for your small business's goods and services will soon become much more accessible. If you are located in North America, you will instantly have access to customers in Europe, Asia, or, for that matter, anywhere in the world. Conversely, your local markets will be much more open to international competition.

Another important technology advancing global markets has been the development of free, Internet-based voice and video communication services, such as Skype. In addition, business websites describing the enterprise and its products and services as well as social media, such as Facebook, Twitter, and Linked-In, are important resources for the promotion of products and services in international trade. A well-designed website provides valuable information about a business and its products and services. It can also be designed to facilitate communications with potential customers or clients.

The Internet also greatly facilitates market research. Market statistics are available and frequently free, if you know where to look for them. For example, the US Department of

---

[21] "B2B e-Commerce Market Worth $6.7 Trillion by 2020; Alibaba and China the Front Runners" Forbes November 6 2014.

Commerce's International Trade Administration's website lists detailed statistics for all imports and exports of goods, the WTO and United Nations collect and publish world trade statistics, and websites maintained by many foreign government statistics agencies also regularly collect and publish trade statistics. In addition, business websites provide a wealth of information about business products and services. Newspapers and business magazines discussing trade issues published anywhere in the world are available online and can be translated using easily accessible free software, such as the Google translate app.

What all this means is that technology is quickly changing market research and marketing, accelerating the globalization of markets for goods and services. As a small business, you must either use this new technology to your advantage or risk being destroyed by it.

### *Tool 3: Work Your Personal Network—*
### *"It's the People, Stupid!"*

A key to Bill Clinton's successful campaign in 1992 to unseat then president George H. W. Bush was an unrelenting focus on the economy. This was captured by Clinton's injunction to himself: "It's the economy, stupid!" There is a similar mantra you should follow as you look for new international opportunities for your small business: "It's the people, stupid."

For most small businesses, particularly small businesses providing services, personal contacts are the principal method of generating new business. This applies to international business as well as business in your domestic markets. The prototypical sales executive is passionate about his or her product or service and is able to communicate its advantages to potential customers. He or she is an extrovert and enjoys socializing with others in his or her industry, and he or she is self-confident and not overly bothered about the inevitable rejection by many potential customers. (But don't despair if you are an introvert - partner with a "sales" personality or concentrate on Internet sales.)

The "comfort zone" for selling is, of course, selling to existing customers, and experts say that this and referrals from existing customers are the best sources for new business. There is already an ongoing business and personal relationship that can be further developed for additional business. What is much more challenging are so-called "cold calls"—contacting a potential customer or client with whom you have had no prior relationship. We all have been on the receiving end of cold calls from everyone from stockbrokers to real-estate agents and roofing contractors. Even if we are interested in buying the products or services offered, the cold call is an intrusion, and we are usually annoyed. Cold calls are usually unproductive. There are other ways to meet potential international business partners that are much more useful. These are discussed in tool 4.

How can you be an effective sales person in international markets? I have met many good small-business sales executives in my career, but three stand out. I will call them Tom, Steve, and Bob. They all had personal characteristics that made them excellent at promoting their products and services in international markets and "getting to yes."

Tom was educated as an engineer and had been a senior executive with a multinational company involved with buying and selling ferroalloys to supply the steel industry. He left to start his own small international metals and minerals company doing the same thing. The business depended on his personal relationships with buying executives of the large steel firms buying ferroalloys for their production needs and his personal relationships with foreign producers of various ferroalloys. Tom's company would buy ferroalloys from foreign suppliers and sell them to domestic purchasers in the United States. Although his company was small, with only a handful of employees, the transactions were large in value—typically millions of dollars. Financing was usually by a letter of credit (L/C) opened by the ultimate buyer or a chain of L/Cs, but the financial risk was still considerable. Logistics issues—shipping ferroalloys from developing countries such as South Africa and China— were also significant. However, Tom exuded great confidence and personal charm. When he dealt with customers or suppliers, they felt that he was personally interested in them. He was comfortable traveling to Turkey, Siberia, or other remote locales to explore new supplier relationships and spend as much time and money as was needed to develop those relationships. His business was successful because of the relationships he was able to build.

Steve had a similar career path to Tom's. A former college football player, he was a naturally gregarious person. In his earlier career, he was a sales executive for a large insurance firm. Subsequently, he was a senior executive and then CEO of an international insurance and logistics firm, working in the UK and Hong Kong. He then joined a smaller insurance firm, providing insurance-based customs guarantees, and also worked all over the world as an insurance consultant. People enjoyed being around Steve. He was always very convivial and enjoyed socializing, golfing, and hunting with his clients. Like Tom, his business was successful because of his deep technical understanding of his business and the personal relationships he was able to build.

Like Tom, Bob had been trained as an engineer. Bob's father had founded a small business in Detroit serving the automotive industry. The business's products were various chemical compounds for improving welding efficiency. Patents or trade secrets did not protect the products, so they could, in theory, be "reverse engineered" by competitors. However, the business's "brand" was well known, and much of the value added related to the technical advice that Bob and his employees provided to customers. Like Tom and Steve, Bob was completely knowledgeable about his products and business, and he enjoyed being around people and developing personal relationships. Bob made it a point to participate actively in various industry trade associations and trade shows, traveling frequently to meet with customers in foreign countries.

Key characteristics these three executives shared made their businesses successful in international markets. They all had in-depth knowledge about their products or services; they all were personable and enjoyed meeting with international customers or potential customers; they developed and nurtured long-term social contacts with key business associates; and they were all self-confident and not overly troubled when a new business possibility did not work out. In sum, they thoroughly enjoyed competing in the international arena!

But suppose you are an introvert, and you hate everything about meeting people to make sales. Perhaps you are a self-described "nerd" who would rather work out engineering or software puzzles than spend time socializing. If this description fits you, think about having a business partner who will handle the personal contacts part of the business. After all, you can have the best product in the world from a technical perspective, but if you can't sell it, you don't have a business.

### Tool 4: Make New Contacts

Trade shows, international trade associations, and international conferences are great places for your small business to develop new international customers. This is an extension of "It's the people, stupid!" principle discussed in tool 3 above.

Trade shows, trade fairs, or "expos," are exhibitions organized so that businesses in a specific industry can showcase their products or services to potential customers or clients and obtain information about market rivals. Some trade shows are vertically integrated so that suppliers or distributors can also showcase their industry-related products and services. An example of a prominent trade show is the Consumer Electronics Show, or CES, held each January in Las Vegas, where consumer electronics firms from all over the world showcase their newest products. At the CES in 2015, a German automobile manufacturer introduced a vehicle driven totally by a computer; a Danish firm previewed a device allowing a user to control a PC or tablet with his or her eyes; and a US firm introduced the "Hovertrax," a skateboard-like device that transports people quickly and is much smaller and less expensive than a Segway.[22] The 2016 CES introduced, among other things, a UV patch to monitor sun exposure and a health monitor that tracks body vital signs.

International trade shows exist for most sectors of the economy. These are excellent places to introduce your products or services as well as meet potential international customers

---

[22] Sanati, Cyrus. "Our Favorite 8 Gadgets from the Consumer Electronics Show" (Fortune, January 9 2015).

and suppliers. There are literally thousands of these shows each year. Expodatabase.com maintains an interactive listing by business sector and location.

Trade associations can also be an important source of new customers or clients. Most trade associations are local or national in membership, but many are international. For example, the Institute of Internal Auditors is a global association with more than 180,000 members. The International Standards Organization (ISO) is a nongovernmental membership organization dedicated to the harmonization of standards. While official members of the ISO are governments, the ISO works regularly with private-sector stakeholders in the development of standards. International associations specific to international trade include the International Free-Zone Association, the International Association of Duty Free Stores, the International Federation of Freight-Forwarder Associations, and so forth. International professional associations include the Certified Institute of Warehousing and Materials Management, the Institute of Mechanical Engineers, the Institute of Civil Engineers, the International Association of Medical Colleges, the International Association of Professional Translators and Interpreters, the International Federation for Information Processing, the Project Management Institute, and so on.

The Federation of International Trade Associations (FITA) based in Reston, Virginia, claims to be the association of international trade associations with links to 450,000 organizations around the world. FITA provides various resources primarily relating to logistics.[23]

---

[23] www.fita.org

The point here is that there are likely one or more international trade associations relevant to your product or service where you can meet potential customers or suppliers. A quick web search will likely identify associations of interest to you.

Some business membership organizations may also provide useful contacts and information for you to develop sales of your goods and services internationally. For example, World Trade Centers are business membership organizations located in many major cities around the world. World Trade Centers are primarily focused on promoting international trade in their cities and regions; I have made many valuable business contacts through World Trade Centers.

Membership in other local organizations devoted to international trade issues can also lead to helpful contacts. Some years ago, I was an active member and officer of a regional trade association devoted to international trade. I met a number of people involved with international transactions through my work with this association who later became clients. Similar groups sponsor networking meetings and educational forums. For example, Vistage International, a US-based, peer-to-peer membership organization of CEOs, business owners, and executives of small- to medium-sized businesses, has membership drawn from a number of developed and developing countries around the world. Vistage provides advice to its members on how to participate in the global marketplace.[24]

---

[24] Go Smart before you Go Global: 5 Steps to Maximize an International Strategy (Vistage White Paper 2012).

### *Tool 5: Use Export Promotion Agencies*

Ronald Reagan famously said that the nine most terrifying words in the English language are "I'm from the government, and I'm here to help." With due respect to President Reagan (who, after all, did end up leading the very organization that he criticized), government export promotion agencies *can* help small businesses with international trade transactions. However, some caution is advised when using them, as the quality of service may vary at times, and your confidential business plans may risk disclosure.

For both economic and political reasons, many national governments have export promotion policies. In advanced economies, this frequently includes government agencies that provide various types of assistance to exporters or prospective exporters. In the US, the focus is typically on small- and medium-sized businesses. Assistance provided may include detailed information about selling products and services in specific foreign markets, assistance with financing export transactions, business-to-business links, foreign market information, and even, in some cases, the government subsidization of exports. (WTO agreements make direct export subsidization by WTO members illegal, but this prohibition may not be enforced against LDCs.)

In the United States, the Global Markets Unit of the Commerce Department's International Trade Administration has primary responsibility for export promotion. This is carried out through the US Foreign and Commercial Service (USFCS). The USFCS maintains a staff of trade professionals in more than one hundred offices around the United States and in embassies and consulates in more than seventy-five nations. USFCS's services to exporters fall into four broad categories:

trade counseling, trade matchmaking, market intelligence, and commercial diplomacy.[25] In addition, the Commerce Department has published a useful guide to exporting, which is now in its eleventh edition.[26]

Trade counseling services include helping exporters develop an exporting business plan; determining any export licensing requirements that might be applicable; assisting in compliance with product standards, certification requirements, and sanitary and phytosanitary requirements; and dealing with any intellectual property or legal issues. Trade counseling also includes assistance with documentation and customs requirements, tariff rates and import fees, advice regarding payment options, trade finance, and insurance.

Trade matchmaking includes helping small exporters identify potential trade partners, arranged meetings with prescreened buyers, and participation in official trade missions and foreign trade shows. USFCS also may feature exporters on its websites and include them in its catalogue of US suppliers sent to over four hundred thousand foreign business firms.

Market intelligence includes obtaining information from the more than one hundred thousand country and industry market reports prepared by USFCS; industry specific trade data and analysis; and market research and background reports regarding potential trade partners.

Commercial diplomacy includes obtaining US government assistance in overcoming foreign trade barriers to exports and advocacy regarding foreign government procurement bids.

---

[25] http://www.trade.gov/cs/services.asp
[26] US Commercial Service. "A Basic Guide to Exporting." 11th ed. 2015.

Commerce's International Trade Administration also operates the Trade Information Center (TIC) that provides export counseling to businesses and individuals by Internet (http://selectusa.commerce.gov/investment-incentives/trade-information-center-tic) and by telephone. Trade professionals who have expertise in various foreign markets and industry sectors staff the TIC. They provide counseling on everything from access to foreign markets to resolving transactional problems.

The Small Business Administration (SBA) is also an important federal government source for advice regarding international trade transactions. In contrast to the USFCS, SBA provides assistance regarding import transactions as well as export transactions. SBA may provide export loans. SBA's SCORE program matches volunteer business counselors with small businesses in need of business advice, and this includes advice regarding international trade transactions.

The Export-Import Bank of the United States (Ex-Im Bank) is an independent federal agency that supplements private sector financing by providing loan guarantees, export credit insurance, and direct loans to finance exports. Ex-Im assumes credit and country risks that the private sector is unwilling to undertake. It claims that more than 85 percent of its transactions benefit small businesses. However, some congressional critics claim that most Ex-Im funding goes to Boeing and other large exporters and that there is no need to continue this program. Funding for the Bank ended in mid-2015 but was then renewed at the end of 2015.

State and local governments can also be a source of export promotion assistance. Many states, such as Virginia, California, New York, and Illinois, maintain export promotion agencies that provide assistance to businesses domiciled in the state. Frequently, these programs are at least partially funded by the federal government.

The US Embassy economic officers in some of the countries where I have worked have also been an excellent resource for recommendations regarding local attorneys and other service providers. In addition, when doing business in countries where there are political, health, or other security risks, registering with the Embassy by e-mail when you arrive gives you immediate access to the latest security information.

In my experience in with working with government officials, cold calls are difficult, although this may be improving with a proposed reorganization of the USFCS. I've made my share of cold calls, and you sometimes end up with a very knowledgeable, dedicated official who will spend as much time as necessary to share his or her knowledge. Other times, you end up talking to a junior civil servant who is not that knowledgeable and does not want to be bothered with your problem. If you can get someone you already know in the government who knows the relevant officials concerned, or a congressional office, to make the first call for you, your chances of ending up with a competent, eager-to-help government official will be much higher.

---

### Uncle Sam Comes to the Rescue!

A small equipment manufacturer located in California was bidding on a contract in the Czech Republic. Their bid had to arrive at the customer's address at a specific date. They arranged for an express courier to make the delivery, but unfortunately, the courier misdirected the package, and it could not be delivered on time. Fortunately, the manufacturer found out about the problem and was able to contact the US Embassy in Prague. The bid was transmitted to the Embassy electronically, and they agreed to hand carry the bid to the customer for it to be timely submitted.

### Tool 6: Visit Them

Visits to prospective clients, suppliers, or customers in other countries are more difficult to arrange than similar visits in your home market for several reasons. First, there is the problem of justifying the time and expense of an international trip. Your small business may not have a regular budget or other resources for such trips. Second, there are frequently significant cultural differences that you must navigate. These will be discussed in tool 7. Third, more informal means of business meetings, such as golfing outings or attending social or sporting events, are usually not realistic options. This means that international business visits end up being shorter and more structured than similar visits in your domestic markets. But despite these obstacles, there is no substitute for a personal visit to an international customer or potential customer—it signals both interest and an investment in the relationship. It is also a great opportunity for you to find out much more about the future needs of the customer or potential customer as well as for them to ask questions about your product or service and evaluate you as a business partner.

Some years ago, when I was working as consultant for an international consulting firm now based in the Netherlands, we were interested in bidding on a new large US Agency for International Development (USAID) project in Jordan. However, another consulting firm had been doing the work in Jordan for the previous ten years. Our marketing strategy was to field a fairly sizeable team of experts to meet with local businesses and government officials as well as USAID and US Embassy officials. The purpose was two-fold: first to obtain up-to-date information about issues that would be addressed by the proposed project; second, to showcase the technical experts and senior executives who would work on the project. We spent about ten days in Jordan doing this—a substantial investment of time and money. Ultimately, our bid was successful in large part because of the information gathered and the impressions the technical and managerial personnel left during the many face-to-face visits.

Bob, the business owner of a welding accessory business mentioned earlier, told me about his selling trips to Japan, emphasizing the need to making repeated visits and develop relationships to be successful. In one instance, a Japanese colleague predicted they would make the sale at the nineteenth hole of a golf course after the third beer. This proved to be correct, but the customer, an executive with a large Japanese multinational, said, "We can do it, but we can't go in the front door. We must go in the side door."

Looking back over my career, I regret not having made more client and prospective client calls to international businesses. These visits should be well planned in advance. Ask yourself what you hope to gain from the visit. Make a list. Do the potential benefits exceed the cost? Even if you don't make a sale or sign up a new supplier, you may be able to obtain valuable information about new customers and suppliers, trends in the industry, and new products or services that will make the visit worthwhile.

## Tool 7: Handle Cultural Differences

"Culture" is a set of shared values, beliefs, and practices that are characteristic of a particular national or ethnic group. Language, religion, and ethnic compositions are important components of a national culture. But even nations such as Canada and the United States or Sweden and Denmark, which share the same or very similar language, religious backgrounds, and ethnic compositions, have disparate cultures.

Academics have attempted to analyze cultural differences that can affect international business into various components. Geert Hofstede, a Dutch scholar, is perhaps the most recognized theorist in the field. Hofstede proposes four factors to explain cultural differences: power distance; individualism/collectivism; uncertainty avoidance; and masculinity/femininity.[27]

> ### Aphorisms Can Reflect Cultural Differences
>
> United States: "The squeaky wheel gets the grease!" "Time is money!"
>
> Japan: "The goose that honks is shot!" "The nail that sticks up is hammered down!"
>
> China: "If you want one year of prosperity, grow grain; if you want ten years, grow trees; if you want one hundred years, grow people!"

Power distance has to do with the distribution of power in a society. High power-distance societies, such as Russia or Saudi Arabia, put a great emphasis on social structure. Lower power-distance societies, such as Australia or Israel, are aggressively egalitarian. Individualism/collectivism reflects the relative importance of the individual in society. Individuals are much more important in American culture than in Japan or China. Uncertainty avoidance relates to the degree with which a member of a culture is willing to deal with ambiguous or risky situations, such as engaging in entrepreneurial activities. Portuguese may be much more averse to changing jobs and participating in start-up businesses than Singaporeans. Lastly, masculinity/femininity relates to characteristics such as aggressiveness, competitiveness, assertiveness, and bottom-line performance versus supportive personal relationships, quality of life, and employee well-being. Japan is

---

[27] Hofstede, Geert (2001). *Culture's Consequences: Comparing values, behaviors, institutions, and organizations across nations* (Sage, 2nd ed.).

a very "macho" culture (from its samurai traditions), whereas Sweden is a very supportive culture.

Other scholars have emphasized cultural differences regarding "pace" (differing concepts of time); communication; and personal space.[28] In America, "time is money," and the failure to arrive for a business appointment on time is a major *faux pas*. This is also generally true in northern Europe; however, in France, sometimes you will be asked when making an engagement if you mean "English time" or, in other words, a precise time. In other parts of the world, the concept of time is more flexible. It may be more important to talk with a relative you meet on the street than to be on time to an appointment. The Spanish word "mañana" literally means tomorrow in English, but it can also mean some time in the future.

While Americans are generally direct when communicating, this is not true in some other cultures. Directness can be interpreted as rudeness. A Japanese businessman may reply "yes" to an American's question but means only that he heard the question, not that he agrees in substance. Different cultures also have different concepts of personal space. When conversing, Americans are most comfortable at arm's length, whereas Arabs and Latin Americans are most comfortable much closer and may interpret an American backing away as rejection.

Over the course of my international business career, I have had many encounters with cultural differences. Some of them are recounted here in the hope that they will help you with your international trade transactions.

---

[28] Copeland, Lennie and Lewis Griggs. *Going International* (Random House 1985).

Much to my amusement, on my first trip to Kazakhstan in 2002, I saw large billboards advertising "Barf" soap in large Cyrillic letters. It turns out that "barf" in Farsi and Tajik means "snow," connoting purity. Of course, in American slang, "barf" means vomit, so its use to advertise a soap product in the English-speaking world would not be advisable.

A widely circulated but apparently untrue story involves General Motor's supposed problems in marketing the Chevy Nova in Latin America. While it is true that "no va" in Spanish means "doesn't go," "nova" in both English and Spanish connotes newness, and GM did reasonably well selling the Nova in Latin America. The auto industry, however, has had legitimate naming problems. Rolls Royce had to change "Silver Mist" in Germany when it found out that "mist" may connote manure. Ford had a similar problem with "Pinto" in Portugal, where "pinto" may be slang for a small male organ.[29]

The list of linguistic and cultural faux pas committed when attempting to introduce a product into a different culture is long. Some years ago, Japanese exporters attempted to market baby soap in the United States called "Skinababe." They also tried to introduce a hair product called "Blow Up." The message is that brand names and advertising should always be reviewed carefully for appropriateness in a different culture.

### Colors and Symbols May Have Different Meanings in Another Culture

Green, a color used in the US to suggest spring and growth, is frequently used in food product, supermarket, and country club logos. However, in the Middle East, green is the color of Hamas and Islamic militants and is used in their battle flags.

---

[29] See Copeland and Griggs, *Going International*, supra, p. 62.

In the United States, white is universally used for wedding dresses, whereas in East Asia, it is the color of death and is used for funerals. Red connotes good fortune in China and is widely used in restaurants and hotels. In the United States, by contrast, red implies financial loss ("you're in the red") and its use for marketing in financially related business communications is uncommon. On the other hand, the color red is widely used for product "trade dress"; Coca-Cola's ubiquitous red cans are one example.

The meaning of symbols also differs across cultures. The okay symbol in the United States involves touching the thumb and first finger. However, this has a vulgar meaning in some other cultures. The number eight is considered to be lucky in China, and some Chinese will go to great lengths to include eight in their phone numbers and addresses. Conversely, the number thirteen is considered to be unlucky in the United States, and some buildings omit the thirteenth floor. Portraying the image of a saint or prophet is completely acceptable in Western cultures and can even be considered high art, whereas portraying the image of Mohammad or other prophets is considered to be blasphemy in Islamic cultures. As is the case with translations, the message is that colors and symbols identified with a product or service in one culture must be reviewed carefully for appropriateness in other cultures.

### Russian Management Style

People of my generation recall Soviet premier Nikita Khrushchev angrily banging his shoe on a table during a United Nations meeting in October 1960. His behavior was uncouth and unacceptable by Western standards, but it was only a slightly more exaggerated example of what I will call the

Russian management style, which is employed to intimidate subordinates and negotiators and to show who is "tsar."

In September 2004, I led an international consulting team that had just arrived in Moscow to begin work with Russian Customs on a World Bank project. Our first meeting was reminiscent of a Cold War meeting, with the Russian side lined up on one side of a long conference table and our consulting team and the World Bank's representative lined up on the other side. I had been asked to present my work plan. Part of the work involved assisting Russia to prepare for WTO membership. When I started presenting that part of the work plan, the woman who led the Russian delegation stopped me, literally puffed up, and angrily said, "We have no interest in the WTO! Take that out of your work plan!" This stopped us in our tracks because assisting with WTO issues was part of our consultancy contract; I exchanged dismayed looks with the World Bank representative.

As it turned out, WTO membership was very sensitive domestically for Russia at the time. We were able to complete the WTO-related consulting during the course of our work by describing it as "customs modernization" rather than as WTO related. After many delays, Russia ultimately became a member of the WTO in August 2012.

### Communicating with Asians

A Chinese friend once told me, "Americans are glass people." This was not a compliment. What she meant was that Americans show others what they are thinking, their inner emotions, in ways that can result in disharmony. This is not considered polite in China and East Asia. Americans have sometimes called Asians "inscrutable" because they conceal their true emotions and may smile even when they are nervous or angry. But this is consistent with Confucian and Buddhist principles of living harmoniously with others. It is a "loss of face" to show your emotions and create disharmony.

The Asian businessman's desire to maintain harmony can cause serious communications problems with someone from a Western culture. For example, in answer to a direct question from an American business executive, a Japanese person may say "yes" but really mean "maybe" or even "no." The "yes" may mean only that the Japanese person heard the question, not that he or she agrees. This communication issue can sometimes lead to disaster when Americans inquire of Asian partners how business plans are proceeding. Not wanting to cause disharmony, the Asians may say everything is fine when, in reality, they are experiencing significant problems.

Business etiquette is particularly important in Japan, which is still very much a traditional, hierarchical society. Even in this Internet age, business cards play a prominent role, and their presentation and use must be done in a respectful manner. It is not considered polite to make notes on business cards or forget to take them after a meeting. Dress and appearance follow strict norms—dark business suits and white shirts with an appropriate tie. Facial hair is frowned upon. Shaking hands and other touching of bodies is not generally practiced. Almost all Japanese business executives are male, and they may have difficulty relating to female executives from Western countries.

Sometimes Japan's hierarchical society benefits its exporters. In Japan, customers have a particularly high social status. While in the United States, we sometimes say the consumer is "king"; in Japan, they say consumers are "kinger," meaning they are the most important people in the commercial chain, even more important than the "king." This has led Japanese business to focus intently on meeting the needs of customers.

During my first business trip to Beijing some years ago, I was personally picked up at the airport and constantly taken to lunches and dinners. I was grateful for the hospitality but was also somewhat puzzled by it. After all, I was only scheduled to be in Beijing for a short time for a conference. Why were they giving me so much attention? As it turns out, this is a more or less standard practice in China. And there is a good reason for it. Chinese don't want to do business with anyone unless they have confidence in him or her as a person. Confidence is built through social engagements. On a lesser scale, this is no different than Western business executives who use the golf links to assess the character of potential business partners. Do they cheat at golf? If they do, they will probably cheat in business.

> ### Character on the Links
>
> "I like the guys who play 18 holes and never once put the ball in the hole. Every hole they pick up their ball or knock it away if it's within 7 feet or so. And to top it off, they take several what they call mulligans. Oh, and I almost forgot, they move their ball 2 or 3 times before each shot to improve their lie. And then of course, they shoot somewhere in low 80s. I can't understand how anyone can play a full round of golf and never hole out once. I thought that was the main objective of the game." —Anonymous

In contrast to an American, who will schedule three or four days to fly to China on business, negotiate, and sign a contract, the Chinese will take as much time as necessary to assess the character of the Westerner before entering into a business relationship. Character is much more important to them than contract terms. This clash of cultures can produce much frustration for an American who is worried that "time is money." The American becomes irritated because after endless lunches, dinners, and other social engagements, seemingly no progress has been made with negotiating a contract. On their side, the Chinese can be concerned that the American has become impatient and irritable—disharmonious behaviors not acceptable in East Asian culture.

What this means for you when you do business in East Asia is you must be prepared to invest sufficient time and money to build relationships with our potential Asian partners. You won't be able to establish a viable business relationship otherwise. And don't count on contract clauses to protect your interests. In East Asia, relationships are important; legal agreements are less so. If there is a business problem, you will be expected to work out an equitable arrangement based on your personal relationship and not be a stickler about the terms of the written agreement.

> ### *Do You Really Know the Language?*
>
> *Vietnamese friends told me the story of a newly minted British Embassy official who arrived in Hanoi to take up his duties. He was very proud of his Vietnamese language facility having just graduated from language training. He tried to use his knowledge to buy food at a local market and so embarrassed the shopkeeper that she closed her shop and went home!*

### *Respect for Authority*

Another cultural difference between the West and East Asia can be the degree of respect for and deference to authority. Recently, when carrying out a legislative consulting assignment in Ulaanbaatar, Mongolia, I tried to organize my work so that there would be "buy in" from local stakeholders. To do this, I proposed that local stakeholders actually draft the legislation with my technical assistance. This process had worked very well in other developing countries, such as Nigeria, and had, from my point of view, the important benefit of developing more democratic processes. Much to my surprise, the senior Mongolian official with whom I was working was furious. He practically threw my proposal at me, shouting, "You are the international expert. I expect *you* to write the legislation incorporating international best practices! I'm not interested in the opinions of the stakeholders!" My subsequent attempts to explain my methodology were futile.

The absence of democracy and inclusiveness in the business-decision process and deference to authority may, at times, be fatal. Several recent aviation accidents involving commercial aircraft operated by East Asian and Middle Eastern pilots apparently involved the reluctance of subordinate flight officers to challenge the authority of and decisions made by the senior pilot. One of the reasons for the widespread employment of Americans and other Westerners as commercial aviation pilots in Asia and Africa is their cultural willingness to challenge authority.

Excessive deference to authority can give the wrong impression in more individualistic cultures. Recently, when flying from Lisbon to the United States, I was seated next to a young Portuguese woman who had been selected for a work-study internship at Disney World. She told me that in Portugal, it was impolite to ask questions of professors in class. I explained to her that, unlike Portugal, in the United States, "the squeaky wheel gets the grease," and students are expected to challenge their professors with questions. If they don't, their professors may assume that they are not fully engaged with learning or not very bright.

## *Time May be Relative*

Einstein famously illustrated the relativity of time when explaining his general theory of Relativity by comparing one minute sitting on a hot stove with an hour talking to a girlfriend. The time with the girlfriend can seem to go by in an instant, whereas the time sitting on a hot stove may seem like an eternity.

Some years ago, I arranged a business dinner with Swedish and Peruvian colleagues. We were to meet at a restaurant at six in the evening for cocktails and then dinner. I arrived at the restaurant about five minutes late, and the Swede was standing at the door, impatiently looking at his watch. I apologized for being delayed in traffic. Our Peruvian colleague, however, didn't make an appearance until nine thirty. He said that no one could possibly have arranged for dinner as early as six, so he assumed that he had mistaken the engagement for nine and that it was polite to arrive half an hour after the appointed time. He then said that nine thirty was still too early for dinner for civilized people, but he would sit with us for cocktails. Needless to say, the meeting got off on the wrong footing and never fully recovered.

Although North American and Western European concepts of exact time are becoming much more prevalent in the business world, in large parts of the world, the concept of appointment time is still much more flexible. A Latin American or Arab may decide that talking to a close friend or family member is more important than punctually keeping a business appointment, and they may show up for an appointment much later than scheduled or not at all. They may also be very flexible about when work is delivered. This is acceptable in their culture but not in Western culture.

Even some Europeans are not always punctual with meeting times or work assignments. Some years ago, I worked on a project where I was supervising an Austrian technical expert, a former government official. He was a very pleasant and knowledgeable professional, and I enjoyed his company. However, he always seemed to have an excuse as to why he did not come to meetings or submit his work on time. Eventually, after many reminders, when I insisted that his work be delivered by the end of the month, he told me in a group meeting that it would be impossible, and he required at least a year to complete it. This was completely at odds with our work plan, so we had no alternative other than to terminate his employment. I surmised that in his previous professional work for government, he had never been responsible for adhering to a precise schedule for delivering a complex work product, and he balked at being required to do this in the private sector.

## Collective vs. Individualist

Years ago, when I was a US Treasury Department official, I scheduled a meeting on a trade issue with the representative of a Japanese business firm. When he showed up for the meeting, he came with five colleagues—everyone from his senior manager to the company driver. They all crowded into my small office. I later understood that this is how meetings are conducted and business decisions are reached in the Japanese culture—by a collective process. Because of Japan's unique history, Japanese business values collaborative decisions. This does not mean that the opinion of the driver is on a same footing as the opinion of the senior manager, but it does mean that everyone is involved in the process, and decisions are based on group consensus.

Swedish culture today can also be very collectivist. The business people I worked with in Sweden invariably worked for large firms. They expressed puzzlement as to why Americans leave secure employment for start-up ventures. A Swedish scholar with a libertarian bent, Johan Norberg, has pointed out that business innovation in Sweden seems to have died out in recent years, possibly because of a collectivist mentality.

Other societies are more individualistic, and one person, a "lone ranger," may make all key business decisions. Americans and Australians are examples. Think of the many high-tech entrepreneurs in the United States who started their work in basements or garages by themselves or with only a couple of colleagues. They did not take their ideas to existing multinational businesses and subject them to a collective process. They headed off into the unknown themselves, obtained financial backing for their ideas, and, in some cases, created completely new industries.

### Meeting Rituals

Cultural differences can manifest themselves in meeting rituals. In the Middle East, meetings always seem to start with coffee or tea, pastries, and small talk. This is considered a sign of hospitality. Recently, when I was working in Jordan during Ramadan, a meeting host apologized profusely for not being able to offer me food and drink before the meeting. In Russia, alcohol frequently plays a role in meetings, and there can be vodka toasts at the beginning and end of a session. In North America, business meetings may revolve around a social occasion, such as golf or a business lunch. In China, as in Japan, presenting business cards is essential, and small talk about family and weather is expected before getting to the substance of the meeting. It is impolite to show impatience or anger.

In Germany, business meetings usually follow a prearranged agenda. Hyperbole regarding products or services is frowned upon. In formal meetings, the highest-ranking person may enter first. In contrast to individualistic and informal America— where during the introduction, an executive is likely to say, "Just call me Pete"—professional titles and last names are used. In Brazil and other countries in Latin America, business people often stand very close and use frequent physical contact during meetings. This can be disconcerting for Americans who are used to maintaining arm's-length distance. In the United Kingdom, if, during a meeting, a British executive taps his or her nose, it means that the matter to be discussed is strictly confidential and should not be shared with others. Among Indians, it is considered extremely rude to use your left hand to eat (the left hand is reserved for other bodily functions). Once when having dinner with Indians, I mistakenly reached for food with my left hand and was promptly struck on my left arm by the host!

Meetings in Kazakhstan tend to follow the Russian meeting culture. As team leader of a group of consultants, I recently made a formal presentation in Kazakhstan to the chief of a government agency seeking approval of our final consulting report. The presentation took place in a large paneled conference room with tables arranged in a rectangle, with the center of the rectangle filled with fresh flowers. Bottled water and microphones were arranged before each seat. After all the agency office directors and department heads had been seated, the chief entered the room dramatically through a sliding panel in the wall. I started my PowerPoint presentation, but he continually interrupted using the Russian-style management method discussed above to challenge my presentation. His underlings, who had already reviewed and approved our report, sat meekly without saying a word during his performance. As it turned out, one of his department heads wanted us to undertake additional work that we believed was beyond the scope of our contract, and the chief was trying to browbeat us into doing the additional assignment without an additional fee. Fortunately for us, within a few weeks after this meeting, the chief was replaced as a result of government reorganization, and our report was quickly approved.

---

### The Dinner Meeting Faux Pas

A good friend of mine had just completed a short consulting project in Yemen, a difficult and dangerous place to work. His Yemeni counterpart invited him for a dinner meeting to his home and also invited a number of other Yeminis, all men. After dinner, my friend said to his counterpart: "Please thank your wife for the delicious meal." Everyone fell silent with embarrassed expressions. It was improper to refer to the host's wife, who was not present, and in any event how would the Canadian consultant know which one of the host's wives had cooked the meal?

---

My similar meetings with agency chiefs in Nigeria have been much less formal and friendly, and this is a reflection of Nigeria's family and tribal cultures, emphasizing hospitality. People seem to wander in and out of formal meetings, and agency chiefs usually go out of their way to be gracious to international consultants.

## Is It Corruption or Is It Their Culture?

Doing business in a corrupt society is extremely difficult for businesses in North American and Western European countries because of ethical concerns and national and international legal prohibitions on bribery. The prevalence of corruption is an important issue to consider when deciding whether to do business in a foreign market.

Transparency International, an international NGO, publishes a corruption perceptions index annually. In 2014, it ranked Denmark least corrupt out of 175 countries surveyed and Somalia and North Korea worst. Nigeria is ranked 136th, tied with a number of other countries. Nigeria is widely regarded as a corrupt business environment by Westerners because bribes and kickbacks to obtain business are relatively common and frequently requested. However, some Nigerians have a different moral and cultural perspective; they feel a particularly strong obligation to their extended family and tribe and will go out of their way to make sure that family and tribe benefit from financial transactions if at all possible. In their view, it is unethical not to take care of extended family and tribe.

We will discuss the national and international legal prohibitions regarding bribery in chapter 6, which covers navigating government regulations. Generally speaking, bribery proscribed by law involves making a payment to a government or corporate official in order to obtain business or get them to take some other action that benefits you financially. However, other conduct may have similar results but not be deemed bribery. For example, if an American business flies Chinese executives to Disney World for a two-week education program and pays all their expenses, this may be a tax-deductible business expense in the United States, even if the Chinese sleep four to a room to pocket the *per diems*. If the American business also builds a hospital for the local community where the Chinese business is located, this also may be tax deductible. However, the "education" of executives and the charitable contribution of building a hospital may have the same effect on obtaining business as an illegal bribe.

If you are asked for a bribe in a foreign country, probably the most culturally insensitive, relationship-killing thing you can do is to react angrily and tell your counterpart, "That's unethical and illegal!" A better approach is to say nonjudgmentally and in an even tone, "Our laws and our business policy prohibit that" and then ask them to suggest other means for accomplishing your business goals.

## Holidays

When traveling internationally, it is important, when planning your schedule, to take important local holidays into account. In Middle Eastern countries, not much business takes place during the month of Ramadan, and it is not advisable to plan business trips for that period. Throughout the former Soviet Union and Eastern Europe, March 8, International Women's Day, or *Zhenski dyen* in Russian, is a very big holiday. Women are given flowers, candy, and general appreciation. Local lore is that men should spend at least two weeks' pay on the women in their lives.

In countries influenced by Persian culture, *Noruz*, or Persian New Year, is a major festival that has been celebrated for thousands of years. It marks the first day of spring, the spring equinox. Celebrants may dress in fantastic costumes that are reminiscent of the garments worn by magicians and witches in European fairy tales. In East Asia, Chinese New Year, or *Tet* in Vietnam, is celebrated at times that vary from the end of January to mid-February, depending on the lunar calendar. Usually. this major holiday involves a week off from work.

In Eastern Orthodox countries, Christmas is determined by the Julian calendar and now falls on January 7. Some countries with substantial Orthodox Christian populations observe January 1–10 as a national holiday. Each country also has its own "national" holiday commemorating national independence. These fall at different times throughout the year.

### Additional Comments about China and India

Businesses based in China and India are increasingly important partners for small businesses located in other parts of the world, so a few additional comments about cultural characteristics relating to those two countries are important. "Face" is important in both cultures; therefore, disagreements should be handled tactfully. Both cultures greatly respect and defer to elders. Both Chinese and Indians are relatively individualistic, despite living under communist and socialist governments. On the other hand, the Chinese tend to be more respectful of authority than Indians. "It is not easy to get Chinese employees to challenge their leader's ideas. Contrast this with India, where, if you are placed in a room with young professionals, you may have a tough time saying much, as everyone is likely to have an idea and will want to beat the others to expressing it first."[30] Western business executives may view Indian partners as more creative but Chinese partners as better at execution.[31] Chinese are generally punctual, whereas to Indians, time may be more flexible.[32]

### Use Cultural Differences to Your Advantage

If you are properly prepared and sensitive to cultural differences, you can use them to your advantage in forming and maintaining business relationships. Be respectful of local

---

[30] Gupta,Anil, Girija Pande and Haiyan Wang, *The Silk Road Rediscovered: How Indian and Chinese Companies Are Becoming Globally Stronger by Winning in Each Other's Markets.* Josey-Bass 2014, pp. 65–66.
[31] Ibid.
[32] Ibid.

culture and customs, but don't try to become a local—you will be seen as insincere. Your foreign partners will be interested in your culture and customs, and sharing them as equals should put your business relationship on sound footing.

### Tool 8: Know How to Negotiate International Transactions

We all think we know what negotiation is and how to negotiate; after all, as business people, we may be involved with business negotiations almost every day. But negotiating with international business partners presents additional challenges. Your prospective partners may be from a different culture. They may have different expectations about the benefits they hope to derive from a business relationship. Their native language is also likely different. They may be located on another continent thousands of miles and many time zones distant, making communications with them and sales trips much more challenging. For these reasons, it is important to give careful thought about how to approach international trade transaction negotiations *prior* to commencing negotiations.

### Deal with Culturally Driven Negotiation Tactics

In North America and Western Europe, the negotiation of prices for goods or services may be limited. Vendors may publish price lists for their merchandise and not be willing to negotiate special deals. Service providers, such as lawyers, doctors and accountants, may have a nonnegotiable fee schedule that they follow. Price lists and fee schedules may occasionally be discounted as a "sale," but these discounts are usually available to all similarly situated customers and clients. Competition laws may prohibit price discrimination between customers. However, the situation is quite different in other parts of the world. Everything is negotiable, and local culture may determine how negotiations take place.

Gerald Williams, a law school professor who teaches negotiation tactics, tells a story about living in Kabul, Afghanistan, prior to the Soviet invasion in 1979. Each day, he would go to the local market to buy vegetables. The routine with the merchant was always the same. The merchant would start with a high price, then engage in chitchat about family. After a low counter offer by Williams, the merchant would say, "Well, since you are now a family friend, I'll give you the special price," which ended up being lower than the initial offer but higher than Williams' counter. After some weeks of this time-consuming routine, one day, Williams said to the merchant: "Look, I come here almost every day to buy vegetables. I know the price is usually such and such in Afghani currency. Let's save time, and I'll pay you that." The merchant was so upset that he told Williams to leave his stall and never come back.

The lesson from this story is that if you are negotiating with a business person in a traditional society, you should be scrupulous about respecting your counterpart's culture and following their local customs for reaching a deal, including a number of offers and counteroffers as you get to know you counterparts personally. In the Middle East, this may entail sitting in a tent, drinking endless cups of tea, and eating roast lamb with your fingers. In Vietnam, this may involve eating exotic foods, such as snake's heart or pigeon's head. In Russia, it may involve going to a banya (sauna) with your hosts, being beaten with birch sticks afterward, and then eating zakuska (snacks) and drinking vodka.

My friend Bob, who owns a welding accessory business, told me about negotiating a business deal in Japan. After lengthy negotiations, the Americans made their final offer. The Japanese side did not respond. The Americans decided that no deal was possible, checked out of their hotel, and called a taxi to the airport. When they got to the lobby of their hotel, the Japanese side was waiting for them with a signed contract. It turned out that the Japanese had wanted a deal all along, but, knowing that Americans are impatient, they were delaying agreement until the Americans left to be sure they had the best possible price.

But the "get the lowest price at all costs" approach can be counterproductive when it is in your interest to build a long-term business relationship with a foreign customer or supplier. One example of this is an international metals-and-minerals trading company, whose business was primarily based on "best price"—obtaining the best purchase price for the metals and minerals purchased in foreign countries and obtaining the best sales price for the goods from customers in North America. However, an important additional consideration for this small business was maintaining good relationships with both suppliers and customers. A "take every last dollar on the table" approach, leaving no profit for the other party, would have motivated foreign suppliers and domestic customers to look for other business partners.

### Prepare Thoroughly; Ask Probing Questions

It is important to prepare well before any serious international business negotiation. This involves asking and answering some hard questions. Ask about the business. Ask for financial statements if they are available. Who is management? Are there hidden investors whose reputation is questionable? Who are the competitors? Why do *they* say they want to do business with you? The more forthcoming they are, the more information you will have for the negotiation and the more confidence you will have with them as a future business partner. However, you likely will have to make at least one trip to visit them to obtain detailed information.

## Questions about International Suppliers

If you are negotiating with suppliers, are there other international firms that could also supply the product or service you plan to purchase? What are the terms of supply agreements concluded between the prospective supplier and its other clients? Are there significant price differences for the goods or service between the foreign market in question and North America? Does your prospective supplier have a good business reputation and treat its employees and workers in accordance with international standards? You may be able to obtain some of this information through government sources, membership in trade associations and other groups, or research from the country in question.

There may also be hidden reasons why an international supplier of goods or services may want to do business with you. For example, perhaps a Chinese steel company will sell to you at a low price because most of their production is sold at higher prices in other markets, meaning that even with the low price to you, they can cover their marginal cost of production. (We will discuss liability for "dumped goods" in chapter 6, which covers navigating government regulations.) Perhaps a Bangladesh garment factory wants to manufacture your clothing products because they would like to copy your up-to-the-minute fashion styles for other markets. Perhaps a German consulting firm wants to use a joint venture with your consulting firm as a first step to entering the North American market. Perhaps an Indian high-tech firm wants to use association with your high-tech business to market their products in third-country markets. You should probe to uncover hidden motives before entering an agreement.

## Questions about International Customers or Clients

If you are negotiating with international customers or clients, will a sales arrangement with one customer or client preclude sales to others in that market? What is the prevailing price for your product or service in the foreign market? Can North American products or services command a higher price than comparable local products or services? Is your prospective customer or client financially sound, and does it pay its obligations on time? Does your prospective customer or client have a good business reputation and treat its employees and workers in accordance with international standards?

There may also be hidden reasons why a foreign customer or client wants to do business with you. They may expect you to finance their domestic sales of your products by giving them very favorable financial terms. They may hope you will invest in their business. They may want to move money and other assets from a politically risky environment in their home country to North America, or, even worse, they may want to launder money obtained from illegal activities. Or they may hope to obtain a business visa for entry into the United States or Canada for themselves and their dependents.

### *Build Relationships*

Building mutual trust is essential for the establishment of a long-term business relationship with an international trade partner. The time to do this is before negotiations begin. Ask yourself how a productive relationship can be developed. Think of the relationship as separate from the business results you hope to achieve.[33] Negotiations experts Roger Fisher and Scott Brown make a number of recommendations about building relationships for more effective negotiations. These include pursuing relationships and negotiating goals independently; not making relationships contingent upon agreement; not trying to "buy" a better relationship through concessions; being unconditionally constructive; learning how your prospective business partner sees things; always consulting before reaching a decision; being wholly trustworthy; and using persuasion, not coercion.[34]

Tom, Steve, and Bob, the very effective small business managers whom I previously mentioned, all put these relationship-building principles into practice when negotiating international trade transactions. They always went to lengths to let their prospective partner know that they had a high regard for him or her as a person, independent of any possible business deal. They never tried to "buy" a relationship by giving unjustified business concessions. They almost always maintained a constructive attitude, even in the face of difficult negotiations and other business problems. They went out of their way to empathize with their international partners and almost always consulted with them prior to making a decision that affected the relationship. Lastly, they were trustworthy and used persuasion and facts, rather than coercion, in business negotiations.

An important part of building relationships is having staying power. The people doing business with Tom, Steve, and Bob knew that they were there for the long haul. They were not

---

[33] See Fisher, Roger and Scott Brown, *Getting Together: Building Relationships as we Negotiate.* Penguin 1989.
[34] Ibid.

after a one-time deal, after which they would disappear. Even if a particular deal did not work out, they took care to maintain their business relationships, separating personal relationships from specific trade transactions.

The antithesis of this "building relationships" approach is the negotiator who loves confrontation and wants to win at all costs. He or she may win one battle, but the other side is unlikely to do business with him or her in the future. Ron Shapiro, a highly successful sports agent and attorney, tells the story about working with a lawyer who viewed negotiation as combat:

> He often got what he and his client wanted. But he only got it once. Nobody wanted or could afford to deal with him twice because he left nothing on the table. *Winner take all. Why take a share of the profit when you can take all of it? Why have investors when you can have sole control? Why pay commissions? Why give concessions to a union when you can break the union? Why not squeeze all the suppliers to rock bottom?...*My partner literally destroyed the other side, and he reveled in it.[35]

Needless to say, there is no attempt of a businessperson who views negotiation as combat or a zero-sum game to build relationships, and long-term productive relationships resulting from a "combat" approach to negotiation are extremely unlikely.

---

[35] Ron Shapiro and Mark Jankowski, "The Power of Nice: How to Negotiate So Everyone Wins—Especially You!" (Wiley 1998), pp. 1–2.

### *Craft a Win-Win Solution*

> The best way to get what you want is to help
> the other side get what they want.

—Ron Shapiro, sports agent

Win-win negotiations are negotiations where each party achieves its important objectives, and the negotiation is value-creating, rather than a zero-sum, bargaining-over-positions process. In other words, through collaboration, probing, and "brainstorming," the negotiators identify options for mutual gain that were not apparent at the beginning of the negotiation.

Once you have properly prepared and built a solid relationship with your prospective business partner, it is time to start the negotiations in earnest. And the basis of a good outcome is a win for each party. To be a successful negotiation, each party should meet at least some of its objectives.

Ron Shapiro, in his book *The Power of Nice*, tells the story of the lengthy negotiations for Cal Ripken Jr.'s baseball contract. When the negotiations started, Shapiro, representing Ripken, and the Orioles baseball team were far apart on the length and dollar value of the contract. The team was adamant about controlling players' salaries to maintain fiscal responsibility. On the other hand, Ripken wanted a contract that reflected his fair-market value as a star baseball player. In addition to being fairly compensated based for his performance, Ripken wanted a contract that recognized his contributions to the community, aided his outside business ventures, and provided for financial security after his baseball career. This led to the Orioles offering post-career compensation guarantees that increased the overall value of the contract but did not raise his compensation during his playing career. They also agreed to give him merchandising rights. In addition, the team offered special accommodations at the baseball stadium to provide security and privacy for his family. After a lengthy and thorough exploration of each side's real interests, a deal was reached.

## Know Your Best Alternative to a Negotiated Agreement

Knowing your best alternative to concluding a business deal protects you from being too accommodating to the positions of the other side in negotiations.[36] If you are not able to conclude a contract to sell your goods and services for acceptable terms with your present negotiating partner, are there other potential customers in the foreign country where you want to do business that may be more amenable to agreement? This should be investigated prior to entering negotiations. Otherwise, after investing time and incurring expenses in connection with negotiations you may be too committed to concluding an agreement at any cost.

## Negotiating with State-Owned Enterprises

Negotiating with State-Owned Enterprises (SOEs) can present a special challenge. An SOE is a legal entity that undertakes commercial activities on behalf of its owner—a government. SOEs are common in many developing countries, including the BRIC countries (Brazil, Russia, India, and China). If you are negotiating business with an SOE in China, for example, you should realize that the primary goals of the SOE may *not* include the maximization of revenue and profit. Instead, the primary goals of your potential SOE business partner may be job creation, industrial development in a particular region,

---

[36] Roger Fisher and Scot Brown, supra.

technological development, providing low-cost inputs to other sectors of the economy, or other societal goals. This may not be a problem if your trade transaction involves a straightforward sale of goods or services, but it can result in a serious conflict of expectations if your business with the SOE involves a more complex relationship, such as a distribution arrangement or joint venture.

### Tool 9: Find a Good Local Representative

Whether you plan to buy or sell goods or services in a foreign market, obtaining the assistance of a good local representative is likely essential. The local representative will be able to obtain valuable market information for you, arrange meetings with potential customers or suppliers, and assist with business negotiations. He or she will be your eyes and ears in the foreign market.

### Exporting Goods: Indirect and Direct Sales

Goods can be sold in a foreign market either indirectly or directly. If goods are sold indirectly, an intermediate business, such as an export management or export trading company, purchases your goods and assumes all responsibility for finding foreign buyers, shipping the goods, and receiving payment. The main advantage of the indirect approach is it enables small businesses to enter international markets while avoiding the complications, risks, and additional financial commitment required for direct sales. The disadvantages are that the intermediary realizes some of the profit to be made from selling to the foreign consumer, and you have no direct contact with your foreign customers.

Most exporters prefer direct sales to foreign markets. The advantages of direct sales include higher potential profits, greater control over the export process, and a closer relationship with the foreign market or markets and its consumers. The disadvantages are that more business resources are required, and the business assumes the risk of losses connected with foreign sales.

For direct export sales, finding the right local representative can be crucial. The type of local representative selected will depend on the nature of the industry involved and business practices in the specific export market. You should become familiar with the different types of local representatives available in a foreign market.

A foreign sales representative is the equivalent of a manufacturer's representative in the United States. The "rep" markets your product to potential buyers in the foreign market using your samples and literature. He or she normally works on a commission basis and may "rep" complimentary product lines as long as they do not directly compete with each other. An agreement with a foreign sales representative will, among other things, be exclusive or nonexclusive, specify his or her compensation (usually a sales commission), state whether the representative has the legal authority to bind your firm, and define his or her territory.

A foreign distributor typically purchases exported goods and resells them to retailers for a profit. Distributors do not sell to ultimate consumers. A distributor usually provides support and service for the product and carries an inventory and a supply of spare parts. Distributors may handle a range of noncompeting but complimentary products. A relationship with a distributor is normally established by contract, frequently with an initial trial period to assess performance.

Another export option is direct sales to foreign retailers, although this option is mainly limited to sales of consumer products to major retail chains. Direct sales to foreign retailers may allow higher sales prices by elimination of distributors, but as a practical matter, sales to foreign retailers will probably require the use of local sales representatives.

Lastly, direct sales to **end users** may be an option if your product is one that is purchased by a foreign government or a major foreign business or sold to foreign consumers on an Internet platform.

### *Exporting Services*

A good local representative may also be essential when exporting services. Some years ago, when I was working for an international inspection company, the firm wanted to sell its inspection services to the government of Ecuador. However, it had no presence or other contacts in that country. Because of the political and legal issues involved with a commercial contract with a foreign government, I decided to look for a highly respected and well-connected local lawyer as our representative. I obtained recommendations from an American colleague who had frequently done business in South America, flew to Quito, and interviewed several candidates. One in particular seemed appropriate, and we retained him as our local representative. He and his firm subsequently did an excellent job representing the company with the government of Ecuador.

Your local representative doesn't always have to be a lawyer or commercial agent. Recently, a small consulting firm that I was associated with wanted to bid on providing services to the customs administration of Kazakhstan (called the Customs Control Committee). I had previously worked as a consultant in Kazakhstan, and I had remained friendly with the owner and manager of a translation service that also provided services to Kazakh Customs. Through the translation service, we were able to obtain information that helped us win the services contract with Kazakh Customs.

### Importing Goods and Services

A foreign representative or buying agent can also be essential to importing goods or services. Importers frequently purchase goods from buying agents located in foreign markets. These businesses act as agents for importers in selecting vendors, reviewing samples, consulting regarding product design, and facilitating manufacturing of products. Normally the importer pays the agent a commission for her services. If the relationship is properly structured, in accordance with customs valuation procedures (discussed in chapter 6) a buying commission is not included in the dutiable value of the imported goods.

### Tool 10: Never Break a Rice Bowl

In China, "breaking a rice bowl" means destroying someone's means of livelihood. An important business ethic in China is to never break the rice bowl of a business partner. This requires adjusting business relationships in order to protect the economic interests of your trading partner. Chinese and many other East Asian trade partners expect this; this is why they are so careful to assess the character of potential business partners through lengthy meetings and social engagements prior to entering into a business relationship. To have long-term success in the business of international trade transactions, you must treat your foreign business partners with respect and take care not to "break their rice bowl" through overly one-sided business deals.

A careful vetting of prospective foreign business partners for ethical business conduct will also be important to your long-term business success. Do they cut corners when producing products or services? Are they corrupt? Is their workers' health and safety adequately protected? Illegal business practices, defects in products or services, and substandard treatment of workers by foreign business partners may adversely affect your business, even if you think you have insulated yourself through exculpatory contract clauses, arms'-length transactions, or by trading through a middleman. The recent tragedy in the Bangladesh garment industry is one example of how illegal practices and substandard treatment of workers can adversely affect supposedly independent business partners.

Bangladesh, a country located between India and Burma, is the largest exporter of garments in the world after China. However, working conditions for garment workers have been generally poor. In April 2013, more than 1,100 garment workers died when a factory building collapsed because of defective construction and management misfeasance. Most of the approximately 2,500 rescued cannot work because of injuries and trauma. The workers had been forced back into the building by management despite obvious structural problems.

As it turned out, this tragedy "blew back" on the many international clothing companies that had purchased garments from Bangladeshi producers either directly or through middlemen. These firms incurred substantial direct costs connected with the compensation of victims and incalculable indirect costs in lost business reputation. Efforts are underway now in Bangladesh to improve factory safety standards, increase the minimum wage, and permit the organization of garment-worker unions. But these efforts, although commendable, are too late for the workers killed and injured and may not rehabilitate the business reputation of the international clothing firms involved.

## *Takeaways for Chapter 2*

- Your product or service is ready to compete internationally if it is in demand, because it is unique, or it is in demand because of low price.
- E-commerce has leveled the international playing field for small businesses; B2B and B2C international sales have soared.
- Work your personal network to make sales.
- Attending trade shows and participating in business membership organizations will help you make international sales.
- Take advantage of government export promotion assistance.
- Be sure to visit your customers and potential customers.
- Be aware of cultural differences and use them to your advantage.
- Develop your negotiating skills.
- Use local representatives.
- Always act ethically.

# Chapter 3

# How Do You Make Sure You Get Paid?

Trust but verify. (doveryai no proveryai)

—President Ronald Reagan quoting a Russian proverb

There is no point in selling your goods or services in international commerce unless you are going to be paid their agreed value. Conversely, there is no point in paying for goods or services provided by an international vendor unless the goods or services will be delivered at the time promised and in the quality and quantity agreed. This chapter discusses some of the problems you can encounter in being paid or receiving the goods or services you contracted for and how to protect yourself against these problems.

## *The Problems*

The business world is full of con artists who promise to pay you for goods or services delivered and then do not meet their payment commitments. The business world is also full of firms that promise to deliver goods or services and then, after having been paid, fail to deliver the quality or quantity agreed or at the time required. Nonperformance can be fraudulent when a business never had any intention of delivering promised goods or services or for paying for goods or services received. Nonperformance can involve "sharp practice," as when businesses "renegotiate" after receiving the promised goods or services. I recount some of my experiences with these problems in chapter 9: The Author's Journal.

Most often, even when the transaction is legitimate and the parties all mean well, the failure to pay for goods or services received and the failure to deliver goods or services as promised may result from poor management, inadequate communications or unanticipated events. The seller miscalculated the time needed to deliver the goods or services. The requirements of the buyer were not adequately communicated in the agreement. Unexpected but foreseeable events, such as an equipment breakdown or a strike delaying production of goods or the loss of a key consultant required to provide services, prevent fulfillment of the agreement.

All these problems of nonperformance can increase when buyers and sellers are located in different countries. Communications and logistics are more complicated. Legal systems differ. Different cultures can give rise to misunderstandings. The process of payment for goods and services may be more complex. To be successful in international business it is important to be aware of these problems and to protect yourself against them.

### The Solutions: Four Steps to Improve Your Chances of Receiving Payment

As a small business, you probably can't afford to have a lawyer on staff to be involved in every business transaction. However, there are four steps you can follow that will greatly enhance your chances of receiving payment for goods and services delivered to your customers. These same procedures will also greatly enhance your chances of receiving the goods or services you paid for. These steps are as follows:

1. Craft an enforceable agreement.

2. Maintain good communications with your trading counterpart.

3. Control your goods and services until payment.

4. Provide for an effective dispute resolution process.

### Step 1: Craft an Enforceable Agreement

You will greatly increase your odds of being paid in full and on time for your goods or services if you have entered into an enforceable *written* international transaction agreement. This is probably the most important single step to assure payment. Reducing an agreement to writing clarifies possible ambiguities.

> An **agreement**, or contract, is an exchange of promises between two or more parties with respect to a specific subject or thing. For an agreement to be valid, the parties must be able to contract (for example, be of legal age and be an authorized representative of the principal); there must be lawful consideration (something of value given by both parties); and there must be assent of the contracting parties. The form of an agreement may be oral, in writing, or under seal (notarized) with witnesses.

From my experience, verbal promises made during negotiations sometimes turn out to be puffery—promises made to induce you to agree that your counterpart does not include in a written agreement. Sometimes when you question your counterpart about the absence of a provision you thought had been agreed to, they will apologetically say, "Oh, yes, management said we couldn't do that" or, "Our lawyers told us not to include that." I recently had this experience. I had agreed verbally to undertake a consulting engagement for one hundred days in a foreign country. However, when I received a draft of the written contract, the time had been reduced to thirty-five days, and my proposed compensation had also been reduced. When I brought this to my counterpart's attention and said I wouldn't undertake the engagement unless the original terms were reinstated, the contract was changed to reflect the original understanding.

### *Employ Sound Negotiating Tactics*

One-sided agreements are much more likely to break down than agreements that have been carefully negotiated and where both sides derive significant advantages if the agreement's terms are carried out. If a negotiator browbeats the other party into one-sided concessions, that party will likely look for any excuse to renegotiate or terminate the agreement. However, frequently a solution that protects the interests of both parties can be negotiated. As an example, when I was a director for a metals-and-minerals trading company, we concluded an agreement with a South African supplier that provided for a low purchase price, protecting our interests in the event that the resale price was also low, but also paying a percentage of our resale price above a fixed dollar level to the South Africans in the event that prices in the US market increased.

A systematic approach to business negotiations includes recognition of culturally driven negotiation tactics, thorough preparation designed to uncover all your potential business partner's interests, building relationships, developing a win-win solution, and knowing your best alternative to a negotiated agreement. Negotiating tactics are discussed in chapter 2.

### *Make Sure All Provisions Are Expressed Clearly in Writing and That the Agreement Is Enforceable*

Perhaps the most frequent mistake when entering into international agreements for the sale of goods or services is to not express clearly the agreement in writing. Frequently, agreements are reached during a business meeting at which the parties verbally agree on terms. But unless all the terms are reduced to writing, there are possibilities for misunderstandings. Moreover, depending on the applicable law, verbal agreements may be unenforceable. This is the case in the United States where, as a general rule, all commercial agreements exceeding five hundred dollars must be in writing. Therefore, don't assume you have an enforceable agreement until it has been reduced into writing and signed by the parties.

An important additional requirement for an enforceable agreement is that the person signing a written agreement for his or her business be legally authorized to represent the business. Sometimes negotiators will use this to their advantage in negotiations, as when a sales representative concludes a verbal contract and then says, "My vice president says we can't agree to such-and-such term." Some automobile dealerships are notorious for this tactic.

In some countries, an agreement is not enforceable unless it is "sealed" by the parties (the authorized signers sign with their corporate seal), and their signatures are then notarized. I was amazed when working in Kazakhstan about the number of notary offices I saw in major cities. There was one on almost every block. The reason was that all business and government documents had to be notarized to have legal effect. Why this is still required in countries like Kazakhstan in the twenty-first century is a mystery. It may be that notaries have sufficient political power to prevent modernization of the formality requirements.

For international agreements, an official language or languages of the agreement should usually be specified to avoid misinterpretation. For example, an agreement could provide that English is the official language or that English and Chinese are the official languages. This, of course, is not an issue if all parties to an agreement use one official language. International organizations, such as the World Trade Organization, may specify that several specific languages are official languages. (In the case of the WTO, the official languages are English, French, and Spanish.)

A typical problem that can create ambiguity in a written agreement is the so-called "battle of the forms." For example, if your customer uses purchase invoices that contain standard terms and your business uses sales invoices that also contain standard terms, these standard provisions can conflict. If there is a subsequent dispute, it may then be difficult or impossible to determine which provisions will apply. Issues of this sort can be resolved when the written agreement is entered into by carefully reviewing the boilerplate terms and then specifying the terms agreed to by both parties by signing them and deleting the inapplicable terms.

### When Possible, Provide for the Applicable Law

For international trade transactions, each nation has a somewhat different law of contracts and agreements that may be enforceable or unenforceable based upon the particular law applied. What is an enforceable agreement in the United States may not be enforceable in China or Japan. Similarly, what is an enforceable agreement in India may not be enforceable in Russia. The easiest and best way to resolve this issue is to insist in your written agreements that the law of the country in which you reside will be applied to interpret the contract. For example, if your business is located in the United States, the contract may provide that "the law of the United States, the State of New York, shall apply to the interpretation of this contract and any dispute arising from the contract shall be resolved in the courts of New York."

Unfortunately, insisting that the contract be interpreted and enforced according to your local law is not always possible. As a small business, you may not have the bargaining power of your supplier or customer in a foreign country; therefore, they may insist as a condition of the contract that their local law be applied to interpret it. If this is a "take it or leave it" condition, then you may have no choice other than to accept the provision or walk away from the potential contract. However, if the parties agree, a compromise may be possible, such as selecting the laws and dispute-resolution process of a neutral third country prominent in international business— for example: "The law of Switzerland shall apply to the interpretation of this agreement and any dispute arising from this contract shall be resolved by arbitration in Zurich, Switzerland under the Rules of Arbitration of the International Chamber of Commerce."

### *Different Types of International Commercial Agreements*

There are a variety of international commercial agreements. In addition to contracts for the international sale of goods and services, there are agency and distributorship agreements, franchise agreements, licensing and technology transfer agreements, joint ventures, natural resource concession agreements, and so forth. Each type of agreement is designed to accomplish a particular business objective. Since this book focuses on transactions involving goods and services only, these two types are discussed. However, if the international trade transaction you plan involves a technology transfer, the selection of a local representative, or a joint venture, these other agreement types are applicable.

- ### *Contracts for the International Sale of Goods*

Agreements for the sale of goods are by far the most common type of international trade transaction. In 2013, merchandise exports amounted to about $18.8 trillion, roughly 25 percent of world GDP.[37] As outlined in chapter 1, world trade in goods has grown rapidly as tariffs and nontariff barriers have been reduced and modern technologies have lessened transaction costs.

For the international sales of goods, an international convention, the United Nations Convention on Contracts for the International Sale of Goods (CISG), provides uniformity regarding applicable law for the businesses when both parties are domiciled in states that are contracting members or the rules of private international law otherwise result in its application. In addition, parties not residing in a CISG contracting state may follow CISG provisions by choice. As of early 2016, the CISG had 84 contracting states, including the United States and all major trading economies except for the United Kingdom. Because of the importance of CISG for international trade transactions for goods, its provisions are summarized here. For details, consult the specific terms of the CISG.[38]

---

[37] WTO statistics (2014).
[38] http://www.uncitral.org/pdf/english/texts/sales/cisg/V1056997–CISG-e-book.pdf

The CISG provides that a contract of sale does not have to be in writing and may be proved by any means, including witnesses. (However, as previously discussed, oral agreements frequently lead to enforcement problems.) A proposal to conclude a contract constitutes an offer, if it is addressed to a specific person, is sufficiently definite, and indicates the intention of the offeror to be bound in case of acceptance. A proposal is sufficiently definite if it specifies the goods involved and fixes or makes provisions for fixing prices and quantities. An offer becomes effective when it reaches the offeree. An offer may be withdrawn if the withdrawal reaches the offeree before or at the same time as the offer. An offer, even if irrevocable, is terminated when rejection reaches the offeror.

A statement made by the offeree or other conduct by the offeree indicating assent to an offer is acceptance. An acceptance becomes effective at the moment assent reaches the offeror. A reply to an offer indicating acceptance but containing additional provisions is not an acceptance but a counteroffer. However, if the counteroffer does not materially alter the terms, it is an acceptance unless the offeror promptly communicates an objection. If he or she does not object, the terms of the contract include the additional terms in the counteroffer.

A breach of contract by one of the parties is fundamental if it results in such detriment to the other party as to deprive him or her of what he or she is entitled to expect under the contract unless the breaching party did not foresee and a reasonable party in the same position would not have foreseen such a result. A contract may be modified or terminated by agreement of the parties. However, a contract in writing that provides for modification or termination only in writing may not be otherwise modified or terminated unless a party's conduct indicated modification or termination, and the conduct was relied upon by the other party.

The seller is obligated to deliver the goods and hand over related documents. Delivery of the goods must be at the time specified in the agreement or, if the time is not specified, at a reasonable time after the conclusion of the agreement. Delivery must take place as indicated in the agreement or, if not specifically indicated, by placing the goods at the buyer's disposal at the seller's place of business. The goods delivered must conform to the quantity, quality, and description set out in the agreement and must be packaged as required in the agreement.

The buyer loses the right to object to lack of conformity of goods with the contract if he or she does not give notice to the seller specifying the problems within a reasonable period of time after discovering the problem. The seller must deliver goods free from any rights of a third party. However, for intellectual property claims, this obligation of the seller is not applicable if the buyer knew or should have known about third party claims or the seller relied on technical specifications provided by the buyer.

If the seller fails to perform any of his or her obligations under the agreement, the buyer may require specific performance by the seller, fix an additional reasonable period of time for performance, declare the agreement voided, reduce the contract price if goods do not conform to the contract, or refuse to accept the goods.

If the buyer fails to perform any of his or her obligations under the agreement, the seller may require the buyer to pay the price, take delivery, or perform the other provisions of the agreement. In addition, the seller may declare the agreement voided when the buyer's failure to perform amounts to a fundamental breach of the agreement.

Loss or damage to the goods after risk has passed to the buyer does not discharge the buyer from making payment for the goods unless the loss or damage is the result of an act or omission of the seller.

Damages for breach of agreement by one party consist of an amount equal to the loss, including loss of profit, by the other party. However, such damages cannot exceed the loss that the breaching party foresaw, or should have foreseen, at the time the agreement was concluded. If a party fails to pay the price for the goods, the seller is also entitled to interest on any claim for damages.

Preservation of the Goods: If a seller is in possession of the goods after the buyer has failed to pay the price or otherwise accept the goods, the seller must take reasonable steps to preserve them, and he or she is entitled to retain them until the buyer reimburses his or her additional expenses. If a buyer is in possession of the goods and intends to reject them, he or she must take reasonable steps to preserve them, and he or she is entitled to retain them until reimbursed for his or her reasonable expenses.

- *Contracts for the International Sale of Services*

International trade in services is less significant in volume than trade in goods, but developed countries, such as the United States, have a comparative advantage in services trade and export substantially more services than they import. According to WTO statistics, exports of services amounted to about $4.6 trillion in 2013. Transportation and travel services accounted for the largest amount.

No international convention exists that sets forth rules regarding agreements for the international sale of services. This is understandable in view of the wide variety of service agreements, which encompass everything from accounting and financial services to medical, educational, software, and Internet providers; transportation and tourism; construction contracts; management services; consulting; and so forth. Generally, the enforceability of these agreements depends on the intent of the parties as expressed in the agreement. However, in some instances, such as management and consulting contracts, standard forms have evolved.

> ### International Chamber of Commerce
>
> The International Chamber of Commerce, or ICC, is a global business membership organization that has developed a variety of trade tools to assist international trade transactions. These include Incoterms, arbitration rules and procedures, ATA carnets, certificates of origin, documentary credits, and model contracts.

### Review of Agreements by an Attorney and Model Contracts

If an agreement for the international sale of goods or services is of a high value, it is prudent to have it drafted, or at least reviewed, by a qualified attorney. A good rule of thumb for doing this is if the agreement's value will represent a significant percentage of your business's annual revenue. However, it is usually not cost-effective for small businesses to use legal services for small or routine international transactions. The best way for a small business to handle drafting agreements for routine international transactions is to develop a model agreement for its business containing standard terms. The model should be reviewed and revised by a qualified attorney before being used.

The International Chamber of Commerce is one source for model agreements for the international sale of goods or services. The ICC publishes a model international sales contract, a guide to negotiating and drafting international commercial contracts, a model international franchising contract, a model international trademark license, a model agency contract, and other helpful models. Of particular assistance, the ICC has developed what are known as Incoterms; these define the respective rights and obligations of the seller and buyer regarding deliver of goods. There are currently eleven Incoterms ranging from Ex Works (EXW), where the buyer assumes all transport, insurance, duty and other obligations, to Delivered Duty Paid (DDP), where the seller assumes all obligations required to deliver to the buyer's place of business. Free on Board (FOB) and Cost, Insurance, and Freight (CIF) are well-known INCO terms used for water transport.

Other sources of model agreements include the United Nations Commission for International Trade Law (UNCITRAL), which has compiled international trade transaction contract terms, the International Trade Centre in Geneva, which has published model contracts for small firms doing international business, and formbooks published by legal scholars.[39]

### Step 2: Maintain Good Communication

Good communication with your international trade partner is essential to the success of international trade transactions.

---

[39] See, e.g., Goldsweig, Shelly B. and David M. Battram. *Negotiating and Structuring International Commercial Transactions.* American Bar Association 1991.

This includes frequent contacts with your counterpart's management about existing and prospective transactions and your business relationship in general. I have seen many situations where after making a sale or concluding a contract, communications dry up. This results in sellers not being aware of subsequent developments in the buyer's business that can affect transactions, and buyers not being aware of difficulties being experienced by the seller in carrying out contracts.

If communication is inadequate, the first time a buyer may know about problems in providing goods that have been ordered or services that have been purchased is when goods or services are not delivered at the time provided for in the agreement, or they are delivered but not as was specified in the agreement. Conversely, the first that a seller may know about financial or other problems experienced by the buyer is when goods or services have been delivered, and the payment required in the agreement is not made.

Continuous communication between partners serves to prevent performance breakdowns or at least provides advance warning when difficulties develop. In international transactions, cultural differences can present particular challenges regarding maintaining good communication and receiving appropriate updates. For example, in some Asian cultures, there may be a "loss of face" in communicating difficulties in meeting production and shipment schedules. In this situation, telephone calls or even personal visits may result in statements saying that everything is okay when it is not. It may be necessary to "read between the lines" in some situations by persistent questioning and/or relying on third party information to be fully informed about a foreign partner's activities.

One option to foster good communication is to provide for periodic progress reports in agreements for the international sale of goods or services. Another option is to designate communication counterparts in an agreement that will be held responsible for agreement updates. Third parties may also be useful in obtaining information about your foreign business partner. A third party can be a credit reporting agency, your company's representative in the foreign country in question, an Embassy official who has responsibility for aiding the business interests of your country, a logistics provider—such as a customs agent or freight forwarder who is familiar with your foreign partner's business—trade associations, or other customers or vendors also doing business with your foreign partner.

I learned my lesson about maintaining good ongoing communication with a client early in my career as a lawyer. After leaving a position at the US Treasury Department and starting a law firm with several other lawyers, I was fortunate in being retained as the lawyer for a major US producer of tubular products. Our client wanted us to bring a trade action against imports of tubular products from Japan. We were eventually successful in obtaining an antidumping order imposing additional duties on the imports. However, if I had maintained better communications with our client, I would have become aware that their business situation had changed, and they were no longer interested in maintaining trade restrictions on imports from Japan. They ended up discharging me as their lawyer and hiring different legal counsel whom they believed was more appropriate for their new business realities. Thus, my inattention to good communications cost me a valuable client.

Later, I put my hard-earned lesson to use when I was the project manager for a consulting project in Russia. I knew from the beginning of the project that the Russians would be difficult clients and that we would not be paid unless they approved of all aspects of our work. To minimize difficulties, I prepared detailed monthly status reports and presented them at meetings with our client so they would be fully informed about our progress. I made sure that the Russians signed each monthly status report, acknowledging that they had read it and agreed with progress to date.

As it turned out, we had a number of difficulties when carrying out the assignment. In each instance, we notified our client promptly about the difficulty and obtained their assent for our corrective actions. In addition, during the status meetings, our client had many comments about our work, ranging from the inadequacy of translators we were using to providing data for an economic impact analysis that the contract required us to perform. We ultimately completed the contract successfully and were congratulated for our work. This was due in no small part to the communication system that we established at the beginning of the project.

### Step 3: Control Your Goods and Services until Payment

It is important to maintain control of your goods and services for as long as possible to assure payment. There are a number of methods that may be employed to accomplish this.

- #### Controlling Your Exports and Imports of Goods

Cash payment in advance. For an exporter, the most risk-free transaction is to require cash payment in advance of shipping the goods to a buyer. This, of course, is the riskiest transaction for the buyer because the buyer has not inspected the goods to assure that they conform to the agreement, and the buyer incurs the expense before receiving the goods at his or her place of business in his or her foreign country. For goods shipped by ocean freight, it may be weeks before the goods are received by the buyer.

A contract requiring cash payment in advance for goods can utilize any one of the eleven Incoterms that relate to the seller's and buyer's responsibilities regarding transport and insurance costs and government requirements and charges. For example, if the sale is Ex Works (EXW), the seller's responsibility is only to make the goods available for pickup by the buyer at the seller's designated place of business. If the sale is Free on Board (FOB), the seller is responsible for delivering the goods on board the vessel designated by the buyer at the named port of shipment. At that point, the buyer owns the goods and assumes all liability for the cost of freight, government charges, and insurance to cover casualty loss. If the sale is Cost Insurance and Freight (CIF), the seller is responsible for delivering the goods onboard the designated vessel at the named port and also for paying the costs and freight to the port of destination. Although the risk of loss passes to the buyer when the goods are on board, the seller is also responsible for insuring the goods against loss. If the sale is Delivered Duty Paid (DDP), the seller is responsible for delivering the goods at the buyer's designated place of business and for paying all expenses in connection with the shipment, including import duties and taxes in the country of delivery.

Probably the two most commonly used Incoterms are Delivered at Place (DAP) and Free Carrier (FCA). DAP means that the seller delivers when the goods are placed at the disposal of the buyer on the arriving means of transport ready for unloading at the named place of destination. The seller pays the expenses and bears the risk of bringing the goods to the place of destination. FCA, in contrast, means that the seller delivers the goods to the carrier or another person nominated by the buyer at the seller's premises or another named place. The risk passes to the buyer at that point. If you are the importer buying from a major multinational firm you may be better off buying DAP and taking advantage of the seller's ability to obtain low freight rates. If you are an exporter, FCA is generally advantageous because no expenses or liability are assumed for transit shipments.

In cash payment in advance transactions, the buyer can reduce the risk of goods not conforming to the agreement by personally inspecting the goods prior to shipment. This, however, may entail significant international travel expenses. As an alternative to personal inspection, a buyer can retain an independent international inspection company to inspect the goods prior to shipment, conduct any necessary tests, and issue a report regarding whether the goods conform to the agreement. These firms maintain offices and agents in most countries throughout the world to carry out inspection work. Inspection companies usually guarantee their services in the event that subsequent defects in the quality and quantity of the goods are discovered.

Cash payments may be made by credit card for small transactions, but the normal method is by international wire transfer of funds from the bank of the buyer to the bank of the seller. Exporters should provide clear routing information to the importer so that the importer can make appropriate arrangements with the transmitting bank. When this is not done, a transaction can be jeopardized.

The buyer paying by credit card for goods will incur an international transaction fee that will be a small percentage of the amount of the transaction. In the case of payment by wire transfer, the sender of the transfer (buyer) will also incur a fee.

Be very cautious about accepting currency for a cash payment. Cash payments using large sums of currency may indicate money laundering or other illegal funds. This problem is discussed in chapter 6. Cash payments received over ten thousand dollars have to be reported to the Internal Revenue Service (IRS) in the United States (most other countries have similar requirements). This can be done electronically. Customs administrations routinely screen for travelers carrying cash amounts exceeding ten thousand dollars, and the failure to report cash transported on passenger customs entry declarations may lead to confiscation of the money and additional penalties.

> ***Rising Franc Upends Daily Life in Swiss Borderlands***
>
> "Switzerland's decision [in January 2015] to lift the cap on the franc sent the currency flying 40 percent against the euro and roiled financial markets world-wide."
>
> —Wall Street Journal, February 22, 2015

Another issue relates to the currency used in the transaction. If the seller is located in the United States, and the buyer insists on using a currency other than US dollars, the seller risks a loss if the currency specified in the agreement depreciates against the US dollar between the time of the agreement and the time of payment. The small business seller can protect him- or herself against currency fluctuation in a number of ways. First, the seller can demand cash in advance, and the current spot market rate will determine the dollar value of the foreign payment. (A spot transaction is when the seller and buyer agree to payment using that day's exchange rate and settle within two business days. This is not always foolproof. While most exchange rate changes take place over a period of time, when I was working in Kazakhstan in 2014, the Central Bank suddenly devalued Kazakh currency by about 15 percent without notice.

Second, the seller can enter into a foreign exchange forward contract by selling a set amount of dollars at a preagreed exchange rate with delivery up to one year in the future. There are no fees or charges for forward contracts, but the seller must deliver the currency promised, regardless of whether the buyer pays on time or not.

Third, the seller can purchase a foreign exchange options hedge for a fee, which gives the seller the option to deliver an agreed upon amount of foreign currency at a set exchange rate during the life of the option.

Because cash payment in advance may not be acceptable for many buyers, alternative payment methods that minimize risk for the seller have evolved. These include letters of credit and documentary collections. In addition, export credit insurance and factoring may be used to protect against losses from open account sales.

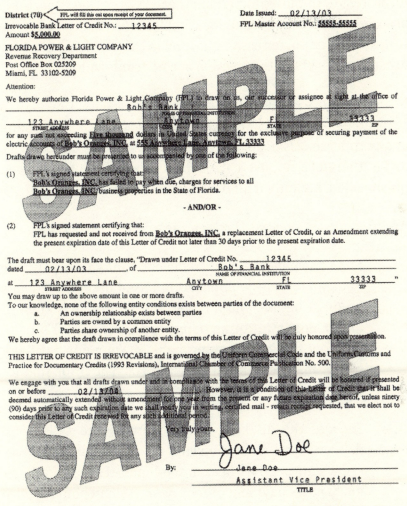

IRREVOCABLE BANK LETTER OF CREDIT

District (70) ◄ *FPL will fill this out upon receipt of your document.*                Date Issued: __02/13/03__

Irrevocable Bank Letter of Credit No.: __12345__                FPL Master Account No.: 55555-55555

Amount $5,000.00

**FLORIDA POWER & LIGHT COMPANY**
Revenue Recovery Department
Post Office Box 025209
Miami, FL 33102-5209

Attention:

We hereby authorize Florida Power & Light Company (FPL) to draw on us, our successor or assignee at sight at the office of
_____Bob's Bank_____
__123 Anywhere Lane__        __Anytown__        __FL__        __33333__
NAME OF FINANCIAL INSTITUTION
STREET ADDRESS        CITY        STATE        ZIP
for any sum not exceeding Five thousand dollars in United States currency for the exclusive purpose of securing payment of the
electric accounts of Bob's Oranges, INC, at 555 Anywhere Lane, Anytown, FL 33333

Drafts drawn hereunder must be presented to us accompanied by one of the following:

(1)    FPL's signed statement certifying that:
Bob's Oranges, INC, has failed to pay when due, charges for services to all
Bob's Oranges, INC, business properties in the State of Florida.

- AND/OR -

(2)    FPL's signed statement certifying that:
FPL has requested and not received from Bob's Oranges, INC, a replacement Letter of Credit, or an Amendment extending
the present expiration date of this Letter of Credit not later than 30 days prior to the present expiration date.

The draft must bear upon its face the clause, "Drawn under Letter of Credit No. ___12345___

dated __02/13/03__, of _____Bob's Bank_____
NAME OF FINANCIAL INSTITUTION
at __123 Anywhere Lane__        __Anytown__        __FL__        __33333__ "
STREET ADDRESS        CITY        STATE        ZIP

You may draw up to the above amount in one or more drafts.

To our knowledge, none of the following entity conditions exists between parties of the document:
a.    An ownership relationship exists between parties
b.    Parties are owned by a common entity
c.    Parties share ownership of another entity.

We hereby agree that the draft drawn in compliance with the terms of this Letter of Credit will be duly honored upon presentation.

THIS LETTER OF CREDIT IS IRREVOCABLE and is governed by the Uniform Commercial Code and the Uniform Customs and
Practice for Documentary Credits (1993 Revisions), International Chamber of Commerce Publication No. 500.

We engage with you that all drafts drawn under and in compliance with the terms of this Letter of Credit will be honored if presented
on or before __02/13/04__. However, it is a condition of this Letter of Credit that it shall be
deemed automatically extended without amendment for one year from the present or any future expiration date hereof, unless ninety
(90) days prior to any such expiration date we shall notify you in writing, certified mail - return receipt requested, that we elect not to
consider this Letter of Credit renewed for any such additional period.

Very truly yours,

*Jane Doe*

By: _____Jane Doe_____
_____Assistant Vice President_____
TITLE

Form 991R (Non-Stocked), Rev. 7/98

Letters of Credit (L/Cs). For exporters, L/Cs are the most secure form of payment after cash in advance. An L/C is a guarantee by the buyer's bank that payment will be made to the exporter as long as the terms and conditions stated in the L/C have been complied with and all required shipping documents have been presented. The buyer pays his or her bank a fee, usually a percentage of the value of the transaction, for this service. L/Cs protect both the exporter and the importer. The exporter is assured of payment if he or she complies with the terms of the L/C, and the importer is safeguarded in the event the goods or other aspects of the transaction are nonconforming.

In theory, L/Cs can be revocable or irrevocable. However, a revocable L/C can be changed or cancelled by the issuing bank at any time, so it is basically worthless as a protective device and is, therefore, not used. An irrevocable L/C can be changed or cancelled, but only if all parties give their consent.

An L/C transaction goes through the following steps:

- First, the buyer applies to his her bank for an L/C. The bank analyzes the application based upon the buyer's credit situation, and if it approves, it prepares the L/C and sends it to an advising bank. The buyer's bank is known as the "issuing bank." (Your normal bank officer may be unfamiliar with L/Cs. The trade finance departments of major banks will have this expertise.)

- Second, the advising bank contacts the seller and delivers the L/C to the seller. At this point, the buyer knows an L/C has been issued, and the issuing bank guarantees payment as long as the seller complies with all terms and document requirements. If the seller is unfamiliar with the issuing bank, he or she may require a confirming bank—a bank he or she is familiar with in his or her country. The confirming bank, for an additional fee, then adds its guarantee to that of the issuing bank. Typically, the confirming bank is also the advising bank.

- Third, after receiving the L/C, the seller ships the goods and provides all required documents to the advising bank. The advising bank normally pays the draft and then forwards all documents to the issuing bank for collection.

There are a number of different types of L/Cs. When an L/C is transferrable, the payment obligation can be transferred to one or more second beneficiaries. This is of particular importance to agents, brokers, trading companies, and other middlemen who may be concerned about attempting to collect an unsecured commission or fee.

A middleman may not have enough capital to buy the goods from the seller before he or she resells to his or her ultimate customer. He or she can solve this problem by having the ultimate customer open a transferrable L/C. The middleman can then have part or all of the L/C transferred to the seller. The confirming bank pays the supplier when the goods are shipped, and he or she furnishes conforming documents.

> ### *What Are Trade Documents?*
>
> Depending on the destination and the type of goods, a number of documents may be required for international shipments. These can include airway bills, bills of lading, commercial invoices, consular invoices, certificates of origin, inspection certificates, dock and warehouse receipts, shipper's export declarations, export licenses, export packing lists, and insurance certificates. For an explanation of these documents and examples, see "A Basic Guide to Exporting," US Department of Commerce, http://export.gov/basicguide/eg_main_017244.asp.

The middleman can then substitute his or her own invoice and receive the difference between the L/C amount opened by the buyer and the L/C amount transferred to the seller. This is his or her commission or fee for arranging the deal.

Revolving L/Cs may be used for ongoing transactions. Revolving L/Cs involve a credit line being restored to its original amount each time it is drawn down by a shipment. A standby L/C is used not to pay for specific shipments, but as a guarantee in the event a particular shipment is not paid as required by agreement. After parties gain confidence in their business relationship through cash in advance payments or regular L/C transactions, shipments can proceed on an open account basis, with a standby L/C providing a guarantee in the event of default. This is a less expensive option than opening a new L/C for each transaction.

L/Cs are not cheap. Banks typically charge a percentage of the dollar value of the transaction, and the fee may also vary with the complexity of the underlying transaction. In addition, as might be expected, the governing rules of interpretation for L/Cs favor the banks, so their obligations are limited in scope. I recall one instance when the confirming bank refused to pay because the L/C spelled "China," "Chine," a typographical error. It takes time and effort to sort out this sort of mistake, and in the meantime, the bank holds all funds.

Documentary Collections. Documentary collections (D/Cs) involve the collection of payment by the banking system. When the goods are shipped, the exporter sends the relevant shipping documents to its bank, and these documents are then sent on to the importer's bank (collecting bank) with instructions for payment. D/Cs are based upon a bank draft that requires the importer to pay the face amount either at sight (documents against payment) or on a specified date after the delivery of the goods (documents against acceptance). The draft gives instructions indicating the documents required for transfer of title to the goods. Since payment for the goods is not received until the goods are delivered to the buyer, the Incoterms used may be those where the seller bears the cost of transport, insurance, and government fees required to deliver the goods to a port terminal or place in the country of importation (DAT or DAP).

D/Cs are simple, fast, and less costly than L/Cs and ownership (title) to goods is retained for ocean shipments. However, D/Cs are riskier for an exporter than L/Cs because the banks do not verify the accuracy of documents nor do they guarantee payment. If the buyer reneges, the seller may have to dispose of the shipped goods in the foreign country or incur the expense of reimported them.

**Open Account**

From the buyer's perspective, purchasing goods on open account with payment typically due anywhere from thirty to ninety days after receipt is the most favorable way to conduct international trade transactions. The buyer's capital is not tied up; in fact, if terms are ninety days after delivery, the buyer may have already sold the goods and received payment by the time he or she has to pay the exporter. Moreover, if there are any problems with the quality or quantity of the goods, the buyer can refuse payment until the problems are corrected. From the seller's point of view, however, selling on open account in international trade transactions is the riskiest arrangement. The seller, in effect, provides financing to the buyer until payment is made. However, in very competitive markets the seller may have to sell on open account to get the business.

There are several ways that a seller may be able to protect against losses when selling on open account. First, and most important, the buyer's creditworthiness should be checked out through local sources in the country of importation. Sources for doing this include local lawyers and business associations, credit reporting agencies, and embassy commercial officers. Bank references can also be requested.

Second, obtaining export credit insurance should be investigated. Export credit insurance can provide protection against both commercial losses and political risk when selling on open account. Premiums are individually determined based upon risk factors and can be lower for experienced exporters. Multibuyer policies cost less than single-buyer policies. However, commercial insurers may not cover risks in certain countries, a substantial "deductible" may mean that considerably less than 100 percent of a potential loss is insured, and insurance rates may be high. The Ex-Im Bank currently maintains an export credit insurance program that may operate in countries where commercial insurance is not available. Products must be shipped from the United States and contain at least 50 percent US content, and military products are not eligible.

> ### Getting Paid for Machinery Exports
>
> A small manufacturing firm based in California sells its manufacturing equipment in more than fifty foreign countries, including many developing countries. Sales prices are in the lower six-figure range; currency specified is always in US dollars. Their normal terms of sale are 40 percent cash in advance and the balance by L/C payable on presentation of the bill of lading. Occasionally, the payment of the advance can be a problem because of currency controls in the customer's country. Terms are CIF or CFR. After the equipment is delivered, the firm sends a technician to the customer to train their employees and correct any equipment problems.

Third, export factoring may be an option. A "factor" is a bank or financial firm that purchases invoices or accounts receivable of exporters at a cash discount from face value. The factor assumes the risk of payment by the foreign buyer and handles collections. This allows small exporters to eliminate the risk of nonpayment in return for discounting receivables. However, factoring is generally more costly than export credit insurance, and it may not be available for sales to some developing countries.

### Controlling Your Exports and Imports of Services

Currently, about 20 percent of international trade is trade in services. There are many different types of services provided in international trade. However, the WTO divides international trade in services into four types or modes:

1. Cross-border supply, or services provided from one country to another: These are services provided where both the provider and user remain in their home country, and the services are provided by telephone, e-mail, or some other means of communication. Examples include a lawyer in the United States sending advice to a client in Italy or a call center in India providing product technical advice to a consumer in Canada.

2. Consumption abroad, or firms or consumers making use of services in another country: Examples include traveling from the United States to Italy for tourism and traveling from the United Kingdom to India for medical services.

3. Commercial presence, or a foreign business setting up branches or subsidiaries to provide services in another country: Examples include Citi Bank establishing a branch in Zurich, Switzerland; or Munich Re reinsurance establishing an office in New York; or United Airlines establishing a sales office in Beijing.

4. Individuals traveling from one country to provide services in another. Examples include consultants, lawyers, teachers, software designers, and interpreters.

National governments impose a variety of restrictions on the provision of international trade in services, particularly on mode 3, commercial presence, and mode 4, individuals traveling from one country to another to provide services. These restrictions are discussed in chapter 6: How Do I Navigate Government Regulations?

Because of the wide variety of international agreements for the provision of services, it is best to employ a qualified lawyer to assist in the preparation of an agreement that will increase the likelihood of prompt payment for services provided. However, there are model agreements that may be helpful. The International Trade Centre's publication *Model Contracts for Small Firms* is one source.

There are a number of provisions that I can recommend from my experience for inclusion in an international agreement for the provision of services. First, if you are the service provider, consider negotiating an initial "retainer" payment from your client of 10 percent to 15 percent to fund start-up costs for providing the service. Retainers demonstrate the commitment of the client to your services and also recognize your commitment to promptly providing the services. Second, rather than providing for one fee at the end of the project, if the project is lengthy, break it into four or five components and require that a progress payment be made after the completion of each segment. For lawyers, it is frequently customary to bill services on a monthly basis. If so, this should be specifically provided for in the agreement. Third, the agreement should permit the service provider to suspend services in the event that periodic payments by the client are in arrears. Fourth, the client's and the service provider's responsible officials for the agreement should be specifically named in the agreement and regular communications provided for regarding the status of work and administrative matters. Fifth, in the event of problems, the applicable law and an efficient dispute-resolution process should be specified.

In situations where there are doubts about the ability or willingness of the client to pay, the agreement can also include a requirement that the client post a financial guarantee with a third party that will compensate the service provider in the event of a default. Banks and insurance companies regularly offer these performance guarantees. Conversely, if the client requires assurances regarding the performance of the service provider, the service provider may also be required to post a performance bond. This is frequently required for construction contracts.

### Step 4: Provide for an Effective Dispute-Resolution Process

The first three steps discussed in this chapter—crafting an enforceable agreement, maintaining good communications with your trading counterpart, and controlling your goods and services until payment—are designed to minimize problems regarding your trading relationships. But on occasion, problems will occur that will have to be resolved by some sort of dispute-resolution process. If you do not provide for a specific dispute-resolution process in your agreement, you may be at the mercy of the processes provided by a foreign legal system. You may be subject to legal action in the courts of the foreign country in which your trading partner resides and have the case determined by a judge not knowledgeable about your business and naturally sympathetic to the claims made by his or her local national. Step 4 explains how you can avoid this very undesirable situation.

### Dispute Resolution by Mutual Consent: Adaption, Renegotiation, and Mediation

Contract adaption refers to the inclusion of terms in an agreement that permit the agreement to conform to changed conditions or circumstances without automatic termination or the need for renegotiation. Short-term agreements usually do not require adaptation, but longer-term agreements require flexibility in view of likely changed underlying circumstances. A *force majeure* clause that automatically suspends performance obligations in the event of a war or natural disaster is one example of contract adaption. Another example might be an agreement that calls for performance in a particular currency, but that currency ceases to exist because the country adopts the euro or US dollar as its currency. These situations can be dealt with by including a "variation and change" clause that permits the parties to alter materials and specifications based on changed circumstances; a "price escalation clause" that permits the seller to maintain her profit margin in the event of unanticipated increases in materials costs; a "tax clause" that protects against changes in government tax policy that affects the agreement; and similar provisions.

Renegotiation means the voluntary adjustment of an agreement to preserve the business relationship. The obligation to renegotiate can be included in an agreement, but if one of the parties is recalcitrant, renegotiation will not succeed. If your business partners are located in China or other East Asian countries, they will likely expect you to renegotiate in the event of changed circumstances to accommodate the business relationship. This is the principle of "never break a rice bowl" discussed in chapter 2.

Mediation means a negotiation facilitated by a neutral third party. Mediation can be either informal or formal, involving the use of established procedures, the exchange of information, and the issuance of a written opinion by the mediator. Mediation is essentially a structured, guided negotiation where the neutral mediator promotes fact-finding, the creation of options, and, if successful, a negotiated resolution. The obligation to mediate before taking other dispute-resolution action can be included in an agreement. However, the result of mediation is not enforceable; therefore, if there is no realistic hope of a negotiated solution, mediation can just delay ultimate resolution of the dispute.

### Dispute Resolution by Adjudication: Arbitration and Court Litigation

Litigation is rarely a satisfactory experience for a business. It is expensive, time consuming, and the outcome is uncertain. Moreover, participation in trade litigation can antagonize customers and business affiliates. Nonetheless, in some circumstances, litigation is the only alternative available to collect money owed, to enforce contract or intellectual property rights, or to correct an unfair trade practice.

Bear in mind, however, that litigation is the "nuclear option" in a business relationship. Once you enter on that path, it is unlikely, in my experience, that you will continue any sort of business or personal relationship with your adversary in the future. In my career, I have been personally involved with litigation regarding the distribution of business gains or losses twice— once in connection with losses on a long-term real estate lease and once in connection with the distribution of profits from a trading company. I was successful in one case and lost the other. My adversaries in both instances had previously been close business associates and personal friends, but after the litigation, we never had contact again.

If despite all the precautions previously suggested in this chapter, it becomes necessary to litigate to assert your business rights, you will be in a much better position if you have provided for this eventuality in your international trade-transaction agreement. This is like a chess game: If the other side knows that you are well prepared for litigation and have a winning position, they may concede.

Arbitration is the preferred method of resolving international business disputes by litigation; arbitration is a binding determination by an independent and neutral tribunal regarding the rights and obligations of the parties. However, arbitration does not operate completely independently of national judicial systems since determinations and awards by arbitrators may have to be enforced in a court. Arbitration is voluntary in nature, and the parties must agree to arbitrate their dispute. This agreement is found either in the underlying business contract or in a subsequent agreement after a dispute arises.

Resolving disputes by arbitration has a number of advantages over resolving disputes in the courts, particularly for international trade transactions. Arbitration is usually much faster than court litigation, avoiding congested court dockets. Arbitration is normally confidential, so, in contrast to court proceedings that are usually public, the nature of the dispute and business confidential information, such as trade secrets and financial data, can be shielded from public view. Of particular importance, the arbitrator or arbitrators (if the parties select more than one arbitrator) are usually selected based upon their expertise in the industry or with the business transaction concerned, and, therefore, do not have to be educated regarding the commercial realities underlying the transaction. Also of great importance, the arbitration proceeding can take place in a neutral third-country site, eliminating perceived unfairness when a dispute is resolved in the courts of one of the parties or when one party has to travel to the home country of the other party. Lastly, rules regarding arbitration proceedings are generally less formal and more flexible than court rules of procedure.

More than 150 countries, including the United States and almost all major trading states, are currently parties to the United Nations New York Convention on the Recognition and Enforcement of Foreign Arbitral Awards (the New York Convention). The New York Convention provides that final arbitral awards made in a contracting state will be enforced in another contracting state. This means that if you win an arbitration award and the arbitration took place in a state that has signed the Convention, the award can be enforced in any other state that has signed the Convention. This is of great significance if it becomes necessary to enforce an arbitration award in the court of a foreign country.

UNCITRAL, the United Nations Commission for International Trade Law, has developed rules for international commercial arbitration in an attempt to promote uniformity among the various arbitral bodies around the world. UNCITRAL rules cover all aspects of the arbitration process. These rules have been widely employed. They can be used by private commercial parties, in disputes between private investors and states, and also in state-to-state disputes.

The International Chamber of Commerce (ICC), based in Paris, has been and remains the most widely used arbitral body. The ICC maintains a Court of Arbitration in Paris and applies its own rules or UNCITRAL rules, depending on the decision of the parties. Other arbitral bodies include the American Arbitration Association, the London Court of International Arbitration, the Hong Kong Arbitration Centre, the Singapore International Arbitration Centre, and a number of others. However, parties to arbitration also have the option of conducting arbitration independent of established arbitral bodies, so-called "ad hoc" arbitration.

To require arbitration pursuant to ICC rules, the ICC recommends that the following language be inserted in international contracts: "All disputes arising out of or in connection with the present contract shall be finally settled under the Rules of Arbitration of the International Chamber of Commerce by one or more arbitrators appointed in accordance with the said Rules."

The ICC also recommends that the parties may wish to stipulate the law governing the agreement (for example, "the law of the United States, the State of New York shall govern this agreement"), the number of arbitrators (under ICC rules the options are one or three), the place of arbitration (this should be mutually convenient for all parties to the agreement), and the language of arbitration (this should be English or another language familiar to all the parties).

ICC arbitration proceedings can be briefly summarized as follows: A request for arbitration is registered on the day it is received by the secretariat. As soon as the request is complete and filing fees are paid, a request is sent to the other party or parties. They must reply within thirty days. Before transmitting the case to the tribunal, the secretariat fixes an amount for the advance on costs. Once the advance is paid, the case file is transmitted to the tribunal (the arbitrator or arbitrators selected). The tribunal then prepares terms of reference that determines the scope of the litigation and convenes a case management conference to determine dates and procedures. The parties and arbitrators are free to determine the rules of procedure relating to document production, cross-examination, and so forth. After the last hearing, the proceedings will be declared closed, and the tribunal will notify the secretariat and parties of the date when it expects to submit a draft award to the court. The court reviews all awards. Once approved, the award is signed by the arbitrators and notified to the parties.

The alternative to arbitration is, of course, litigation in national courts. If you think you have leverage vis-à-vis your trading partner, you can try to get him or her to agree to resolve disputes in your nation's court. For example, assuming that your business is located in New York state, a sample clause providing for litigation in your home jurisdiction follows: "Any dispute that arises out of or in connection with this contract shall be resolved pursuant to the laws of the State of New York, United States of America in any court in the State of New York that has jurisdiction over the parties."

However, the problems with this approach are significant. First, your foreign business counterpart is unlikely to agree to such a one-sided dispute-resolution provision, and your attempt to obtain it could adversely affect your business relationship with it. Second, even if your counterpart does not object to dispute resolution in your home jurisdiction, in the event of a subsequent dispute, it may be difficult to obtain service of process over their foreign business. Courts in the United States and elsewhere require that a plaintiff complete proper service of process against all defendants so that the court may be sure that the defendant is aware of the claims and can respond to them. The Hague Convention, ratified by the United States and more than sixty other countries, provides, more or less, standard procedures for doing this. However, procedures for service of process in countries that have not ratified the Hague Convention may vary widely.

Third, even if you are successful with serving process on the foreign business and you ultimately prevail in court on your claim against them, the judgment then has to be enforced. If the defendant has no assets in the country where the judgment was issued, this entails requesting a foreign court to enforce the judgment. The judgment of one nation's courts has no effect by itself in another state. Moreover, for political and policy reasons, a foreign state's court may be reluctant to enforce the judgment of another state. Imagine, for example, the reaction of a US court to an attempt to enforce the judgment of a court in Saudi Arabia, ordering recovery of the dowry paid by the family of a husband's third wife to the husband when the husband had left his wives and fled the country!

The general principles of international law applicable to requests to enforce foreign judgments are that the court can review the foreign judgment to determine whether (1) the foreign court that issued it had proper jurisdiction, (2) the defendant was properly notified (service of process), (3) the court proceedings involved fraud, and (4) the judgment is contrary to the public policy of the country in which enforcement of the judgment is sought. Notably, some foreign courts have been reluctant to enforce monetary judgments issued by courts in the United States against their nationals on grounds that the amounts of damages awarded in the United States are excessive.

If you are a small business, the costs, delays, and uncertainty involved with litigation and the damage to business relationships are normally prohibitive. However, the situation is different for major multinational enterprises. Large businesses usually have lawyers on staff and may enter into retainer agreements with outside law firms. They look at litigation as another regular business expense and may aggressively use lawsuits to enforce intellectual property rights and the terms of business contracts.

To sum up, if you are small business, you should plan your international trade transactions so that you avoid resolution of disputes by litigation. It is a costly, risky, and time-consuming option that is also likely to destroy your future business relationships with your opponent and other businesses influenced by your opponent.

### Takeaways for Chapter 3

- Make sure that your agreement with your customer is in writing and that it clearly provides for all terms of sale, the language of the agreement, and the applicable law.
- Take care to maintain good communications with your customer after the agreement is concluded.
- Keep ownership of your goods or services until you receive payment through requiring payment in advance or using letters of credit or other trade finance instruments. You may also use other safeguards to assure payment for your goods or services.
- Provide for an effective dispute-resolution process, but employ litigation only as a last resort.

# Chapter 4

# How Do You Protect Your Intellectual Property in International Trade Transactions?

Intellectual property has the shelf life of a banana.

—Bill Gates

Intellectual property is the oil of the twenty-first century.

—Mark Getty

Today we live in an information age, and even standard consumer products and agricultural commodities have significant intellectual property (IP) components. About two-thirds of the value of large manufacturing businesses in advanced economies, such as the United States, is attributable to intangible assets embodying intellectual property. IP-intensive manufacturing industries include, among others, pharmaceutical and medical manufacturing, chemical products production, semiconductor and electronic instrument manufacturing, and machinery manufacturing.[40] Service

---

[40] Economics and Statistics Administration and US Patent and Trademark Office. "Intellectual Property and the US Economy: Industries in Focus." March 2012, pp. 35–38.

industries are also highly intellectual property reliant. IP-dependent service industries include, among others, software publishers, financial and insurance firms, management and technical consulting, and business support services.[41]

Since your intellectual property is likely critical to the success of your small business, it is essential that you protect it in international trade transactions. This starts with first identifying your intellectual property and then taking appropriate steps to protect it in both domestic and foreign markets.

### What Are Intellectual Property Rights?

Intellectual property rights include patents; copyrights; trademarks, service marks, and trade dress; industrial designs; trade secrets; and geographical indications. The owners of intellectual property may be granted exclusive rights by the government or by law to use their IP for specified periods of time. IP rights may be traded or licensed to third parties, normally in return for compensation that can be either an outright payment or periodic fees or royalty payments. The laws of the United States and of most other sovereign nations govern IP rights within their respective borders. In addition, treaties administered by the World International Property Organization (WIPO) and the WTO

***R&D, 2013***

(billions of US dollars)

World: $1,700

United States: $470

EU: $345

China: $336

Japan: $160

All other: $390

Source: OECD

---

[41] Ibid.

have established minimum international standards. These IP rights can frequently be used in combination to prevent products and services from being copied and then exploited by competitors. The different types of IPR are discussed below.

## Patents

Patents are granted for the invention of new products, processes, or organisms. They may also be granted for designs and plants. In order for an idea to be patentable, it must be new, "nonobvious," involving an inventive step, and have a potential industrial or commercial use. When a patent is issued, it

> ### Three Types of Patents
>
> There are three types of patents are 1. utility patents for a new and useful process, machine, or article; 2. design patents for a new ornamental design for an article of manufacture; and 3. plant patents for new varieties of plants. asexually produced.

provides the patent holder with the exclusive right to sell the invention or prevent its unauthorized use for a specified period of time. In the United States, this is normally twenty years. This temporary monopoly is intended to reward the inventor and to encourage research and development. However, in order to obtain a patent, the applicant must publicly disclose all the technical details of his or her invention along with test data and other relevant information. In some cases, this can be a disincentive to pursuing a patent application because competitors are informed about an invention and can design around it. Without patent protection, major industries, such as pharmaceutical and semiconductor manufacturers, would not exist as we know them today because they would not have the financial incentive to invest substantial R&D funds to develop new products.

In the United States, the US Patent and Trademark Office (USPTO) grants patents.[42] The patent application process usually is complex, lengthy, and expensive, and the assistance of legal counsel is advisable.

## Trade Secrets

A trade secret is any type of information that has economic value because others do not know it. Examples include customer lists and pricing; blueprints; or methods, techniques, or processes. In the United States, state laws protect trade secrets. Most states have adopted the provisions of the Uniform Trade Secrets Act. Foreign countries have their own versions of trade-secrets laws. In contrast to patents, the protection of a trade secret originates with the creation of the trade secret. There is no application or registration process. Moreover, there is no time limit on a trade secret. However, the trade secret holder must take steps to keep it secret. It does not expire unless unauthorized third parties learn the trade secret. However, if a third party learns the trade secret by fraud, it doesn't expire, and the holder can sue the unauthorized party.

Perhaps the most famous example of a trade secret is the formula for producing Coca-Cola. After Dr. John Pemberton invented Coca-Cola in 1886, the formula was kept a close secret. Before 2011, the formula was on deposit at what is now SunTrust Bank, but in December 2011, the company moved the secret formula to a vault at the World of Coca-Cola exhibit in Atlanta, Georgia. Coca-Cola goes to great lengths to safeguard the formula; reportedly only a handful of insiders know all the ingredients.

---

[42] See www.uspta.gov.

## *Copyrights*

Copyrights protect original expressions of authorship, including books, articles, music, movies, sound recordings, computer software, architectural plans, databases, and industrial designs. In contrast to patents, a claim that the idea is original or novel is not necessary. It is the expression of the idea rather than the underlying idea itself that is being copyrighted. The policies underlying copyrights protection are similar to those underlying patent protection. The creators of original literary, artistic, musical, and technical works should be rewarded for their efforts and also protected to encourage further creativity. Under the Copyright Act authorship is generally protected for the life of the author, plus 70 years for personal works or 120 years from creation for corporate works. Copyrights can be acquired in the United States without registration. However, registration provides *prima facie* evidence of a valid copyright and provides other advantages in the event of litigation. In the United States, copyrights may be registered with the Copyright Office of the Library of Congress.[43]

The symbol © signifies that someone is claiming copyright protection, but it is not necessary to show the symbol on a work for protection to be effective. Registration of the work with the US Copyright Office is also not required, but it provides public notice of the copyright's existence. Registered works may be eligible for statutory damages and attorney's fees in the event of successful infringement litigation. Registration with the Copyright Office is also necessary before the work can be registered with CBP.

---

[43] See www.copyright.gov

Without copyright protection, the entertainment industry as we know it today would not exist—authors would have little financial incentive to write new books; movie studios would have no financial incentive to invest millions of dollars in producing new works; and musical composers and singers would also have more limited financial incentives to create and perform new music.

## Trademarks, Service Marks, and Trade Dress

Trademark rights allow the seller of a product using a distinctive name, mark, or symbol to market that product and prevent others from using confusingly similar names or marks that may mislead a consumer as to the source of the product. The trademark permits a clear identification of the source of the product and product quality. A trademarked product may command a higher price in the market because of perceived higher quality; examples include Rolex watches and Prada shoes. Generic names of commodities cannot be trademarked.

A service mark differs from a trademark in that service marks are used for the advertising of services. There is generally no package on which to place a trademark. An air carrier can paint its service mark on its aircraft or a motion-picture company can use an image and a sound, such as MGM's lion and lion's roar.

Trade dress refers to the visual appearance and packaging of a product; its packaging signifies its origin to consumers. To have protection, a trade dress must not have a function other than to identify the product to consumers and also be inherently distinctive or have acquired a secondary meaning that indicates the source of the product to the public. Examples include a restaurant's distinctive décor and layout as well as the distinctive and nonfunctional aspects of golf club design.

In the United States, trademarks, service marks and trade dress are protected by both federal law (the Lanham Act) and by state law. Rights are acquired through use and through registration with the US Patent and Trademark Office. A trademark never expires as long as it continues in use (but to keep it registered, it may be necessary to file affidavits of use and periodically renew the registration). Stella Artois, a Belgian beer, incorporates a trademarked horn symbol of a predecessor brewery dating back to 1366.

A trademark is a product's "brand." It conveys information about the origin and quality of the trademarked product. It can be an image rather than words; for example, the Nike "swoosh" design is recognized around the world. Or it can be a sound, such as NBC's chimes.

The symbol ™ signifies trademark protection, and the symbol ℠ indicates service mark protection. In the United States, marks do not have to be registered with the US Patent and Trademark Office to obtain protection, but this is advisable because of the possibility of confusing marks. When a mark is registered, you then have the right to use the federal registration symbol ®. Advantages of registration include (1) a legal presumption of ownership of the mark and the right to use it nationwide, (2) the right to use the federal registration symbol ®, (3) the use of the registration as a basis for registering the mark in foreign countries, and (4) the ability to record the registration with US Customs and Border Protection to preclude infringing imports.

## Geographic Indications

A geographic indication (GI) signifies to consumers that a product has originated in a specific region and has the same quality and reputation as similar products originating from that region. Examples are Maryland blue crabs, Florida oranges, or Napa Valley wine. In the United States, the Lanham Act protects geographical indications. Although standards for GI are regulated by the WTO's Trade-Related Intellectual Property Rights Agreement (TRIPS), a conflict has developed between the United States and European Union approach to GI regulation. In Europe, the prevailing approach is that of strict usage of geographical designations. Thus, to call a wine "champagne," it must originate in in the Champagne region of France. Wines that are made by the same method in California or New York cannot bear the name "champagne." Similarly, ham cannot be called "Parma" ham in the European Union's view unless it actually originates in the Parma region of Italy.

> **China Now Leads the World in IPR Applications**
>
> According to the WIPO, in 2013, China led the world in applications for patents, trademarks, and designs. The United States was second in applications for patents and trademarks and sixth in applications for designs. Germany, Japan, and Korea rounded out the top five countries for IPR applications.
>
> —World Intellectual Property Indicators (WIPO 2014).

In the United States, by contrast, the situation is more fluid. On the one hand, a product named Kentucky bourbon whiskey must be produced in Kentucky from at least 51 percent corn. This is similar to the EU approach. On the other hand, geographic names whose usage has become generic cannot be protected. Some US producers argue that "champagne" and "Parma ham" are generic terms in the United States and, therefore, usage cannot be restricted to specific geographic areas. This conflict between the EU and US regulatory approaches is currently the subject of trade negotiations.

In the United States, if a geographic indication is used over time so that consumers identify it with a particular product or service, it may acquire secondary meaning, identifying the source of the product or service. This may qualify the GI for trademark or service-mark protection.

### Infringement of Intellectual Property Rights: An All-Too-Common Problem

IPR infringement involves the violation or misappropriation of an IP holder's rights. Patent infringement involves a third party's unauthorized use of a patent. As one example, a manufacturer of generic pharmaceutical products may "reverse engineer" or copy a drug still subject to patent protection. This may then be combined with trademark infringement if the producer simulates the packaging of the legitimate manufacturer in an attempt to deceive the consumer about the origin of the product and profit from the legitimate owner's reputation and good will. The goods are then known as counterfeit. Needless to say, counterfeit goods, particularly pharmaceuticals, can result in injuries and even death to consumers.

> **Counterfeit Baby-Teething Syrup**
>
> In November 2008, children in Nigeria taking a medicine called My Pikin Baby Teething Mixture began to die. The syrup was counterfeit, with the standard glycerin replaced with cheaper diethylene glycol, which looks, smells, and tastes the same. But diethylene glycol is an industrial solvent, which attacks the central nervous system, kidneys, and liver. The medicine killed eighty-four children before it was pulled from pharmacy shelves.
>
> —NY Times, June 4, 2014.

Copyright infringement involves a third party reproducing and using copyrighted material or work without the consent of the copyright owner. If this is intentional, such as the copying of software, music, or movies for profit, it is known as piracy. When I was working as a consultant in Pristina, Kosovo, there were a number of shops selling pirated movie DVDs at very low prices, usually around one euro each or five euros for six. Some were even current movies that were still in theaters and had not yet been commercially released as DVDs. Piracy of computer software is also widespread in some parts of the world. For example, in Vietnam, a WTO member country, software piracy is currently around 80 percent despite the enforcement efforts of software owners.

Piracy also involves the copying and use of famous trademarks and trade dress, such as Nike footwear or Rolex watches. Traveling around the world, I have seen many examples of this. Unfortunately, some people do not consider this to be a serious offense, even though the producer of the genuine goods is being defrauded of revenue and the circulation of inferior goods is damaging its reputation.

> ### *A Fatal Charger*
>
> On a family vacation to Thailand, a seven-year-old boy forgot to bring along a charger for his Nintendo Gameboy. His father unknowingly purchased a counterfeit replacement charger. The wires in the counterfeit charger were so close together that they became live and fatally electrocuted the boy. His parents found him dead on the floor of the hotel room, gripping the Gameboy in his hands.
>
> —Global Intellectual Property Center

Trade secrets, such as customer information and confidential statistical financial data, can also be the subject of theft. When I was working for an international inspection company. we discovered that a competitor had paid the office trash-removal staff to provide them with our discarded correspondence and other business papers. Later, when I was working as a consultant in Moscow, the Russian government insisted that our consulting firm pay about $150,000 for government statistics that we needed to conduct economic analysis. A Russian colleague subsequently told us that the same information could be purchased from a black-market bazaar in Moscow for a fraction of that amount.[44] This was not an attractive option for a variety of reasons. We eventually renegotiated our contract so that we did not have to undertake the economic analysis requiring the data.

### *International IP Standards*

Although IP laws and the enforcement of IPR are a matter of national legislation and national law enforcement, since the 1880s, a number of international treaties have been negotiated to harmonize IP practices around the world. One of the first international agreements for the protection of IP rights was the Paris Convention of 1883 governing international reciprocal patent filing rights. It was followed by the Bern Convention for the Protection of Literary and Artistic Works of 1886, the Madrid Agreement for the Repression of False and Deceptive Indications of Sources of Goods of 1891, the Madrid Agreement Concerning International Registration of Marks of 1891, the International Convention for the Protection of Performers, Producers of Phonograms and Broadcasting Organizations of 1961, the International Convention for the Protection of New Varieties of Plants of 1961, the Treaty on Intellectual Property in Respect of Integrated Circuits of 1989, and a number of similar agreements. Today, the World Intellectual Property Organization (WIPO), a United Nations

---

[44] This data was not a trade-secret problem because government information was involved, but the principle is the same.

organization, is responsible for administering twenty-six international treaties relating to IP.

Despite the existence of WIPO and numerous international treaties, there was continuing frustration on the part of multinationals in knowledge-based economies, such as the United States, with the reluctance of many countries to adopt high standards and strict enforcement measures for IP rights. As a consequence, when the WTO came into existence in 1995, an agreement mandating higher IP enforcement standards on the part of WTO members was included as part of the WTO scheme. This is the WTO's Trade-Related Intellectual Property Rights Agreement (TRIPS).

TRIPS does not directly provide additional rights for individual IP holder businesses. It is intended instead to raise the standard of IP enforcement in WTO member countries. TRIPS provides for relatively high minimum standards for each of the primary IP rights (patents, copyrights, trademarks and service marks, GIs, trade secrets, industrial designs, and integrated circuit designs). It also includes specific provisions for enforcement at borders and internally, and it also provides for the WTO dispute settlement process to settle IP enforcement disputes between WTO members. In addition, TRIPS provides for the basic principles of nondiscrimination and national treatment for IP rights holders.

TRIPS has been criticized by some as promulgating inappropriate IP standards for developing countries. Developing countries may incur significant costs in raising enforcement standards to the level required by TRIPS and also may lose scarce financial resources as a consequence of increased IP royalty payments. Least-developed country members of the WTO (LDCs) have been given an extension until 2021 to implement TRIPS.

Perhaps the most sensitive TRIPS issue has involved access to patented pharmaceutical products. IP enforcement may keep drug costs too high for many patients in developing countries, thus denying them access to life-saving medications. After much debate, this issue has been temporarily resolved through the authorization of a compulsory licensing scheme permitting developing countries to address health crises such as HIV/AIDS infections. In addition, it is the policy of at least one major pharmaceutical manufacturer to donate pharmaceuticals without cost when there is a need in least-developed countries.

After the advent of TRIPS, the United States, the European Union, Japan, and other advanced economies have continued to press for additional international IP protection through the negotiation of "TRIPS Plus" regional trade agreements and other agreements, such as the Anti-Counterfeiting Trade Agreement (ACTA). Very influential economic interests continue to support increased IP enforcement globally. On the other hand, there are powerful political groups opposing TRIPS Plus agreements. The EU Parliament rejected ACTA in 2012 after widespread protests throughout Europe.

### Specific Steps to Take to Protect Your IP in Trade Transactions

Despite the evolving international IP-protection regime, as a small business, it is unlikely that you will be able to obtain direct assistance from your national government in the event that your IP rights are violated in a foreign country. However, you can at least minimize that possibility by taking a number of steps prior to entering into an international trade transaction. These are

> **Protecting Original Artwork**
>
> An artist in California makes original figurines of clay that she sells on the Internet. They could be easily duplicated and mass produced in China. However, she can protect her creations from duplicate imports by registering her designs with the Copyright Office (www.copyright.gov) and then notifying CBP of her registration. Infringing imports will then be subject to seizure by Customs. She can also protect her works by establishing and using a trademark for her business as well as by signing each work and providing a certificate of authenticity with each sale.

1.     identify and protect your IP in your domestic markets;

2.     investigate the IP climate in foreign markets prior to doing business there;

3.     negotiate an agreement that protects your IP rights;

4.     retain local counsel to register your IP rights with the appropriate authorities; and

5.  regularly monitor your foreign markets for possible violations and take enforcement actions when necessary.

### Step 1: Identify and Protect Your IP in Your Domestic Markets

Every small business has IP that should be protected. Patented inventions are an obvious example. Less obvious are trade secrets, such as customer lists and processes; copyrightable materials such as writings, designs, blueprints, and photographs; trademarks, service marks, and trade dress identifying unique products and services; and geographic origins. If you haven't already identified your IP through consultations with your business's attorney and taken measures to protect it in your domestic markets, this should be your first priority. When you obtain IP protection in your domestic markets, obtaining IP protection in foreign markets is greatly simplified because of international agreements giving mutual recognition to IP rights.

### *A Template for a Small Business IP Audit*

| IP Assets (list products by IP type) | Life of Asset (years) | Extent of Use (percentage of business) | Importance (low, medium, high) | Value ($) to business |
|---|---|---|---|---|
| Patents | | | | |
| Designs | | | | |
| Trademarks | | | | |
| Service marks | | | | |
| Trade dress | | | | |
| GI | | | | |
| Copyrights | | | | |
| Trade secrets | | | | |
| Licenses | | | | |

Protecting your IP involves applying for and receiving patent protection when appropriate; registering trademarks, service marks, trade dress, and copyrightable materials; and vigilantly safeguarding trade secrets. Your employees should be educated regarding the importance of IPR and the measures that must be taken to ensure maximum protection.

### *Step 2: Investigate the IP Climate in Foreign Markets Prior to Doing Business There*

Obtaining information about the existing IP climate in foreign markets has been greatly simplified by the annual "Special 301 Report" reviews by the US Trade Representative (USTR) of the state of IP enforcement around the world. The most recent Special 301 Report can be obtained from USTR's website: www.ustr.gov/.

In the 2014 report, the IP enforcement practices of eighty-two trading partners were reviewed. Of these, thirty-seven were listed on a watch list because of concerns about their IP protection. Algeria, Argentina, Chile, China, India, Indonesia, Pakistan, Russia, Thailand, and Venezuela were included on the priority watch list. Ukraine had previously also been designated as a priority watch-list country, but because of the political and military conflict in East Ukraine, it was removed. Barbados, Belarus, Bolivia, Brazil, Bulgaria, Canada, Colombia, Costa Rica, Dominican Republic, Ecuador, Egypt, Finland, Greece, Guatemala, Jamaica, Kuwait, Lebanon, Mexico, Paraguay, Peru, Romania, Tajikistan, Trinidad and Tobago, Turkey, Turkmenistan, Uzbekistan, and Vietnam were included on the watch list.

*IPR in China*

An examination of the report's findings regarding China indicates the level of detail in these annual reports on foreign IP climate. According to the 2014 report, IP enforcement in China remained the greatest concern because of the volume of trade between China and the United States. US businesses reported serious obstacles to effective protection of all forms of IPR. As a consequence, sales of IP intensive goods and services in China by US firms are disproportionately low compared to comparable foreign markets that provide better IPR protection. The theft of trade secrets is a major concern. These thefts are taking place both inside and outside China through use of the Internet and other methods and are intended to give a competitive advantage to both state-owned and private businesses.

Also of continuing concern is pressure from all levels of government in China on foreign firms to transfer IP to Chinese enterprises. Government permissions, procurement, and tax treatment may be conditioned on requirements to transfer IP. Pressure has been exerted to license technologies and to dissuade foreign firms from pursuing legal avenues to enforce their IP rights.

Protection for trade secrets under existing Chinese law is difficult to obtain. Enforcement problems include constraints on gathering evidence for use in litigation; a problem meeting the criteria for establishing that information constitutes a trade secret; and inadequate criminal penalties. Liability under law is apparently limited to businesses and not individual actors.

Copyright violations also remain a problem. Losses by software businesses resulting from piracy at state-owned and privately owned enterprises remain very high. This gives Chinese firms a cost advantage vis-à-vis competitors that pay for legally acquired software. Online piracy is also a large-scale problem. For example, in 2013 revenue from music sales in China totaled $65.4 million compared to $108.3 million in South Korea, a much smaller country. As a result of the widespread piracy of movies, over 90 percent of revenue from US-origin films comes from box-office receipts compared to 25–30 percent in the United States.

Counterfeit goods are also a major problem in China. Commonly counterfeited goods include food and beverage products, apparel, footwear, consumer electronics products, computers, pharmaceuticals, and auto parts. About 93 percent of the value of all infringing products seized by US Customs and Border Protection in fiscal 2013 originated in China and Hong Kong.

Problems also exist in the area of patent protection. China has begun to severely restrict a patent applicant's ability to

> ### Refusal to Do Business in China Because of Poor IPR Protection
>
> A small machinery manufacturer located in California sells its equipment in more than fifty countries around the world. Patents for its equipment have expired, but the equipment is the subject of trade secrets and also protected by trademark. The manufacturer refuses to do business in China because of concern that its equipment will be reverse engineered and then sold by Chinese firms in the United States and other markets.

provide supplemental information in support of an application. As a consequence, pharmaceutical patent applications have been denied and existing patents invalidated, even though those patents have been award by the US and other national patent offices. In addition, there are concerns about a failure to protect against unfair commercial use as well as unauthorized disclosure of test or other data generated to obtain approval for pharmaceutical products.

## IPR in Other Countries

While the level of detail is somewhat less for other countries covered in the Special 301 Report, the information provided is still sufficient for an assessment of the risks to IP in the countries discussed. Vietnam, a watch list country, is an example. The report acknowledges that Vietnam took steps to improve its regulatory framework to strengthen copyright protection and enforcement, but significant problems remain. Piracy and sales of counterfeit goods over the Internet and in physical markets continue to occur on a large scale. Moreover, book piracy, software piracy (including on government systems), and cable and satellite signal theft are also widespread. Some progress has been made with IP-enforcement actions. However, enforcement agencies have resource problems; coordination between enforcement agencies is poor. Although broad laws criminalizing IPR crimes exist, implementing guidelines have not been issued.

Another example of a watch-list country, somewhat surprisingly, is Canada. As of the date of the 2014 report, Canada had not enacted legislation allowing customs officials to take *ex officio* action[45] to seize pirated and counterfeited goods at the border and in transit. The report also expressed concern about heightened utility requirements for patents, allowing a court to invalidate a patent on utility grounds years after a patent has been granted. Using this criterion, Canadian courts have invalidated a number of patents held by US pharmaceutical companies, finding that the products in question lacked an industrial application, even though the products had been in the market for years.

In addition to the annual Special 301 Report, USTR and the US government collect additional information and complaints about IPR enforcement problems around the world. Details about the level of IPR enforcement in most countries can be obtained from USTR and the country desk officers at the US Department of Commerce's International Trade Administration as well as from commercial officers at US embassies in the countries concerned.

After investigating the amount of IP protection that exists in a potential foreign market, you may decide that the enforcement environment is too risky for you to do business there. When I was working as a consultant in the newly independent country of Kosovo, I noticed that, in contrast with a neighboring

---

[45] An *ex officio action* is an action taken by the power of someone's office. In this case, since Canadian customs did not have *ex officio* powers as provided for in TRIPS, they had to rely on other legal authority to seize pirated and counterfeited goods.

country, none of the franchise food multinationals, such as McDonald's, Subway, or Burger King, had outlets in Kosovo. One of the reasons for this may have been a decision by these firms not to do business in Kosovo because of a poor level of IPR protection.

### Step 3: Negotiate an Agreement That Protects Your IP Rights

Chapter 3 discusses the importance of having a clear, enforceable written agreement with your foreign trade counterpart. That agreement should normally provide protection for your IPR.

The provisions protecting IPR in the agreement will depend on the type of IP involved. For example, if you intend to license your patent and other IPR for the payment of a royalty, your agreement may contain a grant of rights clause; a grant back to licensor clause regarding a license to use modifications or improvements; a clause where the licensor warrants that she is the sole owner of the patents involved; a clause providing for royalty payments; a confidentiality clause providing that the licensee will keep confidential all information disclosed to it by the licensor; a quality clause specifying that goods manufactured according to the agreement shall meet specific quality specifications; a noncompetition clause specifying that the licensee shall not make goods that compete with the goods subject to the license agreement; an infringement clause requiring the licensee to notify the lessor of any possible IP infringement and assist the licensor in prosecuting an infringement; and a term and termination clause.

If the agreement is a distribution agreement for goods subject to trademarks, your agreement may include clauses pertaining to the use of trademarks (possibly granting the distributor a nonexclusive, nontransferrable right to use the supplier's trademarks); a clause requiring the supplier to register the trademarks; a clause preventing the distributor from removing patent numbers, trademarks, trade names, or other identifying marks affixed to the manufacturer's products; and an infringement clause requiring the distributor to promptly notify the supplier of any use of confusingly similar marks by third parties that may constitute an infringement.

> ### The "Overreaching" Distributor
>
> An IP lawyer and international IP consultant told me about encountering a big problem with distributors trying to register the trademarks of licensors at their national trademark office in their own name. If they are successful, this can give them considerable leverage vis-à-vis the licensor.

If the agreement is one for the provision of services, your agreement may include clauses that provide that the purchaser of the services will own any copyrighted materials created as a consequence of the agreement. A sample clause follows:

> All writings, books, articles, computer programs, databases, and other material of any nature whatsoever that are subject to copyright protection and reduced to tangible form in whole or in part by the provider of services in the course of this Agreement shall be considered a work for hire. The service provider understands and agrees that the client may itself and permit others to reproduce any provided publications and materials through, but not limited to, the publication, broadcast, translation, creation of other versions, and quotations therefrom, and may otherwise utilize the service provider's

work and material. During this agreement and thereafter, the service provider agrees to take all actions and execute any documents that the client may consider necessary to obtain or maintain copyrights, whether during the application for copyright or during the conduct of an interference, infringement, litigation, or other matter. The service provider shall identify any and all materials it intends to exempt from this provision prior to the use or development of such materials.

All reports prepared and data collected during the service provider's employment by the client shall be considered the property of the client and shall not be reproduced, disseminated or discussed in public other than for the authorized purposes of this Agreement. All findings, conclusions, and recommendations of the service provider shall be considered confidential and proprietary.

Needless to say, this is not the time or place for amateurs. You should employ a qualified IP lawyer to help you draft contract language appropriate for the protection of your specific IP rights in the context of the specific trade transaction.

### Step 4: Retain Local Counsel to Register Your IPR with the Appropriate Authorities

If you have significant concerns about protecting your IPR in a foreign market you plan to enter, you should register your IP with the appropriate authorities. All WTO member countries and most others have agencies responsible for registering and enforcing patent rights, copyrights, and trademarks. In the United States, this is the US Patent and Trademark Office (USPTO) and the US Copyright Office. In China, the State Intellectual Property Office (SIPO) is responsible for the registration of patents, the Trademark Office is under the State Administration on Industry, and Commerce (SAID) and the National Copyright Administration (NCA) registers copyrights. In Barbados, the agency responsible for IPR is the Corporate Affairs and Intellectual Property Office (CAIPO). In Brazil, the National Industrial Property Institute (NIPI) is responsible for IP except for copyright. Copyright registration is not required, but rights holders may register at various accrediting institutions. In Japan, patent and trademark registration is the responsibility of the Japan Patent Office (JPO) in the Ministry of Trade and Industry (MITI), and copyrights are the responsibility of the Japan Copyright Office in the Ministry of Education, Culture, Sports, Science, and Technology.

As you can see from these few examples, there are a wide variety of agencies in countries and regions around the world that are charged with the responsibility of registering and enforcing IPR. Even though these agencies may comply with international IPR standards, local laws and procedures differ. Of course, business is conducted in the local language of the country involved. It is therefore essential that you retain a local IPR lawyer to register your rights.

International agreements can shortcut the registration process with regard to patents and copyrights. The Patent Cooperation Treaty (PCT), administered by WIPO, makes it possible to seek patent protection for an invention simultaneously in countries that have acceded to the treaty by filing a so-called international patent application in the applicant's home country. The PCT application fixes the application date in all contracting states. The international application is then subjected to an international patent search carried out by one of the patent agencies appointed by the treaty. This results in an international search report that may affect the patentability of the claimed invention. The report may be followed by a preliminary international examination. Subsequently, the relevant national or regional patent authority issues or denies the application. As of early 2016, the PCT had 148 contracting states.

Obtaining copyright protection has also been simplified under international agreements, such as the Berne Convention and TRIPS. In most countries, registration is not required. However, in a small number of countries, the works of foreign nationals receive little or no protection. Copyright protection ultimately depends on national law, so before publishing a work, it is essential to investigate the legal requirements and protection available in the specific foreign markets where the work will be published.

You can obtain recommendations for a foreign IPR lawyer from a variety of sources. Your local IPR attorney in your home country can obtain recommendations through his or her contacts and then handle the matter for you. A second option is to request recommendations for IPR attorneys from your embassy in the country concerned. A third option is to delegate the responsibility to your trade partner in the country. However, you should be cautious about this option, as your trade partner may not always represent all your interests. Fourth, for important cases, you probably should travel to the country concerned and personally interview and retain the IPR lawyer. This will ensure the clearest communication about the rights that you want to have protected and the state of local IPR law.

### *Step 5: Regularly Monitor Your Foreign Markets for Possible Violations and Take Enforcement Action*

Some years ago, I worked as a consultant to Morocco's Customs and Excise Administration to help them implement the IPR border agency procedures of TRIPS. While working in Morocco, I met with local representatives of multinationals, including Nike, Microsoft, and the Motion Picture Association. These local representatives of multinationals were actively defending their respective brands and copyrights in Morocco by surveying major markets for counterfeit goods and reporting suspected violations to customs and other government authorities. Unfortunately, small businesses usually do not have the sources of these major multinationals to monitor foreign markets for IPR violations.

Under TRIPS, WTO members must provide for civil and administrative procedures for the enforcement of IPR. Courts must be authorized to issue injunctive relief to stop infringement and order the payment of damages in appropriate cases. In addition, TRIPS provides that border agencies can exclude infringing imports. In accordance with TRIPS' border agency procedures, holders of trademarks and copyrights can register their IP rights with customs, and in many countries, patent rights can also be registered.[46] If customs then suspects imports of counterfeit goods, it will suspend importation and notify the local representative of the mark or copyright owner and give them an opportunity to examine the suspected goods. If they determine the goods are infringing, they have a period of time to file a complaint with an appropriate court. If the goods are found to be infringing, the court normally will order destruction of the goods or other appropriate remedies.

---

[46] In the United States, exclusion of goods by CBP for violating patent rights must be pursuant to an USITC order.

Frequently, consumers in foreign markets will know from the low price and shoddy quality that branded goods are fakes. However, in some cases, this may not be readily apparent, and counterfeit equipment parts or pharmaceuticals can lead to disastrous consequences. A midsize US manufacturer of air brake equipment for trucks, buses, and other commercial vehicles was experiencing counterfeiting problems with its products in the US and foreign markets.[47] Sophisticated counterfeiting made it difficult for consumers to detect fake parts until they failed. An added complication was that heavy equipment parts are usually sold through distributor outlets and repair facilities, so the parts are frequently removed from their packaging. To deal with the problem, the manufacturer instituted an IPR enforcement program that included circulating trademark usage guides to dealers and distributors, conducting customer and industry IPR awareness campaigns, exhibiting genuine and counterfeit parts side by side at trade shows, and instituting patent and trademark infringement actions when appropriate.

Small businesses do not have the resources to monitor foreign markets for IPR violations to the same degree as major multinationals. However, there are a number of cost-effective steps that can be taken to counter IPR violations. Your first line of defense should be your foreign representatives and customers since their business—the resale and servicing of your goods—also depends on your IPR. You could consider requiring your representatives and customers to monitor their market for IP infringement as part of your agreement with them.

---

[47] See Global Intellectual Property Center. "Intellectual Property Protection and Enforcement Manual. Global Intellectual Property Center." 2009.

If you have registered your IPR in the foreign market, the lawyer who was responsible for handling the registration could also be tasked with periodic checks to assure that your IPR are not being violated. Active participation in trade-association groups that among other activities monitor IP violations for members is another option to consider. Lastly, any unusual decline in sales in a particular market should be investigated as possibly being tied to competing counterfeit products.

### Is It Parallel-Market Trade or Gray-Market Trade?

Parallel-market or gray-market products are genuine, branded products that have been diverted from the normal distribution channels and then are imported normally without the knowledge or consent of the owner of the IP. These products are usually sold at lower prices than those offered by authorized distributors. Trade in these goods is usually limited to popular, high-margin branded products that are relatively easy to ship.

Today there are many consumer goods that are subject to parallel market trade. Automobile manufacturers, for example, tend to segment the world into national or regional territories with different price structures depending on the demographics and economy of the region and the competitive position there of the manufacturer. American-brand automobiles, such as Ford, tend to sell for premium prices in Kazakhstan, and small international businesses have developed shipping US-used autos, usually in good condition, to Kazakhstan to be sold. As another example, some US auto dealerships arrange trips for Americans to Germany that involve both tourism and the purchase of a new German-made automobile. Typically, the automobile is purchased for a lower net price in Germany than in the United States, is driven in Europe by the "tourist," and then imported into the United States.

Sometimes the international arbitrage in used automobiles results from local regulations. In Japan, rigorous road tests, rapid depreciation standards, and strict environmental laws lower the value of used automobiles. Used Japanese vehicles are then sold around the world, particularly in other left-hand traffic countries and in developing world nations. I have seen many of these used Japanese autos operating in countries such as Myanmar, Nigeria, Liberia, Sao Tome, Jordan, Kosovo, Kazakhstan, Cambodia, and Laos.

> **Prosecutors Drop Cases on Buyers of China-Bound Luxury Cars**
>
> Small businesses were exporting tens of thousands of new luxury cars a year to China and "selling them for a big profit" before Federal prosecutors initiated seizure cases against the traders, claiming that they were straw purchasers with no intent to use the autos. Recently, the prosecutors settled the cases by returning the seized cars and reimbursing the traders for damages.
>
> —NY Times, April 1, 2015

There is also an active parallel market for cell phones, including smartphones. It is estimated that at least 30 percent of all mobile phones sold are sold outside normal distribution channels. The reasons for this include market segmentation, with the introduction of products in some markets before other markets; price differences between markets caused by currency fluctuations or other economic conditions; and different product preferences in different markets. For example, Blackberry smartphones are very popular in Nigeria, but their market share in North America today is small.

Parallel-market sales of computers, software, and other information technology products are also widespread. Studies indicate that manufacturers are losing billions of dollars in profits annually because of this arbitrage.[48]

Those brand owners that are adversely affected by this arbitrage in goods argue that consumers purchasing these products may not have access to technical support or valid OEM warranties. Moreover, products sold outside normal distribution channels could, in fact, be counterfeit (and not "parallel market"), a serious problem particularly for products such as pharmaceuticals. On the other hand, many distributors surveyed believe that it is necessary to purchase genuine products from alternative suppliers in order to remain price competitive.[49] In addition, surveyed distributors frequently claim that they are able to obtain faster delivery from unauthorized sources.

OEMs use various methods to deter trade in gray-market goods. These include

- limiting sales by distributors to specific products and sales regions (presales restrictions);

- taking legal action against distributors that violate these restrictions;

- employing incentive (rebate) systems to track sales;

- restricting price differentials between national markets to a narrow range; and

---

[48] KPMG. "Effective Channel Management is Critical in Combating the Grey Market and Increasing Technology Companies' Bottom Line." 2008.
[49] Ibid.

- monitoring global pricing; and tracking product serial numbers throughout the distribution chain to the ultimate consumer.

Even if you are a small business, you can use these same methods to protect your trademarked goods.

### *Takeaways for Chapter 4*

- Understand the various IP types and how they apply to your business and its products or services.

- Investigate the level of IP protection in a foreign market before doing business there.

- When selling your products or services internationally, be sure to negotiate an agreement that protects your IPR.

- Before doing business in a foreign country, retain local legal counsel to register your IPR.

- Regularly monitor foreign markets for possible IP violations relating to your products or services and monitor your distributors to reduce competition from gray-market goods.

# Chapter 5

## How Can You Minimize Trade-Transaction Costs? Logistics, Global Value Chains and Trade Facilitation

My logisticians are a humorless lot...they know if my campaign fails, they are the first ones I will slay.

—Alexander the Great

This chapter and chapter 6 are about minimizing your trade-transaction costs as you engage in international trade transactions. As you recall from the introduction and chapter 1, transaction costs are those additional costs that you as a business face when you engage in international trade transactions. These include the costs of moving your goods and services, known as logistics costs—which are discussed in this chapter—and the costs of dealing with government taxes, regulations, and other restrictions relating to importing and exporting goods and services—which are discussed in the following chapter. There is an inverse relationship between trade-transaction costs and trade: lower transaction costs result in more trade, and higher transaction costs reduce trade.

Logistics, supply chains or global-value chains, and trade facilitation are essentially three different ways of looking at the same activity—the flow of international trade transactions. Trade facilitation relates to how the procedures and controls governing the movement of goods across national borders can be improved. It looks at the movement of goods across borders from a big-picture perspective and measures how successful economies are in expediting trade transactions. Measurements of trade facilitation include the average time and cost it takes to move goods through international distribution channels in different economies and perceptions of logistics efficiency based on surveys. Looking at the trade facilitation performance of individual countries is important when you decide whether to do business in that country.

Logistics is the management of the flow of goods and related services between the point of origin and the point of consumption in order to meet the business requirements of organizations. In the context of international trade, logistics focuses on the movements of goods in individual trade transactions, so it is the "micro" side of trade facilitation. In addition to moving goods using various modes of transportation, logistics includes related services and information pertaining to shipments, such as packing and containerization, freight forwarding and brokerage services, IT systems, and warehousing. Understanding the cost-effective logistics arrangements to deliver your products and services is critical to successfully conducting international trade transactions. However, for most small businesses, independent logistics professionals, known as freight forwarders, handle logistics arrangements.

Supply chains are generally interbusiness systems involved in creating and moving products or services from suppliers to consumers. They are networks of independent business organizations that are involved in upstream and downstream relationships as well as all the value adding processes and activities required. Supply chains include the physical movements of materials, information flows, and resources, such as freight forwarding, IT, and finance that help supply chains to operate efficiently. Global supply chains can be complex, involving many different goods and services providers, to produce a complex end product such as a jet airplane, smartphone, or laptop computer. Managing your supply chains effectively is necessary to creating value, increasing efficiency, and satisfying the expectations of your suppliers and customers.

A value chain looks at a supply chain from the perspective of value added to products and services at each step of the production and distribution process. Value chains can be a firm-level value chain, focusing on the activities of a single enterprise, or, more typically, an industry-level value chain, including all the various processes involved in producing goods or services in a particular industry. The term "global value chain" is a value chain that extends over two or more countries or economies. It is frequently referenced in connection with the efforts of developing countries to move up a value chain from being only raw materials suppliers to undertaking intermediate processing and service steps.

Although trade facilitation, logistics, and supply chains are normally thought of as involving trade in goods and not services, trade in services frequently require the management of logistics regarding the travel of service personnel and the shipments of related tangible goods supporting service products (IT equipment, computers, publications, and so forth). Moreover, there are important service sector components in supply chains for tangible products. These include logistics providers (for example, carriers, freight forwarders, and warehouse operators), banks and other financial intermediaries, and IT and communications services.

A service-specific supply chain is the network of all service providers necessary to produce the services in question. These supply chains may be international in scope. For example, an accounting firm located in Alexandria, Virginia, may subcontract the preparation of tax returns to a consulting firm in Mumbai, India. It may also employ the services of IT consultants located in Tallinn, Estonia, and an Internet marketing firm based in Toronto, Canada. Moreover, some of its clients may be American citizens working in foreign countries. There are many international service supply chains in the tourism, medical services, legal, and consulting service sectors to name only a few examples.

## 1. Everything You Always Wanted to Know about International Trade Logistics

Your business may produce an outstanding product or service at a competitive price, but unless you can efficiently and economically deliver your product or service to customers, your business will fail. International trade logistics is about how you deliver products and services. Good logistics results in reduced production and distribution costs and increased value to customers.

When I recently asked the president of a small equipment manufacturing business located in southern California that has customers in more than fifty countries around the world how his firm handled shipping logistics, he replied, "It's simple. Find a good freight forwarder." Today, even many major multinational firms have outsourced logistics to freight forwarders, express couriers, and other logistics professionals. Nonetheless, you should have a good comprehension of the

---

### Amazon: A Logistics Business for the Internet Era

Amazon is usually thought of as an Internet B2C business, but in many ways, it is really a logistics service. Amazon provides an Internet platform for consumers to purchase books, movies, and a wide range of consumer goods. However, rapid delivery of products purchased on Amazon's Internet site is essential. Without good logistics arrangements, Amazon's business model would fail. Amazon has reduced delivery time by developing its e-reader, the Kindle, allowing e-books, newspapers and periodicals, music, videos, and other electronic products to be delivered almost instantaneously. A system of strategically located fulfillment-center warehouses and subcontracted logistics arrangements allow tangible products ordered by consumers to be delivered within one to two days. Amazon is now experimenting with the use of drones for even faster deliveries. The handwriting is already on the wall for printed books sold in brick-and-mortar bookstores as sales of books increasingly go to e-books delivered online and hard copies ordered online and delivered through logistics services. At the point when Amazon is able to reduce the shipment time of consumer goods to overnight, or even in hours, many brick-and-mortar retail stories may also lose much of their business.

---

elements of modern logistics because of its importance to the success of international trade transactions. Of particular importance are understanding the roles of the various service providers; the cost benefits of different transportation modes; and the importance of intermodal containers.

### Trade Logistics Providers

To someone new to international trade transactions, the names and functions of the various logistics service providers can seem arcane. The overlap between the different types of service providers can even be confusing at times for a trade professional. So let's take a quick tour of these service providers.

Freight forwarders, also known as forwarding agents, are businesses responsible for organizing international shipments for their clients and assisting clients with the preparation of trade documentation. They typically have corresponding forwarding agents in the destination countries for shipments. Forwarders contract with carriers to move the goods of their clients. They can contract for moving goods on any of the four modes of transit: air, rail, road, and sea. In fact, in most cases, international shipments will be intermodal; that is, the shipment will take place using two or more transit modes. For example, a shipment of pharmaceutical products may be shipped by airfreight from New York to Frankfurt, Germany, and then transferred to a truck for delivery at the customer's place of business in Dusseldorf. Or heavy machinery may be shipped from Chicago by rail to the Port of Long Beach, California, where the containers are placed on a vessel for delivery at the port of Valparaiso, Chile. Once in Chile, the equipment may be transferred to trucks for delivery at the customer's place of business in Santiago.

Freight forwarders can also be nonvessel operating common carriers (NVOCCs). A NVOCC acts as a carrier, issuing its own bills of lading, but does not actually operate the vessels, aircraft, vehicles or railroads on which the cargo will be carried. They frequently consolidate various shipments into full container loads. (A consolidated shipment is a shipment that consists of a number of smaller shipments combined into one loading unit.) In contrast to a non-NVOCC forwarder, NVOCCs are legally responsible for loss or damage to goods during transit.

A freight forwarder normally obtains better shipping rates from carriers than the exporter or importer is able to realize. Their fee usually is the "spread" between the rate that they obtain from the carrier and the rate the carrier would quote the shipper plus an additional fee. In the case of NVOCCs, this spread is even greater because NVOCCs are actually shippers themselves.

As a small business, how can you find a reliable and cost-effective freight forwarder? You can obtain a list of freight

---

### Selecting a Freight Forwarder: Some Questions to Ask

- Are you a member of the national freight forwarder association?
- Do you have appropriate liability insurance coverage?
- Are you certified by customs as an authorized economic operator or the national equivalent?
- Do you specialize in particular commodities?
- Do you specialize in particular nations or regions?
- Are you a member of a network of other forwarders?
- What are your business references (anyone in the same line of business as the hiring company)?
- Obtain information so you can check their credit.
- What IT systems do you use and are they compatible with mine?
- Do you perform customs-brokerage services?
- Do you offer insurance products?
- Do you provide trade advice?
- How do you keep your information on country-specific regulations current?

---

forwarders in your area from the Internet and from freight-forwarder associations. A freight-forwarder professional had the following suggestions in the box above regarding questions to ask.

Customs brokers are agents who clear a shipper's goods through customs. In the United States, Canada, and some other countries (but not the European Union), brokers must be licensed by customs; this usually entails passing a background check and an examination. Typically, customs brokers will fill out and submit import declarations (export declarations are usually submitted by exporters and their forwarders) and required supporting documents on behalf of their clients; advise shippers regarding the appropriate customs classification and valuation of the goods and the applicable duty rate; be present if customs inspects the goods; prepay the customs duties, taxes, and fees assessed on behalf of their clients; and perform all other activities required to clear goods through customs and other border agencies. Some countries require that customs brokers represent all importers and exporters. Customs brokers typically charge a small fee for their service. Frequently, freight forwarders will also provide customs-brokerage services.

Insurance firms provide casualty insurance to shippers in the event that a shipment is lost or damaged in international transit, and they also provide third-party financial guarantees to customs, called "customs bonds," that assure the duties and taxes on imports will be paid in the event of a default by the importer. In the United States, CBP requires that customs brokers and almost all traders post customs bonds, but this is not a requirement in many other countries.

The term "all risks" is used in casualty insurance; these policies cover all losses that are not specifically excluded. "All risk" is somewhat of a misnomer because specific exclusions typically include war, strikes, riots, and other civil unrest. Other exclusions vary from policy to policy, so it is essential for shippers to carefully check the exclusions. A common mistake made by some shippers is to assume that their shipments are insured under the policies carried by carriers or under Incoterms requiring the other party to maintain insurance. However, this is not always the case, as the policies carried by other parties may exclude certain losses.

Freight forwarders may also act as insurance agents by providing these services and may even insure traders under their own umbrella insurance coverage. Insurance providers also make possible a number of special customs procedures, including TIR transit, allowing the shipment of goods by truck through multiple countries without intermediate customs inspections and payment of duties and taxes, and ATA carnets, which facilitate the short-term importation of goods, such as commercial samples and musical instruments used by traveling performers without the payment of duties and taxes.

Carriers are the organizations that actually physically transport goods in international commerce. They include air carriers, trucking firms, railroads, and "steamship services" (the term "steamship" is still used even though ships are no longer necessarily powered by steam). Shipments are documented by bills of lading that contain all relevant information regarding the cargo in question. For airfreight, this is called an air waybill. Carriers publish their shipping rates, and you can obtain them from their websites or from a freight forwarder. The *Journal of Commerce*, a trade publication in the United States, which has very useful information about international shipping, also publishes steamship rates.

## Express Couriers

Express couriers, or express delivery companies, deliver small packages around the world and also perform freight forwarding, customs brokerage, and other logistics services. The major international express couriers are DHL, UPS, TNT, and FedEx. However, there are a number of smaller couriers that also provide international services.

DHL provides delivery services in more than 220 countries and territories and is also one of the largest air carriers worldwide. UPS also operates in about 220 countries and operates its own cargo air and truck service, delivering more than 15 million packages per day. FedEx also operates its own air carrier and truck service and also says it delivers packages in more than 220 countries. TNT provides similar service. All four couriers provide freight forwarding and customs-brokerage services, and they also all have expanded into shipping larger and heavier goods by surface as well as air.

In April 2015, FedEx announced a plan to purchase Dutch-based TNT for $4.8 billion to increase its presence in Europe. However, the proposed acquisition is subject to national competition regulations.

## Postal Services

Surprisingly, an increasing amount of international shipments are now taking place via postal services. The Universal Postal Union, an international agreement administered by the United Nations, establishes the rules of the exchange of mail, including parcels, between its 192 member states. Over 6 billion parcels were delivered by mail in 2012.[50] This included 3.7

---

[50] Universal Postal Union Annual Report 2013.

billion international deliveries. About 60 percent of all postal revenues now relate to parcel shipments, and this percentage is increasing as "snail-mail" letter deliveries decline. The US Postal Service publishes weight limits and prices for international deliveries depending on the country and class of service (global express guaranteed, priority mail express international, priority mail international, and first class package international).[51] The maximum weight per package permitted is 70 lbs. for the global express guaranteed service and less for other forms of service. The Postal Service of the destination country is responsible for collecting any customs duties and taxes due on shipments.

International postal deliveries by small packages is particularly suited to B2C Internet business, where individual customers order products on a business website such as eBay, Amazon, and Alibaba. In 2010, the US Postal Service entered into an agreement with China to provide special services for small packets mailed from China. Packages shipped from China using this "ePacket" service have grown rapidly. Between 2011 and 2012, the number of packages almost tripled, growing from 9.5 million to 26.8 million.

## Customs Warehouse Operators

Warehouse operators are important service providers for many international trade transactions. Frequently, international shipments in transit may be held at a particular location because onward carriage is not available, or customs and other administrative formalities at a border must be performed. In addition, in some cases, goods are shipped to a destination prior to being sold and it is advantageous to the shipper to hold them in a warehouse in the destination country without payment of

[51] http://pe.usps.com/text/imm/immpg.htm

duties and taxes until a customer for them is obtained. In these instances, customs warehouses act as distribution centers in a supply chain.

## Trade Advisors and Attorneys

Additional important service providers are trade consultants and trade attorneys. Trade consultants may provide advice regarding structuring specific trade transactions and also counsel importers and exporters on the proper classification, valuation, and duty rates for their products. Many of them also provide services in connection with trade compliance with various customs and other regulatory agency requirements. Freight forwarders, customs brokers, and express couriers frequently provide trade advisory services for an additional fee. Trade lawyers represent traders in legal proceedings related to imports and exports and also advise their clients regarding the legal aspects of international trade transactions.

## Logistics IT Specialists

Immediate access to accurate information about the movement of goods and services in a global value chain is essential to modern logistics. Networked mobile devices, such as laptop computers and smartphones, access real-time information, allowing managers to monitor the current status of materials resources, goods, and services. Various IT applications support these information flows. These include e-business solutions, such as electronic data interchange (EDI), radio frequency identification (RFID) systems, warehouse management systems, materials requirements planning systems, collaborative planning, forecasting and replenishment systems, and others. Logistics IT specialists provide and service these essential information services.

## Preshipment Inspection Firms

Preshipment inspection (PSI) refers to the examination of the goods for quality, quantity, and value by an independent inspection agency to assure compliance with a purchase order and/or letter of credit. This may be a requirement imposed by contract and, in some cases, by foreign governments. A PSI can be performed during and after production as well as when the goods are packaged and loaded on a conveyance. There are PSI firms that provide inspection services in most countries. These firms issue inspection certificates called "clean reports of findings" (CRF) regarding the goods inspected.

## Third-Party Logistics Providers (3PLs)

Third-party logistics providers are businesses that provide a full range of shipping services, encompassing the activities of freight forwarders, customs brokers, warehouse operators, carriers, and IT specialists. Some freight forwarders and express couriers provide 3PL services for part or all of a client's supply chain.

> **Bill of Lading (B/L)**
>
> A B/L is a document issued by a shipping line giving the details of a shipment of goods, assigning title to the goods, and requiring the carrier to release the goods to the holder of title or another party at the port of destination.

## How Do You Ship Your Goods in the Most Cost-Effective Manner?

Depending on the nature of your products and business, international shipment by postal service, express courier, or multimodal shipment arranged by a freight forwarder may be the most economical method. The factors to consider are cost, time taken, reliability, and the risk of loss, damage, or delay resulting from a particular mode of carriage. In addition, some shipments may, because of their high value or sensitivity to the environment, require special handling. Each trader will have a somewhat different calculation of these factors. Experienced freight forwarders or express couriers can assist you in determining the most cost effect method for your goods. If you are a small business, consider, in particular, employing a small freight forwarder in your region, as they may be more attuned to serving a small business and give you better value for your money.

Most international shipments are transported in containers by ocean freight; it is more economical for relatively bulky, high-weight, low-value goods. Steamship carriage can be scheduled, nonscheduled, or charter. Steamship carriers are either conference lines or independents. The conference carriers compete on a "friendly" basis; they maintain similar standards and charge identical rates. This would be a violation of US antitrust laws in other sectors of the economy, but the ocean carriers are permitted to charge the same rates by law. Carriage-by-charter vessel is usually only cost effective for large quantities of goods. However, a forwarder may, on occasion, be able to place goods on a chartered vessel that has extra space and is willing to carry additional goods for a low rate.

If you are shipping by vessel, the rates may vary markedly depending on supply and demand on a particular route. For example, because of the current imbalance of trade in goods between China and the United States, many containers travel empty from the United States to China. As a result, shipping rates for containerized goods from the United States to China may be low.

Today, air transportation can be one of the most cost-effective means of transporting cargo, particularly for relatively high-value, low-weight goods, such as consumer electronic products, pharmaceuticals, or cut flowers. In addition, when you factor in the savings of transit time and less possibility for losses due to casualty or theft, air transportation may make sense for many other goods. But be cautious about air-cargo service; it can at times be uneconomic, particularly on routes with little or no competition.

A freight-forwarder colleague advises that air shipment by express courier may be a high-cost option if you are exporting products and expect payment on delivery to your foreign customer. She claims that freight forwarders are able to facilitate this sort of transaction more economically through their local correspondents. However, another expert advises against having a foreign forwarder handle collections.

International rail shipments of containers can be very cost competitive and result in faster delivery times than shipment by vessel. For example, China-Germany rail service via Kazakhstan and Russia on the Trans-Siberian Railway was recently inaugurated, and one train per week is expected in 2015. The trip takes about fifteen days.

## Shipping Containers: The Big Steel Boxes

Prior to the introduction of intermodal containers, most goods in international trade had been moved in "break bulk"—cargo in individual boxes, crates, drums, and barrels. This was a labor-intensive process, resulting in delays and significant losses of merchandise from casualty and theft. In port cities such as New York, it is estimated that in the mid-twentieth century, more than 12 percent of all employment was related to maritime freight activities. But starting about fifty years ago, the use of intermodal containers to transport goods revolutionized international trade. Today, more than 90 percent of trade is containerized. As a result, shipping costs and port employment have dramatically declined. Cranes, forklift trucks, side-loaders, and automated handling equipment efficiently handle the movement of containers from different modes of transportation—truck to rail to vessel, or truck to aircraft. Some ports are almost completely automated.

Intermodal containers are large rectangular boxes made of corrugated weathering steel with plywood floors and hinged doors fitted at one end. They are capable of being stacked up to seven units high. For maritime trade, containers have been standardized in nominal eight feet wide by eight feet, six inches high and by twenty-foot or forty-foot lengths. However, there are other

---

### Occasional Problems with Maritime Cargo

- Delay and diversion, particularly involving consolidated shipments. (NVOCCs may consolidate shipments one or more times to get better rates.) This happens frequently to small exporters looking for the lowest cost and importers relying on the foreign exporter to make shipping arrangements.

- A request from the freight forwarder to pay again for freight or for additional costs. (Sometimes this may be due to a consignee NVOCC not having paid the overseas consignor.)

- The shipment involves less than container load or coloaded cargo and a problem with another shipment in the container causes delay.

Shippers should keep track of who has custody of their shipment at all times and the identity of all NVOCCs involved. In the United States, the Federal Maritime Commission's (FMC's) Office of Consumer Affairs and Dispute Resolution Services may, in some circumstances, help to resolve shippers' problems. Its website is: http://www.fmc.gov/resources/shippers_or_other_business_entities.aspx

lengths, and taller "high cube" units are also common. At each of the eight corners of a container are castings, or "twist locks," that fasten the containers together during transit. Specially designed refrigerated containers, or "refeers," are used to transport perishable goods. For airfreight, the International Air Transport Association (IATA) has specified standard aluminum container sizes up to 11.52 cubic meters, and major air carriers also have custom designed containers to fit their aircraft.

Container capacity is usually expressed in twenty-foot equivalent units, or "TEUs." This is the cargo capacity equivalent to one standard twenty-foot length container. Each container is given a standardized ISO reporting mark that is four characters long, ending in a U, J, or Z, followed by six numbers and a check digit. This is issued by the Bureau International des Containers et du Transport Intermodal in Paris and is known as the "BIC-Code."

Containers are usually sealed to protect the contents and for efficient shipment. A simple seal may provide not much more than a visual assurance that a container's doors have not been opened. However, more sophisticated seals retain electronic data about the container and its contents on a radio frequency identification (RFID) tag, which can be "read" as a container and its contents moves through the supply chain.

IT systems track the routing of intermodal containers and determine their placement on vessels as well as the most efficient route to move them from point to point. Placement on vessels is particularly important: ships make many stops, and a container scheduled to be unloaded at the final port should not be placed above a container to be unloaded at an earlier destination. Container security systems include motion detectors that trigger alarms to deter intruders and other alarms triggering wireless communications to alert guards. Intermodal containers are also usually shipped under seal.

After a vessel reaches port, the containers are lifted by cranes and placed directly on truck chasses or, in some instances, rail cars. This is known as lift on, lift off, or LOLO. In some cases, trailers are loaded onboard with the chasses, and both units are transported to the destination. This is known as roll on, roll off, or RORO. Exporters can use containers that are owned by shipping companies or they can own or rent their own containers. Normally containers are cleaned, inspected for defects, and then packed, locked, and sealed. When an exporter seals containers, the cargo is described as "under shipper load and count," which means that the shipper, not the carrier, is legally responsible for the cargo description, weight, and number of items.

Today, more than 20 million containers are in constant circulation, carrying goods around the world. They even have utility after they are no longer suitable for carrying goods. Working in Sub-Saharan Africa, I have frequently seen containers used as businesses and homes. And even in developed countries, businesses are using used shipping containers as the underlying structure for modular homes.

## 2. Global Value Chains

As a small business, you will most likely play a role in adding value to a global supply chain through contributing goods or services. For example, you may provide accounting services in the United States for a business that imports clothing from China or you may operate a warehouse, packaging, and distribution facility in Hong Kong that receives container-load shipments of consumer goods from North America, packages the products in individual lots, and distributes them to retail outlets in Hong Kong and China. However, in some cases, your small business may produce the ultimate product or service, and you may incorporate products or services received from other countries in your own global value chain. As an example, my wife's "wearable art" small business purchases materials from Italy, the United Kingdom, and Japan and incorporates these materials into end products for sale in North America.

> ### Apple's Global Value Chain
>
> Because of volume, Apple is able to obtain large discounts on parts, assembly, and air freight. Its operational expertise gives it a major competitive advantage. As one example, a few years ago, when most computer makers were still shipping their products by sea, Apple bought up all available air cargo space to make sure its new products would be available for the holiday market. Products were shipped directly from Chinese assembly plants to consumers. Apple's engineers worked closely on site with suppliers and assemblers, translating prototypes into mass-produced products. The focus is on a few product lines with a minimum of customization.

The more complex global value chains involve inputs of goods and services from a variety of countries and economies, with manufacturing and distribution then also taking place in multiple countries. For example, Apple's iPhone 6 is designed in California. Suppliers for components are currently located in thirty-one countries, although suppliers are always changing depending on commercial realities. As of the end of 2014, 349 suppliers were located in China, 139 in Japan, 60 in the United States, 42 in Taiwan, 32 in South Korea, and 24 in the Philippines. Germany led European countries with thirteen suppliers. Components are shipped to China, where they are assembled into the end product. Finished iPhone 6s are then distributed throughout the world. Apple has been repeatedly acknowledged as having the most efficient supply chain management of all multinational firms.

## Free Zones

Special economic zones, or free zones, are frequently an important component of global value chains. These are enclaves that are physically within the borders of a particular nation, but they are outside that nation's so-called customs territory. This means that goods can be moved into and out of zones, stored there, and processed or manufactured without the application of import duties and valued added and other sales taxes; other national laws, however, still apply. Zones usually have enhanced infrastructure, such as modern roads, good electrical and other utility access, and industrial parks. This is of particular importance in developing countries that otherwise may not have a preexisting infrastructure suitable for foreign investment. Some zone programs, particularly in developing economies, provide additional financial incentives for investing in zones, such as income-tax reduction or forgiveness.

In the United States, free zones are known as foreign trade zones (FTZs). They have become an essential component of global supply chains for many businesses. In 2013, there were 177 active FTZs in the United States, housing 289 active production operations and employing approximately 390,000 people.[52] The value of shipments admitted into zones amounted to $835 billion. About 65 percent of goods admitted were "domestic status" merchandise, meaning that they were goods either made in the United States or that had already been imported and had duties and taxes paid. Production

---

[52] US Department of Commerce. "75th Report of the Foreign-Trade Zones Board to the Congress of the United States." 2013.

operations amounted to $571 billion, or 68 percent of zone activity, and warehousing/distribution operations amounted to $264 billion. The largest industries involved in zones were oil refining, automotive production, and the pharmaceutical and machinery/equipment sectors.

China has a particularly large and successful zones program. Starting in the late 1970s, China established special economic zones (SEZs) in its coastal cities as a means to apply free-market principles and provide modern infrastructure and tax incentives designed to attract foreign direct investment (FDI). In contrast to the US zones, which are primarily import oriented, China's zones are primarily designed to facilitate manufactured exports. Other economies have relied heavily on zones to attract FDI and boost trade. As examples, Ireland pioneered zones starting in 1959 in order to industrialize its economy; the Mexican *maquiladora* program has successfully attracted manufacturing operations from the United States; the Dominican Republic developed zones specializing in assembling garments; Panama developed zones adjacent to the Panama canal to facilitate storage and transshipment; Jordan has developed zones to encourage light manufacturing and facilitate international trade shipments; Dubai has developed large zones to facilitate trade and encourage duty free shopping; and India also has an active zones program.

Developing countries frequently view the establishment of zones as an important instrument of economic development. However, unless zones in developing countries are well integrated into global supply chains with strong backward and forward linkages as well as private-sector ownership and management, they frequently fail. As one example, Senegal established an export-processing zone in Dakar in 1974. However, excessive government bureaucracy and regulation, poor backward linkage (connections with local businesses outside the zone), an untrained workforce, and inadequate infrastructure and high production costs doomed the project. It closed in 1999.[53]

Businesses considering locating their operations in a zone should carefully investigate any user fees and other additional costs that may be associated with zone operations (compared to locations outside of a zone) and make certain that the benefits from zone operations outweigh any additional costs.

When zones are carefully planned and located as an important logistics link in global value chains and are managed on a for-profit basis, they usually succeed. On the other hand, if zones are located in underdeveloped regions that are remote from major transport hubs, operate solely as a government device to aid economic development, have poor backward and forward linkages, and are managed and subsidized by governments, they frequently fail.

## Evaluating and Improving Your Value Chains

Zones can be an important component of your global value chain, but they are only one of many components. Other components include your suppliers, your customers, carriers, freight forwarders, customs warehouses, and your other logistics providers. You should clearly define the value chain or chains that you participate in and then consider how the various linkages can be improved. Taking the time to chart value chains frequently may uncover relationships that were previously unclear. For example, you may have overlooked the significance of insurance providers in facilitating the

---

[53] World Bank. "Special Economic Zones: Performance, Lessons Learned and Implications for Zone Development." 2008.

movement of your goods. Or you may have been unaware of the importance of the location of distribution centers. When you chart a services value chain, it may make you more aware of cost savings that could be derived by obtaining certain services in a foreign country. In conclusion, careful analysis of your value chains may lead to increased sales and profitability for your products and services.

## *Primary Value Chain*

## *Support Activities*

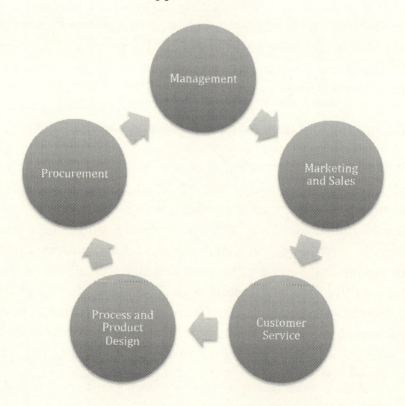

## 3. The Importance of Trade Facilitation

Trade facilitation refers to how border and behind-border procedures relating to imports and exports can be improved. Trade facilitation involves customs administration, port and other logistics efficiency, information technology, and the domestic regulatory environment affecting the movement of goods. However, the main focus is frequently on customs administration. Inefficient and corrupt customs administrations can seriously impair trade transactions, whereas modern, efficient customs administrations facilitate trade.

### The Advent of Modern Customs Procedures

The adversarial and inefficient environment connected to customs administration began to change in the 1970s with the advent of modern IT and communications technologies and a fundamental modification of the relationship between customs and traders. In the Netherlands, Dutch customs and major Dutch exporters, such as Royal Phillips, pioneered a more cooperative relationship that expedited trade and also enhanced regulatory compliance. The new, more cooperative relationship was founded on modern management and tax administration principles, including the application of risk management; use of information technology; post-transaction audits; self-assessment of duties and taxes; and simplified procedures for qualified traders. Customs and legitimate traders became partners in efforts to expedite trade and increase compliance. Traders were no longer excessively penalized for honest mistakes.

This new trade facilitating approach to customs administration also solved a major government resource problem. By the

1970s, international trade was growing rapidly, and developed-country customs administrations simply didn't have the financial resources to employ more customs officers to cope with the increases. The switch to a more cooperative approach, making customs administrations and traders partners, greatly increased administrative efficiency, improved compliance, and solved the resources problem.

Perhaps no procedure is more central to the trade facilitating approach of modern customs administrations than risk management. Risk management applied to customs administration involves statistical prediction regarding whether a particular trader dealing in a specific type of goods is a good compliance risk. Traders who have had past law violations or are dealing with countries or goods that represent compliance risks then have their imports and exports closely examined. Traders who have an unblemished record and are trading with countries and goods that do not represent a high-compliance risk are not regularly examined. However, after trade transactions are completed, traders may have their books and records audited by customs, and if violations are then uncovered, they become subject to fines and penalties. A system of required customs financial guarantees, or customs bonds, assures that traders that are found to have committed infractions will be financially liable, even years after the imports and exports concerned have been completed.

While customs risk-management systems can work without automation, modern IT systems greatly facilitate the application of risk-management criteria. High-risk shipments and traders can be identified for close examination even before goods arrive at a port or airport. Risk management specialists and other senior customs officials can also closely monitor risk-management criteria.

A US customs officer who had been a senior management at a major US port told me about one example of the effectiveness of risk management. A shipment of a large electrical generator valued at several hundred thousand dollars arrived by vessel from Colombia. The shipper was unknown to customs, and the generator was being shipped to what turned out to be a private residence in Miami, Florida. A check of trade statistics showed that Colombia then had no manufacturers or exporters of electrical generators. Exports from Colombia were also considered to be high risk at that time because of the possible smuggling of cocaine and other illegal drugs.

Risk management criteria predicted that the shipment was a very high risk for concealed illegal drugs. The customs agent carefully inspected the generator and also used an x-ray scan as well as narcotics detection dogs but uncovered nothing. Nonetheless, based on risk management, the inspector was convinced there was a likely problem. The final inspection option involved disassembling the generator to examine interior cavities. However, this could result in damage to the import, requiring reimbursement to the importer. If the inspector was wrong, he or she might even have been personally liable for this expense. The inspector finally decided to take this last step and, after doing so, found cocaine carefully hidden in the generator.

Other important elements of modern customs administration include self-declaration by traders and simplified treatment for qualified importers and exporters. Self-declaration involves traders or traders' representatives submitting customs declarations. (A customs declaration is the basic document indicating the type of goods involved in a trade transaction, the quantity and quality, the price or value, and other information required to be reported.) The old system (still used in some parts of the world) involved customs officers inspecting imports and exports and then completing customs declarations. This was inefficient and also created an environment for corruption. Self-declaration is a procedure that had worked well elsewhere in tax administration, and it has proved to greatly increase efficiency in customs administration.

Another aspect of self-declaration is a procedure for voluntarily disclosing infractions of customs law. Under the old system, if a trader unintentionally violated customs regulations, he or she had no incentive to disclose the violation to customs. Whether the trader disclosed the violation or whether customs uncovered it on their own, the penalty would be the same. And usually the penalty would be severe, possibly even the forfeiture of the goods. Under the modern system, traders that voluntarily disclose violations are usually only subject to recovery of any duties and taxes owed with interest and a small penalty. This encourages compliance on the part of traders, and it is consistent with the overall concept of a partnership between customs administrations and the trade.

A centerpiece of modern customs administration is special, simplified treatment for qualified traders. In order to qualify for special procedures, traders must meet a number of requirements: They must have had good compliance records, maintain records in accordance with required procedures, have had their records audited with no significant problems uncovered, meet minimum financial requirements and post financial security, maintain appropriate supply-chain security measures, and have qualified personnel handling trade transactions. The benefits for simplified treatment include the immediate clearance of imports and exports without inspection, the electronic submission of declarations, and the payment of duties and taxes owed on a periodic basis (for example, twice monthly or once a month), physical inspections, when necessary, at the trader's warehouse or other facilities, and the clearance of goods after hours and on weekends.

Simplified customs procedures can be of great financial benefit to traders. As an example, if your business is entitled to simplified treatment and your competitor's is not, you will be able to import and export your goods much more quickly and at a lower cost. This, in turn, will result in lower inventory requirements and carrying costs. Your competitor will not be able to stay in business long if you have such a significant advantage. Complying with customs requirements in order to qualify for simplified procedures thus becomes an imperative for modern traders.

## International Agreements Codifying Modern Customs Procedures

By the later 1990s, modern customs principles and procedures had been so successful in increasing compliance and revenue collection as well as improving administration efficiency and trade facilitation in developed economies that policy makers believed that these principles and procedures should be enshrined in international agreements. The initial effort to do this took place at the World Customs Organization (WCO), an organization based in Brussels, Belgium, that as of early 2016, represented 180 national customs administrations. WCO negotiators amended the International Convention on the Simplification and Harmonization of Customs Procedures, known as the Kyoto Convention, to include the principles of modern customs administration. This "Revised Kyoto Convention" became effective in February 2006. As of mid-2015, 103 countries and economies were signatories, including all major trading economies. However, some developing and least-developed economies have been reluctant to become members because of concerns about the investment required to modernize customs administration and other aspects of trade facilitation. Moreover, no process existed in the Revised Kyoto Convention or the WCO for enforcing treaty obligations in the event that signatories failed to comply with treaty commitments.

Because of these limitations, the WTO decided to negotiate its own agreement on trade facilitation as part of the Doha Development Round Trade Negotiations, officially launched in November 2001. The negotiating process stretched over twelve years, with professional trade and multinational businesses advocating a strong agreement and developing countries opposing an agreement because of implementation concerns and opposition from various vested interests.

In December 2013, a WTO Agreement on Trade Facilitation (TFA) was concluded. The TFA will go into effect once two-thirds of WTO members have completed their domestic ratification process. The key principles of the application of risk management and simplified treatment for authorized traders are included in the agreement. In addition, the agreement covers a variety of areas, including the publication and availability of information; advance rulings; review and appeal procedures; disciplines imposed on fees and charges; procedures relating to the release and clearance of goods; expedited shipments; formalities regarding export, import and transit of goods; and cooperation between customs authorities. Importantly, the agreement provides for phased in implementation and technical support for developing countries and LDCs. In contrast to the WCO's Revised Kyoto Convention, the provisions of the WTO's TFA are mandatory for WTO members, and noncomplying WTO members are subject to the WTO's dispute-resolution process.

Recent regional trade agreements, such as the US-Korea Free Trade Agreement, also include trade facilitation provisions. For example, chapter 7 of the US-Korea FTA contains a number of provisions about customs administration and trade facilitation, including electronic processing, the expedited release of goods, and the application of risk management.

## The Economic Benefits of Trade Facilitation

The economic benefits of improved trade facilitation for individual traders are obvious. Goods move more quickly from the producer through the supply chain to the ultimate consumer. Shipping, demurrage, and warehouse expenses are minimized. Inventory and other carrying costs are reduced. "Just in time" business systems can be adopted. Predictability and transparency of transactions are increased. In addition, there are significant benefits from improved trade facilitation for economies as a whole.

The significance of improved trade facilitation for national economic development should not be overlooked. One economic study led by World Bank economist Simeon Djankov, who later became finance minister of Bulgaria, estimated that for each day the transit time of goods can be reduced, trade volume will increase by 1 percent, and for time-sensitive goods, as much as 7 percent.[54] Other studies have confirmed similar benefits. Small nations such as Singapore, the Netherlands, the UAE, Korea, and Hong Kong (now politically part of mainland China) have relied heavily on international trade driven by improved

---

[54] Simeon Djankov, Caroline Freund, Cong S. Pham, Trading on Time, Review of Economics and Statistics (Nov. 2010).

trade facilitation to vault to the forefront of developed economies. Developing nations such as Ireland, the Dominican Republic, Panama, and Malaysia have also relied on improved trade facilitation to underpin economic development.

Singapore's story is particularly noteworthy. Today, Singapore is one of the busiest ports and financial centers in the world and has one of the world's highest per-capita incomes. But only fifty years ago, after independence from Malaysia, Singapore had a small domestic market and high levels of poverty and unemployment. Per-capita GDP was only a little over five hundred dollars. Half the population was illiterate. To promote development, Singapore adopted investment friendly, pro-free trade policies that resulted in an average of 8 percent growth per year through 1999. Trade facilitation was essential to its development strategy as a logistics hub for Southeast Asia. Today, Singapore is ranked as having among the best trade facilitation in the world.

## Measuring Trade Facilitation

The World Bank has developed two methodologies for measuring the level of trade facilitation for a nation or economy. One of these methodologies is an annual survey called "Trading across Borders."[55] The other is a survey known as the "Logistics Performance Index."[56] A third survey, the World Economic Forum's Global Enabling Trade Report,[57] also evaluates trade facilitation across nations and economies.

---

[55] http://www.doingbusiness.org
[56] http://lpi.worldbank.org
[57] http://www.weforum.org/reports/global-enabling-trade-report-2014

**Country Reports on Trade Facilitation: A Useful Tool for Traders**

Country trade facilitation reports from the most recent LPI or Trading across Borders surveys are useful when evaluating potential problems exporting and importing goods from a specific economy. As might be expected, the leading developed economies rank at the top of the LPI. In the 2014 survey, the top ten economies, in order, are Germany, the Netherlands, Belgium, the United Kingdom, Singapore, Sweden, Norway, Luxemburg, the United States, and Japan.

Looking at Brazil, Russia, India, and China, the four so-called BRIC developing countries that have obtaining notoriety because of the sizes of their economies and their rapid recent development, the 2014 LPI ranks China twenty-eighth out of 160 economies surveyed. India is ranked fifty-fourth. Brazil is ranked sixty-fifth, and Russia is ranked ninetieth. These scores can be unbundled into their components: customs, infrastructure, international shipments, logistics, tracking, and timeliness. So, for example, for international shipments (ease of arranging competitively priced shipments), China ranks 22nd, India 44th, Brazil 81st, and Russia 102nd. This should tell you that you should anticipate some shipment delays and additional costs when doing business with firms located in Brazil and Russia.

In the event that you are considering trading with businesses located in countries such as Bolivia (ranked 121st), Mongolia (ranked 135th), and Iraq (ranked 141st), you should be especially attentive about issues relating to the time and cost of transporting goods. And if you weren't already concerned about political instability in the lowest ranked economies— Afghanistan (158th), the Democratic Republic of Congo (159th), and Somalia (160th)—their LPI rankings provide good reason not to do business there.

### *Takeaways for Chapter 5*

- Consult trade facilitation surveys before deciding to do business in a particular foreign country or economy.

- Understand the roles of the various logistics providers— freight forwarders, express couriers, carriers, customs brokers, insurers, warehouse operators, trade advisers, IT specialists, and PSI and 3PL firms and how to select the logistics providers to assist your business.

- Appreciate the significance of intermodal containers to the expansion of world trade.

- Know the role played by free zones in value chains.

- Know how to chart, evaluate, and improve your own value chain.

# Chapter 6

# How Do You Navigate Government Regulations of Imports and Exports?

If you have ten thousand regulations, you
destroy all respect for the law.

—Winston Churchill

### *Overview of Chapter 6*

This chapter's topic, an overview of government regulations of international trade transactions, is complex. However, your general understanding of these regulations will be key to planning successful trade transactions.

The government regulations discussed in this chapter are examined from the point of view of a business located in the United States or a foreign firm doing business with a US partner. However, the regulations applicable to trade transactions are similar in most economies.

Chapter 6 is divided into three parts: a discussion of regulations affecting trade in goods, a discussion of regulations affecting trade in services, and additional regulations affecting trade transactions. The first part, discussing trade in goods, is subdivided into regulations affecting imports of goods, trade remedies, and regulations affecting exports of goods. The second part, discussing trade in services, is subdivided into regulations affecting the four types of trade in services: cross-border movement of service products; movement of service consumers to the country of importation; establishment of a commercial presence for the provision of services in a foreign country; and the temporary movement of natural persons to another country in order to provide services there. The third part discusses additional government regulations applicable to international trade transactions, such as taxes, government contract restrictions, competition law and prohibitions on bribery, and money laundering.

*Additional information regarding specific government regulations can be obtained from referenced government websites, publications discussing in detail specific regulations and from trade advisers.*

## 1. Regulations of Trade In Goods

### a. Import Regulations

Government regulations of imports and exports, especially the assessment of duties, taxes, and other restrictions, and delays resulting from inspections and other bureaucratic requirements, can significantly increase your trade-transaction costs. This can be a "deal breaker" for international trade transactions, especially if the government regulations are not transparent and subject to corrupt administration. However, knowledge is power when it comes to government regulations. If you understand both the general trade environment in the countries where you plan to do business and the specific regulations applicable to your trade transactions you should be able to assess whether you can profitably do business there.

---

### *Government Regulations as a Deal Breaker*

In 2001, I was working as a consultant in Mozambique, interviewing local businesses that engaged in international trade transactions. At the time, Mozambique, a former Portuguese colony, had recently emerged from a civil war. Its customs administration was dysfunctional. A Mozambique business told me that rather than dealing with Mozambique customs, they smuggled goods across the border with South Africa. They said that although the cost of obtaining smuggled goods was about 45 percent higher than if they imported legitimately, they received the smuggled goods in their warehouses within 48 hours of placing the order, whereas goods processed through Mozambique customs were delayed by a month or longer, and the ultimate costs were difficult to predict because of complex regulations and corruption.

I never recommend smuggling as a business option! In addition to the moral and ethical problems, the ultimate costs could include forfeiture of property, substantial penalties, and prison time. If you encounter an environment like Mozambique's in 2001, you should not do business there.

---

As a small business, you do not need to know all the details of government regulations of trade transactions, but you should know, in general, how customs duties and other border assessments are determined, the border procedures, restrictions and prohibitions that may be applicable, and how in general international trade is regulated. Detailed information on duties and other border assessments and restrictions applicable to your products or services can be obtained from government websites and qualified customs brokers and trade advisers.

Throughout human history, governments have regulated the movement of goods and people between nations. Originally, the main aims of these border controls were to impose duties and other taxes on imports and exports, to prevent smuggling, and to restrict the entry of aliens. Today, a large number of government agencies regulate the imports and exports of goods and services. Some of these agencies, most notably customs and immigration agencies, are physically present on borders and have primary responsibility for border controls. Others, such as agencies regulating food and drug safety, product standards, agricultural products and livestock safety, intellectual property, trade in weapons, and unfair trade practices may enforce their requirements through customs administrations or their own inspectors.

In the United States, the main border agencies are Customs and Border Protection (CBP) and Immigration and Customs Inspection (ICE), both part of the Department of Homeland Security. However, as many as forty-five additional US government agencies also have responsibilities regarding the regulation of international trade and may be involved with border inspections.

The first US Congress created US Customs in 1789 to collect duties on imported goods and prevent smuggling. In its early years, Customs was the primary source of federal government revenue. However, by 1940 tariffs represented only about 6 percent of all tax revenue. Currently, tariffs and other border taxes and fees amount to only a little over 2 percent of all federal government revenue collections. In recent decades, Customs' mission has been primarily law enforcement. In 2003, as part of a government reorganization to deal with the threat of terrorist attacks, Customs was combined with the inspection programs of the Immigration and Naturalization Service (INS), Plant Protection and Quarantine, and the Border Patrol to form US Customs and Border Protection, a component of the Department of Homeland Security (DHS). In addition, the investigative branches of Customs and INS were combined to form Immigration and Customs Enforcement (ICE), also a part of DHS.

---

### Other US Agencies Regulating Trade Transactions

Food and Drug Administration (FDA)–responsible for the safety of food and drug products

Food Safety and Inspection Service (FSIS)–inspects meat, poultry, and egg products for safety as well as correct labeling and packaging

Animal and Health Plant Inspection Service (APHIS)–inspects for pests and disease

Consumer Product Safety Commission (CPSC)–responsible for the safety of consumer products

Bureau of Industry and Security (BIS)–regulates exports for national security

International Trade Administration (ITA)–responsible for trade remedies

Environmental Protection Agency (EPA)–responsible for compliance with environmental standards

National Highway Transportation Safety Administration (NHTSA)–regulates the safety requirements of vehicles

Fish and Wildlife Service–supervises imports of wildlife and wildlife products

Bureau of Alcohol, Tobacco and Firearms (BATF)–regulates the importation of beverage alcohol, tobacco, and firearm products

US Coast Guard (USCG)–safeguards maritime borders

Transportation Security Administration (TSA)–protects transportation systems

## Border Agencies, Single Windows, and Trade Facilitation

Obviously, the regulatory oversight and inspections conducted by these various border agencies in the United States—and comparable multiple border agencies in other countries—can significantly slow the processing of trade transactions. This is being addressed through the development of information technology and single-window systems. The key benefits of a single window system for a nation's border agencies and traders are the following

- There is an improvement of information flows by electronically sharing all information with all stakeholders, including private-sector participants, such as banks and insurance firms, and all relevant public agencies;

- Traders submit standardized information and documents through a single electronic gateway—a single window. This eliminates delays resulting from paper-based document submissions to multiple agencies, improves coordination and cooperation, and increases the accuracy of data.

- Systematic data collection improves the quality of trader profiles and risk-management systems, reducing physical inspections and improving cargo security.

- Trader compliance is improved and duties and fees are collected more quickly, increasing government revenue and reducing corruption.

In the United States, in 2014, the Border Interagency Executive Council (BIEC) was established to improve coordination among border agencies and the trade community. The Executive Order[58] creating BIEC also requires the completion and utilization of a government-wide international trade data system (ITDS) by December 2016. CBP plans to complete implementation of an Automated Commercial Environment (ACE) system by the end of 2016 that will incorporate ITDS and create a "single window" for all trade transactions.

Other nations and customs unions also are developing single-window systems to improve trade facilitation and revenue collection. Singapore, a small island nation that is a logistics hub for Southeast Asia, was a pioneer of single-window processing to improve trade facilitation. Today, Singapore's system, called TradeNet, handles more than thirty thousand customs declarations daily, processes more than 99 percent of permits in ten minutes, and receives all collections through interbank deductions.[59]

As of early 2015, eighteen economies had adopted a single window system that links government agencies electronically, and fifty-five have partial systems. The WTO's Trade Facilitation Agreement urges all WTO members to establish and use single-window processing.[60] In addition, major multinational enterprises and international logistics providers are actively lobbying for rapid implementation of single window systems. This should lead to additional single window system adoptions in the next decade.

---

[58] EO 13659 Feb. 19, 2014.
[59] World Bank. "Implementing trade single windows in Singapore, Colombia and Azerbaijan." 2014.
[60] Trade Facilitation Agreement, Article 10(4).

## Customs Duties, Taxes, and Fees

In contrast to the United States and a few other developed economies, tariffs and other border taxes on imports and exports remain an important source of revenue for many other countries. For example, in 2009, border collections amounted to a little over 12 percent on average for EU countries, 15 percent of government revenue for India, and in the range of 50 percent to 60 percent for some sub-Saharan African and small island nation countries.[61] Kosovo, a new nation, received about 78 percent of all government tax revenue in 2012 from border collections. This higher reliance on border collections by many economies is mainly attributable to the collection of national sales taxes, such as VAT, at the border (and in the case of some developing economies, to an ineffective internal tax collection administration). The United States has no national sales tax.

Because of the reliance of many governments on border collections for national revenue, it is not surprising that they closely scrutinize trade transactions to assure that

> ### Four Basic WTO Rules
>
> The WTO regime establishes four basic rules applicable to international trade. These are:
>
> 1. Tariffs are the only permitted mechanism to protect domestic producers from import competition. Quotas and other nontariff barriers (NTBs) are normally not allowed.
>
> 2. Tariffs are "bound," which means that they cannot be increased except as may rarely be permitted by WTO rules.
>
> 3. All WTO members must give most favored nation (MFN) treatment to goods from other WTO members. This means that a benefit given to one trading partner must normally be given to all others.
>
> 4. WTO members must give national treatment to imports from other members. This means that a nation cannot discriminate in favor of its domestic products after goods have been imported.

---

[61] WCO survey (Jan. 2012).

the correct duties, taxes, and fees are collected. This can result in delays and red tape at borders, creating an environment conducive to corruption unless modern, trade-facilitating procedures have been adopted. International agreements designed to lower tariffs and other trade-transaction costs, and improve trade facilitation, recently culminated with the adoption of the WTO's Trade Facilitation Agreement.

## The International Rules

As previously discussed in chapter 1, there has been a great deal of convergence in the national border regulations since WWII as a result of GATT and, more recently, WTO and WCO agreements. As a consequence, the import and export procedures reviewed in this chapter almost always have a basis in international standards.

WTO and WCO agreements impose standards governing how goods are described for customs purposes, how they are valued for customs purposes, and how a variety of other border procedures relating to international trade—such as import licensing, the application of sanitary and phytosanitary measures, product standards, and the protection of trade related intellectual property rights—must be conducted. In addition, WTO agreements govern the imposition of additional duties or other restrictions resulting from unfair trade practices or imports causing serious injury to domestic producers. WTO agreements also govern trade in services and government procurement. We will briefly discuss these international standards in this chapter.

Customs duties and other border assessments on imports are normally determined based upon three procedures: the description or "classification" of the imported goods, the value for customs purposes of the imported goods, and the origin of the imported goods. Based upon the application of these three procedures, the appropriate tariff published in a nation's tariff schedule is then applied (or no tariff is assessed if the goods are duty free). Proper application of these three customs procedures is also essential for the collection of international trade statistics. And in a few cases, the application of these procedures will lead to the imposition of additional duties and charges, such as antidumping or countervailing duties or safeguards restrictions, or even the exclusion of the imported goods as prohibited merchandise.

## Customs Classification of Goods and Tariff Rates

The "classification," or description of goods for customs purposes, is governed by an international agreement administered by the WCO. This has a forbidding title, "The International Convention on Harmonized Commodity Description and Coding System," but it is usually just referred to as the Harmonized System or "HS." Over two hundred countries currently use the HS. It is a common international, six-digit code arranged in a hierarchical order with rules of interpretation. It is updated by the WCO every five to six years. The 2012 edition is divided into twenty-one sections and ninety-seven chapters. The chapters, in turn, are divided into four-digit "superior" headings and six-digit product codes. An example from the HS—chapter 50, silk—follows:

| Heading | H.S. Code | |
| --- | --- | --- |
| 1. 50.01 | 5001.00 | Silk worm cocoons suitable for reeling |
| 2. 50.02 | 5002.00 | Raw silk (not thrown) |

3.  50.03  5003.00    Silk waste (including cocoons unsuitable for reeling, yarn waste and garneted stock)

4.  50.04  5004.00    Silk yarn (other than yarn spun from silk waste) not put up for retail sale

5.  50.05  5005.00    Yarn spun from silk waste not put up for retail sale

6.  50.06  5006.00    Silk yarn and yarn spun from silk waste, put up for retail sale; silk-worm gut

7.  50.07  Woven fabrics of silk or silk waste

      5007.10    Fabrics of noil silk

      5007.20    Other fabrics containing 85 percent or more by weight of silk or silk waste other than noil silk

      5007.90    Other fabrics

Many countries, particularly more developed economies, expand on this six-digit code to distinguish product variations for both duty and statistical purposes. For example, the United States uses a ten-digit code, adding an additional four digits to the HS nomenclature. The first two additional digits differentiate applicable duties. The last two are only for statistical purposes. A national tariff schedule typically also includes the applicable tariff rate for particular items as well as indicates any regulatory restrictions. The entry from the

Harmonized Tariff Schedule of the United States (2015) for HS 5007.90 (silk, other fabrics) follows as an example:[62]

| Heading/ Sub-heading | Stat. Suffix | Article Description | Unit of quantity | Rate of Duty – General | Rate of Duty – Special | "Column 2" Rate (currently applicable to North Korea, Cuba) |
|---|---|---|---|---|---|---|
| 5007.90 | | Other fabrics | | | | |
| 5007.90.30 | | Contains 85 percent or more of silk or silk waste | m2/kg | 0.8 percent | Free (letters specifying certain countries whose exports qualify because of free trade agreements or other arrangements) | 90 percent |
| | 20 | Not jacquard woven— more than 127 cm in width | | | | |
| | 40 | Not jacquard woven - other | | | | |
| | 90 | Other | | | | |

---

[62] http://www.usitc.gov/tata/hts/index.htm

What you should know about the tariff schedules is that they will determine how your product is described and, therefore, what duty rate and other regulatory requirements will be applied to your imports or exports. Frequently, there may be more than one tariff description that will apply to your goods and, therefore, different duty rates may be applicable. This can, at times, be extremely important to your business, and you should seek advice from a knowledgeable trade consultant or lawyer when planning your trade transactions. It is possible to obtain a binding advance ruling from customs agencies to guarantee that your imports or exports will be entitled to a particular classification and duty rate. The procedure for obtaining these rulings is discussed later in this chapter.

Some years ago, one of my US-based clients was importing a steel product from China that was used in the construction industry. Its proper customs classification was not clear. One option was classification as a basic steel product, which normally took a low duty rate, and another option was classification as a construction industry product, which took a slightly higher rate. Naturally my client opted for the lower duty rate. However, after some years of importing the product, temporary additional duties designed to protect the US steel industry were imposed on basic steel products. These temporary duties were very high and, of course, completely changed my client's costs. We tried to argue to customs that the original classification as a basic steel product was incorrect, but customs had previously accepted this classification and was reluctant to change it.

This case illustrates a basic principle of tariff interpretation. Once goods have been "classified" under at particular tariff number, customs administrations are reluctant to change the classification. Consistency and predictability are frequently valued more highly than technical correctness. Nonetheless, litigating a classification decision may still be worth it to a trader if a change in classification will result in major savings in duties or as a defensive measure against possible penalties claimed for an "incorrect" classification.

In some cases, a new tariff nomenclature must be created to describe a new product or products that have been classified in a "basket category" (a "basket category" is a tariff item that covers goods "not otherwise provided for"). These products must be specifically described, or "broken out," in order to better collect statistics or apply trade remedies. In the United States, the US International Trade Commission has the responsibility for periodically revising and updating the tariff

> ### Some Famous Customs Personalities
>
> • Adam Smith, economist and author of *Wealth of Nations*, was Commissioner of Customs for Scotland.
>
> • Geoffrey Chaucer, father of English poetry, was controller of customs for London.
>
> • Henri Rousseau, the French painter, was a customs officer for twenty-two years.
>
> • Herman Melville, *Moby Dick* author, was a customs inspector for the Port of New York for nineteen years,
>
> • -Chester Arthur, twenty-first President of the United States, was customs collector for the port of New York.

schedule. One of my clients, an association of fencing manufacturers, was able to convince the Commission to add a "break out" to the tariff schedule for particular fencing products that had previously been classified in a basket category. This allowed the association to better track trade trends.

At times, the classification of a truly new and different product must be resolved by a change to the Harmonized System. The

WCO considers these cases and issues a revised and updated HS every five to six years.

For historical and policy reasons, tariff rates vary widely from nation to nation and, in some cases, can be extremely complex. The current version of the Harmonized Tariff Schedule of the United States (HTSUS) contains over ten thousand eight-digit tariff lines.[63] The simple average rate is 4.8 percent. A significant number of tariffs are very low, and 37 percent of tariff lines are free. On the other hand, many tariffs above 25 percent *ad valorem* (of value) are in the agricultural, footwear, and textiles sectors. Although the large majority of US tariffs are ad valorem, about 11 percent of duty rates are specific or compound (A specific duty rate is a specific amount per unit of measurement, such as cents/kg. A compound duty rate is a combination of an ad valorem duty and a specific duty rate). These are concentrated in the agricultural, footwear, and textiles sectors, which have historically been highly protected for political reasons.

The European Union also has a very complex tariff schedule, with over nine thousand tariff lines at the eight-digit level, and tariff peaks designed to protect politically sensitive industries, such as agriculture, footwear, garments, and leather.[64] The simple average rate is 6.5 percent. Around 11 percent of the EU's tariff lines are not ad valorem, mostly on agricultural products. The European Union uses seasonal duties and duties that are reduced if an import's price is above a certain level. The duties on some agricultural products can be extremely high: for example, the duty on preserved mushrooms is 170 percent, and on citrus juice, it is 196 percent.

---

[63] WTO. "Trade Policy Review of the United States of America." December 2014.

[64] WTO. "Trade Policy Review: European Union. July 2015.

In contrast to the United States and European Union, a few economies with a free-trade philosophy have adopted a very simple tariff approach. For example, Singapore applies the ASEAN Harmonized Tariff Nomenclature, containing over 9,500 eight-digit tariff items. However, all goods, except for six beverage alcohol products that are restricted for social reasons, are duty free.

> **Finding the Tariffs Applicable to Your Products**
>
> Most national customs administrations publish their country's tariff schedules on their website (for example, for the US, see http://www.cbp.gov/document/guidance/harmonized-tariff-schedule), and if you already know the tariff classifications of your products under the HS, you can check the applicable tariffs on the national customs administration's website. However, the safest course of action is to verify the classification with a local customs broker or other trade adviser, and if there is any doubt, obtain an advance ruling verifying the classification and duty prior to importing or exporting your goods.

## Customs Valuation of Goods

After determining a goods' customs classification, its value must also be determined, in most cases, in order to calculate applicable duties and taxes and for statistical purposes. The WTO has adopted rules that govern this. They are set out in the WTO's Agreement on the Implementation of Article VII of the General Agreement on Tariffs and Trade 1994, known as the Agreement on Customs Valuation (ACV).

The ACV's main rule is that value of goods for customs purposes should be based on the price actually paid or payable for goods when they are sold for export. This, in other words, is the invoice or contract price. It is known as the transaction value. The transaction value may be adjusted upward for certain expenses incurred by the importer, such as commissions and brokerage (but not buying commissions), packing and containers, assists, royalties, proceeds from a subsequent sale that are paid to the seller, and the costs of transport and insurance.

In cases where transaction value cannot be determined, the ACV provides for alternative valuation methodologies. These are, in the order of preference, the transaction value of identical goods; the transaction value of similar goods, with appropriate adjustments; the deductive value (the first unrelated sale in the country of importation less commissions or the additions for general expenses and profit, the costs of transportation and insurance within the country, and customs duties and taxes assessed); the computed value (the cost of materials, fabrication, general expenses and profit, and other expenses necessary to produce the goods in the country of export); or a fall-back method consistent with the principles of the ACV. When using the fall-back method, customs administrations cannot employ the selling price in the country of importation, minimum customs values (e.g., price lists), fictitious values, or several similar methodologies. At the request of the importer, the order of deductive value and computed value may be reversed.

In the United States and most developed economies, more than 90 percent of imports are routinely valued based on transaction value. However, some developing country customs administrations have found it difficult to apply the ACV for a number of reasons. Frequently, customs personnel are not well trained in applying the principles of the ACV. In addition, many of these countries do not fully employ modern customs investigative procedures, such as risk management and postclearance audits. There is also usually intense pressure on these customs administrations to maximize revenue collections. As a consequence, these administrations may resort to value "uplifts" based upon price lists or other information even though this is not permissible under the ACV. (Price lists, such as Blue Book values for automobiles, can be used as investigation tools to determine whether a claimed transaction value is legitimate, but the dutiable value must ultimately be determined using one of the mandated ACV methodologies.)

It is frequently possible to obtain an advance customs ruling from customs administrations on the methodology that will be used to establish valuation based on the facts presented. This is advisable if there is a concern that the transaction value may not be accepted because the parties are related and the relationship may have influenced the price, the shipment is "on consignment," or for some other reason.

### What is GSP?

The Generalized System of Preferences (GSP) program is an exemption from the WTO's MFN principle that permits developed economies, such as the United States, and other nations to provide duty-free treatment to specified imports from designated beneficiary countries. Under the US program, for goods to originate in a beneficiary country, at least 35 percent of the value must be attributed to the growth, products, or manufacture of the beneficiary country. So-called "import-sensitive" products, such as garments and footwear, are usually excluded from the program. The United States reviews eligibility of countries and products on an annual basis. Congress has periodically renewed the program.

## Origin of Goods

Rules of origin are laws, regulations, and administrative determinations applied to determine the origin of goods. There are two types of rules of origin: nonpreferential and preferential. Nonpreferential rules are used to determine nonpreferential duties, quantitative restrictions, marking, and origin for trade remedies, government procurement, and statistics. Preferential rules are used to determine origin for regional trade agreements and preferential programs, such as the US Generalized System of Preferences (GSP) and the African Growth and Opportunity Act (AGOA).

After the Uruguay Round Trade Negotiations, the WTO planned on adopting an agreement establishing nonpreferential rules of origin and established a work plan to do this. However, an agreement has not been possible because of the differing viewpoints of WTO members. A number of different methodologies are typically used by national governments to determine nonpreferential origin. These include the "entirely the growth or manufacture of a specified country" rule; a change in tariff nomenclature at the four-digit level; an ad valorem percentage criterion; specific manufacturing or processing operations; and the "substantial transformation" rule. "Substantial transformation" refers to a rule developed by US courts providing that if a manufacturing process results in a new and different product, the origin of the new product is where the manufacturing process took place, even if some or all of the inputs were imported materials.

The World Chambers Federation (WCF) and the International Chamber of Commerce (ICC) have developed a certificate-of-origin service through which national chambers of commerce issue nonpreferential and preferential certificates of origin according to specific guidelines. These provide useful proof of origin. However, these certificates are not binding on national customs administrations; they are free to disregard the certificates, conduct an investigation and apply their own criteria.

One of the most contentious cases I handled as a trade lawyer involved a client that fabricated hand tools in the United States from components made in Taiwan. US Customs claimed that the tools should have been labeled "made in Taiwan" because they had not been substantially transformed in the United States, and it brought a civil penalty case against my client, claiming fraud. After an administrative review, the case ended up in federal court. The court eventually threw the case out on procedural grounds. Nonetheless, it was an uncertain and expensive process that could have been avoided if my client had requested a ruling from customs regarding origin before manufacturing and selling the tools.

> ### US Country-of-Origin Marking Requirements
>
> United States law requires that every article of foreign origin or its container be marked to show the country of origin. The marking must be in a conspicuous place and be legible, indelible, and permanent. If CBP finds that goods have not been properly marked, they may be subject to a redelivery notice, liquidated damages, and a marking penalty.

Because of the varying criteria used by different customs administrations in determining nonpreferential origin, it may be necessary to obtain an advance ruling regarding origin if this will be an important issue for the determination of duties or other regulatory requirements. It is also frequently advisable to obtain an advance ruling regarding the qualification of imports for preferential duties.

## The "Other" Border Taxes and Fees

In addition to the assessment of customs duties, CBP also collects other taxes and fees on trade transactions. These include merchandise processing fees (MPF), other "user fees," a harbor maintenance fee (HMF), excise taxes, and small fees collected for other federal agencies. Importers of record for commercial transactions (formal entries) are required to pay a merchandise processing fee of approximately 0.35 percent of the value of the merchandise imported. Duty, freight, and insurance charges are excluded from value. However, many preference programs provide a MPF exemption. User fees collected include agricultural and land border inspection fees and those for customs broker licensing and IP enforcement. WTO rules require that user fees reflect the approximate costs of the services rendered. A harbor maintenance fee is assessed on imports of goods through ocean ports. It is not applicable to air cargo or exports. The current HMT is 0.125 percent of the value of commercial cargo.

Federal excise taxes are imposed on imports of firearms and ammunition, beverage alcohol products, tobacco products, and gasoline and diesel fuel. (Excise taxes are also imposed on certain international services, such as telecommunications and air and ship transportation.) The current excise tax on beverage alcohol products is $13.50 per proof gallon or about $0.21 per ounce of alcohol. Beer is taxed at about $0.10 per ounce of alcohol and wine at about $0.08 per ounce of alcohol. Federal excise taxes on tobacco vary depending on the product. For small cigarettes, the tax is $3.90 per carton.

The customs administrations of many other countries collect national sales taxes, such as VAT, on imports of goods. These frequently are an important source of government income. For example, as of early 2015, Denmark's VAT was 25 percent; the United Kingdom's was 20 percent; Germany's was 19 percent; China's was 17 percent and Mexico's was 16 percent. Canada imposes a Goods and Services Tax (GST) of 5 percent and Harmonized Services Taxes (HST) ranging up to 14 percent, administered by Canadian provinces. National VAT taxes are normally rebated in these countries when goods are exported. Excise taxes on beverage alcohol and tobacco products and other "luxury goods" are also commonly applied on imports.

The WTO valuation methodology discussed above is also used for the assessment of VAT. Thus, even for countries that essentially have a free-trade or low-tariff regime for duties, WTO valuation is important for VAT and statistical purposes. In 2007, I provided technical assistance to Chile's Customs regarding applying WTO valuation methodology and the establishment of advance rulings. At the time, Chile imposed a tariff on most imports of from 0 to 6 percent, but its VAT rate of 19 percent was much more important for border revenue collection.

## Customs Publications and Rulings

When you are considering importing goods from another country the information that your national customs administration provides on its website and through its rulings service can be extremely helpful. Both WTO and WCO agreements require customs administrations to publish their general rules and requirements and to issue rulings on request providing binding advice to traders. The WTO requirements are found in GATT Article X and the WTO's Agreement on Trade Facilitation, articles 1–3. (Article 3 provides for advance rulings; these are written decisions issued *prior* to the importation of goods that bind customs administrations regarding the treatment of goods at the time of importation.) The WCO's requirements regarding publication and rulings are found in the Revised Kyoto Convention, General Annex, chapter 9.

In the United States, CBP maintains an electronic library on its website that includes customs laws, regulations, and instructions as well as prior rulings of general applicability.[65] This allows traders to research precedents regarding previous imports of goods. CBP's electronic resources include the

---

[65] See http://www.cbp.gov/trade/trade-community.

Customs Bulletin and Decisions, a weekly compilation of decisions, rulings, regulations, and abstracts; trade-related Federal Register notices; and publications, directives, and handbooks covering various trade topics.

In addition, CBP issues binding advance rulings regarding imports. A ruling letter may address classification, origin, valuation methodology, the exclusion of merchandise, and many other matters relating to CBP jurisdiction. CBP also issues binding rulings regarding current and past customs transactions. These are in the form of internal advice letters or protest review decisions.

Most other customs administrations in developed and advanced developing countries also maintain customs information on a website and provide for rulings and advance rulings. You can access this information by searching for a country's customs administration's website. (These websites are also frequently obtainable through the WCO's website, http://www.wcoomd. org/en/about-us/wco-members/wco-regional-websites. aspx) However, some LDCs with limited resources have not yet developed websites that provide detailed information and provide for the electronic submission of advance rulings.

Even if a customs broker or other trade professional is assisting you in planning your trade transactions, you should review the online information available about your planned business. At a minimum, you may be able to verify the advice you are receiving, and in some cases, your review may indicate options your consultants have not considered.

## Making Customs Import Entries: Declarations and Accompanying Documents

A customs declaration (also called a customs goods declaration) is an official document used to provide the required details about goods being imported and exported. Declarations are increasingly made in electronic format. This is the primary point of contact between you, as the trader, and the customs authorities. In many countries such as the United States, you have the right to submit your own declaration and the required accompanying documents; in other countries, a customs agent or broker must do this on your behalf.

In a prior era, customs officers would examine the merchandise when it arrived and make decisions about its description (classification), value, and the duties and taxes due. This created significant delays and also fostered an environment where corruption could flourish. Unfortunately, this system still is followed in some developing countries. In contrast, modern customs best practice requires that the trader or his or her representative make customs declarations, describing the goods and their value and calculating the applicable duty and other charges. Customs may subsequently check the information provided, and the trader is responsible for the accuracy of all information submitted. In the event that the information provided is found to be inaccurate, the trader may be subject to increased duties and penalties.

In the United States, when goods are imported, they are known as "entries for consumption." This is a two-part process that requires filing the documents necessary for determining whether Customs can release the shipment from its custody and submitting documents that contain information relating to duty assessment or for statistical purposes. Normally, entries and related documents are submitted electronically.

These documents are the following:

- a Bill of Lading (B/L) or Air Waybill

- an Entry Manifest (CBP Form 7533), Application and Special Permit for Immediate Delivery (CBP Form 3461), or other form of merchandise release required by the port director

- evidence of the right to make entry

- commercial invoice or a pro forma invoice when the commercial invoice cannot be produced

- packing lists, if appropriate

- a certificate of origin, if required

- other documents necessary to determine merchandise admissibility, if required (for example, to fulfill sanitary and phytosanitary requirements).

An entry summary for consumption (CBP Form 7501) must be filed and estimated duties deposited within ten working days of the goods' entry. In addition, a customs bond in an amount sufficient to cover any duties, taxes, and other charges that may be applicable must accompany the entry.

After an entry is presented, it may be inspected, or inspection may be waived. Whether goods are inspected or not is normally determined by the application of risk-management criteria, although inspections for statistical verification purposes are also sometimes performed. On average, about 4 percent of goods imported into the United States are inspected during the entry process.

> **You can obtain CBP forms from the CBP website:** *http://www.cbp.gov/newsroom/ publications/forms.*

The fact that goods are not inspected at the time of importation doesn't let importers off the hook. After importation, CBP may review the documents and, based on that review, request redelivery of the merchandise to CBP for inspection. In addition, importers may be subject to post clearance audits of their books and records. If these subsequent inspections reveal omissions or errors, the importer will be liable for any increased duties and interest on the additional payment. Depending on the nature of the omission or error, penalties may also be assessed. Entries are not final until they are liquidated, which refers to when Customs makes a final determination of duty liability. In the United States, liquidations must normally take place no later than one year after entry of the goods.

The immediate release of goods from customs control on arrival may be authorized in some cases. CBP Form 3461 is used for this purpose, submitted prior to the arrival of the goods. An entry summary must then be filed and estimated duties paid within ten working days of the release of the goods. This procedure is currently limited to goods arriving from Canada and Mexico, articles for trade fairs, and a few other categories of merchandise.

*Commercial Invoices*

Commercial invoices must be signed by the seller or shipper and contain the following information:[66]

- the port of entry to which the merchandise is destined;

- if merchandise is sold or agreed to be sold, the time, place, and names of buyer and seller; if consigned, the time and origin of shipment as well as the names of shipper and receiver;

- a detailed description of the merchandise, including the name by which each item is known, the grade or quality, and the marks, numbers, and symbols under which it is sold by the seller or manufacturer to the trade in the country of exportation, together with the marks and numbers of the packages in which the merchandise is packed;

- the quantities in weights and measures;

- if sold or agreed to be sold, the purchase price of each item in the currency of the sale;

- if the merchandise is shipped for consignment, the value of each item in the currency in which the transactions are usually made or, in the absence of such value, the price in such currency that the manufacturer, seller, shipper, or owner would have received or was willing to receive, for such merchandise if sold in the ordinary

---

[66] Source: Importing into the United States: *A Guide for Commercial Importers* (CBP 2006).

course of trade and in the usual wholesale quantities in the country of exportation;

- the kind of currency;

- all charges upon the merchandise, itemized by name and amount, including freight, insurance, commission, cases, containers, coverings, and cost of packing; and, if not included above, all charges, costs, and expenses incurred in bringing the merchandise from alongside the carrier at the port of exportation in the country of exportation and placing it alongside the carrier at the first US port of entry. The cost of packing, cases, containers, and inland freight to the port of exportation need not be itemized by amount if included in the invoice price and so identified. Where the required information does not appear on the invoice as originally prepared, it shall be shown on an attachment to the invoice;

- all rebates, drawbacks, and bounties, separately itemized, allowed upon the exportation of the merchandise;

- the country of origin; and

- all goods or services furnished for the production of the merchandise not included in the invoice price.

A separate invoice is required for each shipment. However, goods assembled for shipment to the same consignee by one commercial carrier may be included in a single invoice. Commercial invoices should specify whether the production of the goods involved "assists"—that is, dies, molds, tooling, artwork, engineering work, and so forth—not included in the invoice price. If assists are involved, their value and source should be specified.

*Pro Forma Invoices*

If a commercial invoice cannot be submitted when the goods are entered, the importer must file a pro forma invoice at the time of entry. The commercial invoice then must be submitted within 120 days of the date of the entry summary. If the commercial invoice is not submitted within this period, the importer incurs a liability under his or her customs bond.

## Six Useful Customs Procedures

Some useful customs procedures include customs-bonded warehouses, foreign trade zones, transit under bond, ATA carnets, temporary importation bonds, and drawback.

There may be times when you want to postpone making customs entry of goods. For example, if the duties and taxes on importation are significant, as may be the case with beverage alcohol and tobacco products or garments and footwear, or you purchased the goods or obtained them on consignment without having a customer, it may be advantageous to store the goods in a customs-bonded warehouse or foreign trade zone until they are sold. This defers the payment of duties and taxes.

A customs-bonded warehouse is a building or other secured area where goods are stored under CBP supervision and are held under an appropriate bond or financial guarantee. Goods may remain in a bonded warehouse for up to five years from the date of importation. There are eleven different classes authorized. Common bonded warehouses include warehouses owned and leased by CBP; private warehouses for the use of specific importers; public-bonded warehouses for the storage of imported goods; bonded warehouses established for the manufacture in bond and subsequent export of products, such as cigars that are subject to excise tax; and bonded warehouses known as duty-free stores that sell conditionally duty- and tax-free merchandise to international travelers at airports and seaports.

When goods are stored in a customs-bonded warehouse, they may be sorted, cleaned, repacked, or otherwise altered as long as the process does not constitute manufacturing. They may then be exported without the payment of duty or taxes or imported for consumption upon payment of the applicable duty and taxes at the time of importation.

Storage in a customs-bonded warehouse may be particularly useful if the goods are subject to an annual quota. Goods subject to a quota can be imported as soon as the quota opens for the next period. Similarly, goods that may be duty free under a preference program that has expired can be stored until the preference program is renewed.

Customs-bonded warehouses can be used as "just in time" distribution centers in a global supply chain. For example, if your business imports consumer electronic products and sells them on a nationwide basis in the United States, you can defer the payment of customs duties and other assessments until the products are sold to your customers by storing them in a bonded warehouse. These warehouses can be positioned around the country near your major markets to further reduce delivery time to your customers.

Foreign trade zones (FTZs) can be extremely useful trade tools, depending on the nature of your trade transactions. FTZs are the US version of "free zones." They are enclosed areas under the supervision of CBP that are outside the "customs territory" of the United States; therefore, duties and excise and similar taxes do not apply to foreign goods admitted to zones. In contrast to customs-bonded warehouses, goods can be stored in FTZs indefinitely, and FTZs can also be used, with few restrictions, to manufacture new and different products from both foreign and US-origin materials.

Manufacturing in FTZs can result in substantial savings on applicable duties and taxes. This works in part because of so-called "upside down" tariffs—lower tariffs on end products than on the product's component parts. For example, the four-digit tariff applicable to most motorcars is HTSUS 8703, with a "normal" duty rate of 2.5 percent. However, many of the components used to manufacture automobiles are dutiable at higher rates. This permits automobile manufacturers to produce automobiles in FTZs from foreign and domestic parts and pay duties only on the value of the foreign components at the tariff rate applicable to the finished imported product—2.5 percent.

Additional FTZ benefits include duty and tax exemptions on goods brought into an FTZ and then exported, and the elimination of duties and taxes on waste and scrap. Normally, all goods imported are subject to duties and taxes when they are imported. For example, if you are a distributor of wine from Spain, your imports will be classified under HTSUS 2204.10.00 and subject to a duty of 19.8 cents per liter as well as the applicable excise tax. However, if you import the wine into an FTZ, store it, and then export it to Mexico or Canada, no duty or tax will be assessed. Similarly, under FTZ rules, scrap and waste created during an FTZ manufacturing operation is normally not subject to any duty or tax. As an example, if you are manufacturing a chemical product from components that partially evaporate during the production process, you will save the duties and taxes that would otherwise be applicable to the inputs lost in the production process. And if the production process results in scrap that is ultimately discarded, the duty applicable to the scrap will likely be 0. On the other hand, if the scrap has some value, it may be subject to a duty, depending on its tariff classification at the time it leaves the FTZ.

In 2013, there were 177 active FTZs with 289 production operations.[67] About 390,000 people were employed by the over 3,000 firms using FTZs. The value of shipments into zones amounted to over $835 billion. Over $571 billion, or 68 percent, involved production operations, whereas $264 billion, or 32 percent, involved warehouse/distribution operations. Most goods (about 65 percent) admitted into FTZs were of domestic origin. The manufacturing in FTZs normally involved combining domestic origin and foreign origin goods. The main foreign status products received in FTZs were oil/petroleum ($163.6 billion); vehicle parts ($9.3 billion); machinery/ equipment ($5.6 billion); consumer electronics ($5.2 billion); pharmaceuticals ($3.5 billion); ships/boards ($1.2 billion); and chemicals ($1.1 billion).

A particularly attractive feature of US FTZs is that a manufacturer can create an FTZ subzone for its preexisting manufacturing facility if it is close to one of the active "general-purpose" FTZs. A FTZ subzone is a single firm location that is designated for a special purpose, usually manufacturing. A general-purpose zone grantee must apply for subzone status on behalf of the applicant firm. Applications are evaluated based upon the net benefit to the US economy.

---

[67] See US Commerce Department, "75th Annual Report of the Foreign-Trade Zones Board to the Congress of the United States." 2013.

When planning your import and export transactions, you should also consider taking advantage of zone programs in other countries. Other zone programs around the world are called, variously, export processing zones, free zones, free trade zones, economic development zones, maquiladoras, and special economic zones. Active zones are concentrated in China, Korea, the Philippines, Vietnam, Thailand, and other East Asian countries, as well as in India, Jordan, Dubai, and other Gulf countries. Successful zones also exist in Ireland, Panama, Mexico, and the Dominican Republic. Most of these zones are engaged in labor-intensive manufacturing operations, such as for apparel, textiles, footwear, and consumer electronics goods.

Whether it makes sense to use a zone will depend on the nature of your international trade transactions and the specifics of particular zone programs. Some zones in developing countries provide very liberal tax incentives, including income tax holidays, for locating manufacturing operations in their zones. This is the case currently in Dubai and Macedonia. On the other hand, burdensome regulations and administrative costs, the location of zones in depressed areas that are remote from transportation hubs, and an unskilled labor force may make zone operations uneconomic. Generally, zones managed by private businesses have been more successful than zones managed by governments. However, since whether zone managers are public or private entities is frequently determined on a nationwide basis, a potential user may have no choice in the matter if he or she wants to do zone business in a particular location.

## Inward and Outward Processing: An Alternative to Processing in Zones?

Some economies, such as the European Union and Canada, rely on inward and outward processing procedures in lieu of zones to facilitate manufacturing operations. With the exception of the temporary importation under bond procedure (discussed later in this chapter) these procedures are not authorized in the United States. Inward processing refers to a customs procedure that permits the importation of goods for processing and subsequent exporting of the finished products without payment of duties and taxes on the imported goods. Fairly complicated customs administrative procedures apply to inward processing. Import duties and taxes may be charged on waste derived from manufacturing, and the manufactured products must be reexported within a specified period of time. The products produced from this manufacturing are called "compensating products." They may be produced partially from goods originating in the country and from goods previously imported with the payment of duties and taxes.

Outward processing refers to a customs procedure that permits the total or partial exemption from duties and taxes on goods declared for home use, which are obtained by the manufacturing, processing, or repair of temporarily exported goods in free circulation. This exemption is usually partial but is total if repairs are carried out free of charge. Processing usually also includes packing or repackaging of goods. A typical application would be the exportation of a product for warranty repairs.

You should be aware of the possibility of using inward and outward processing procedures if you are engaged in trade transactions with countries that authorize those procedures.

## Transit under Bond

Goods that enter the United States and are intended for domestic commerce do not have to be entered at the port where they arrive. Instead, the importer may direct that the goods be transported under bond to a customs office near their business location or warehouse. This is known as "immediate transportation procedures" and is accomplished by completion of CBP Form 7512. The goods are then placed on a carrier under bond for transportation to the intended destination. At that destination, normal entry processing will occur.

The transit-under-bond procedure, combined with warehouse and FTZ procedures, allows traders to defer the payment of duties and taxes until the final products are delivered to the trader's customer. This permits businesses to more efficiently manage their supply chains.

The same procedure, known as "national transit," exists in many other countries. Depending on the sophistication of the country's customs administration and the availability of financial guarantees, additional controls, such as the production of a license or even a requirement

> ### TIR Transit
>
> TIR transit (TIR stands for "Transports Internationaux Routiers", or in English, International Road Transports) is an international road transit system that facilitates the movement of goods across multiple national boundaries to the country of destination. The TIR system consists of 1. secure vehicles and containers that meet rigid specifications; 2. an international financial guarantee chain consisting of national guarantee organizations backed by international reinsurers; 3. a TIR carnet that serves both as a customs document and assurance of the guarantee; 4. reciprocal recognition of customs controls pursuant to an international agreement, the TIR Convention; 5. controlled access by customs administrations and the supervising organization, the IRU; and 6. electronic monitoring and termination of transit operations.

that the goods be transported under customs escort, may be required. A transit procedure is always followed by another customs procedure, such as importation for domestic consumption or admission to a warehouse or zone.

In contrast to national transit, "international customs transit" refers to transit movements during which one or more borders are crossed in compliance with an international transit agreement. Normally, in an international transit movement, goods move in an approved container and vehicle under customs seal and are subject to a financial guarantee. They are not inspected until they arrive at their ultimate destination. In the event of any discrepancies or losses in transit, the guaranteeing organization is responsible for compensating national customs administrations in transit countries for any losses of duty and tax revenue. A leading example of international transit, used in Europe, the Middle East, and Asia, is TIR transit. TIR transit is currently used in fifty-eight countries. It operates under an international convention (the Customs Convention on the International Transport of Goods under TIR Carnets) and is administered by the International Road Transport Union (IRU).

The TIR system has had continuing problems operating in the Russian Federation. Russia has temporarily continued TIR operations but is considering substituting its own guarantee and transit system.

### Temporary Admission of Goods: ATA Carnets and Temporary Importation under Bond (TIB)

For economic and social reasons, governments may permit the temporary importation of goods without the payment of duties and taxes. These goods can include musical instruments for touring musicians; filming and production equipment for movie producers; exhibitions for trade shows; and samples accompanying sales representatives. However, temporary admission procedures usually require the posting of a financial security and the exportation of the goods, unaltered, within a specified period, usually one year.

An internationally accepted system for the movement of goods under temporary admission through multiple customs territories is the ATA carnet system. The WCO's Customs Convention on Temporary Admission, known as the Istanbul Convention, governs principles applicable to ATA carnets. ATA carnets are both customs declarations and financial guarantees. Frequently, carnets will provide for multiple international stops. Local carnet associations are part of an international guarantee system administered by the ICC. These associations guarantee payment to the customs authorities of the importing country in the event that goods are not exported within the required time period. The United States limits the use of ATA carnets to professional equipment, commercial samples, and advertising materials; other countries may permit additional uses.

Temporary importation under bond (TIB) is a US customs procedure that permits certain types of goods that are not imported for sale or sale on approval to be admitted under bond without the payment of duty. They must be exported or destroyed no later than one year from the date of importation. There are currently fourteen classes of goods eligible for TIB. These include merchandise to be repaired, altered, or processed in the United States (with some exceptions); models of women wearing apparel imported by manufacturers solely for use as models within their own establishments; articles imported by illustrators and photographers solely for use as models in their own establishments to illustrate pamphlets, catalogues, or advertising matter; samples solely used for taking orders for merchandise; articles intended solely for testing, experiment, or review; and automobiles intended solely for show purposes. If you believe that TIB may be a useful procedure for your business, you should discuss TIB's requirements with your customs broker or trade adviser.

## Drawback Refunds of Duties and Taxes on Exported Goods

The United States and many other customs administrations provide for repayment of import duties and taxes paid on goods used in the processing and manufacture of exported products, materials consumed during the manufacture of exported products, and imported goods that are reexported in the same state. This is known as "drawback." The refunding of duties and taxes on export allows domestic producers to offer more competitive prices in international markets. Drawback is a useful procedure when other procedures, such as temporary admission or zone procedures, cannot be used.

In the US drawback system, exporters are eligible for a 99 percent refund of duties and taxes on establishing proof of exportation, information regarding manufacturing in the United States (if any), and information regarding the import entries for which drawback is claimed. An additional feature of the US system is that merchandise of domestic origin that is "commercially interchangeable" with imported products may also be eligible for drawback. Commercial interchangeability means that the goods are identified under the same eight-digit tariff classification. One example of this would be a candy manufacturer that uses both imported and domestic sugar to produce candy bars that are sold in the United States and in foreign markets. As long as all the sugar is consumed, drawback can be claimed for all the imported sugar under the commercially interchangeable principle, even if some of it was used for products sold domestically.

Drawback specialists speculate that billions of dollars of potential drawbacks are unclaimed because businesses are unaware of the procedure. However, the record keeping required by CBP can be complex, and the wait for refunds, at times, is lengthy. (Some traders use an accelerated program for immediate payment, but this increases the risk of audits.)

### b.  Trade Remedies: Safeguards, Antidumping, and Countervailing Duty Measures

Trade remedies are trade policy tools that allow national governments to take remedial action against imports that are injuring domestic producers. Because of globalization and the related reduction and/or elimination of tariffs and nontariff barriers, trade remedies have become increasingly important as a means to protect domestic industries. There are three trade remedies that are authorized under WTO rules: antidumping duties, countervailing duties, and safeguard measures. Because tariff levels are "bound" (fixed) by international agreements and import quotas are normally prohibited, usually tariffs can only be increased[68] and/or quotas employed by using one or more of the three trade remedies provided for by the WTO.

When you plan your international trade transactions, you must be aware of the possibility of trade remedies being applied to your imports or exports of goods. Increased duties or other restrictions resulting from trade remedies can make planned

---

[68] An important exception is that when the "applied" tariff rate is less than the "bound" tariff rate, the tariff rate can be increased up to the bound rate without violating an international agreement.

or current trade transactions unprofitable. These three trade remedies—safeguards, antidumping, and countervailing duty measures—are described below.

## Safeguards

WTO safeguard measures, sometimes called "global safeguards,"[69] may be applied when as a result of unforeseen circumstances products are being imported in such increased quantities and under such conditions as to cause or threaten to cause serious injury to the domestic producers of the product. Safeguard measures can be increased tariffs, quotas, or tariff-rate quotas (a tariff-rate quota increases the tariff after imports reach a certain quota level). Safeguards are designed to give temporary protection to local producers to enable them to modernize production methods and increase economies of scale so that they can become internationally competitive. Safeguards must normally be applied on an MFN basis to imports from all trading partners, including Regional Trade Agreement (RTA) partners. Moreover, the WTO Safeguards Agreement requires that trading partners be compensated for the application of safeguards with equivalent trade concessions. (These can be tariff reductions on imports; tariff increases on exports.).

Use of safeguards usually implicates that country's overall economic and trade policies as well as domestic political concerns. Developed economies and developing countries with a more free-trade orientation generally do not use safeguard remedies, whereas developing countries following

---

[69] GATT Article XIX and the WTO Agreement on Safeguards. RTAs and other WTO provisions (e.g., GATT Art. XVIII c) may provide for special or bilateral safeguards.

an industrial policy designed to foster the development of select local industries are more likely to apply safeguards.

If you are importing goods into the United States or another developed economy, it is unlikely that safeguard measures will affect your trade transactions. On the other hand, if you are exporting goods to developing-country economies, following an industrial policy designed to encourage local manufacturing, such as Indonesia, Turkey, and India, the possibility of safeguard measures being employed against your exports should be considered.

The specific requirements for applying safeguards are discussed below.

*Increased Imports*

An import surge can be an increase in either absolute or relative terms (imports decline, but they take an increasing share of the market for the product) during the most recent representative period of time.

*Serious Injury*

Serious injury means a significant impairment to the domestic industry producing the like product. Factors that must be analyzed in making this determination include changes in levels of sales, production, productivity, inventories, capacity utilization, profitability, and employment. A threat of serious injury requires proof that injury is imminent based upon facts such as rapidly increasing imports, underselling, inventories, and the capacity of the foreign exporters to increase production.

*Domestic Industry*

The domestic producers, or domestic industry, means all the producers of like or directly competitive products located in the country *or* producers who account for the major proportion of the like or directly competitive products. What is or is not a directly competitive product is determined by the evidence and economic analysis.

*Causation*

A causal link between the increasing imports and serious injury must be established by objective evidence. In addition, factors causing injury other than increased imports must be isolated and the injury caused by these factors must not be attributed to increased imports.

*Procedures*

Safeguards measures can be applied only after conducting an investigation in accordance with the procedures specified by the WTO's Safeguards Agreement. This normally requires the adoption of national legislation. Initiation of a safeguards proceeding can be by an industry petition that on its face contains evidence meeting the requirements for safeguards or by the national government acting on its own initiative.

The procedures must include reasonable public notice of a safeguards investigation to all interested parties, publication of a detailed analysis of the case, and an opportunity for interested parties to present their views to the investigators and at any public hearing. The WTO must be promptly notified of the initiation of an investigation and of its outcome.

## Remedies and Duration of Relief

The maximum duration of safeguard relief is four years, but it can be extended for an additional four years if a new investigation shows that its continuation is necessary and the industry is adjusting to import competition. LDCs can extend relief by an additional two years. Safeguard measures must be progressively liberalized after the first year, and any measure imposed for more than three years must be reviewed at midterm.

In contrast to antidumping and countervailing duty remedies, safeguard remedies must generally be applied on an MFN basis; that is, the remedy is applied to all WTO member countries. However, if members of a regional trade agreement are excluded from the investigation, they may also be excluded from the remedy.

## Provisional Remedy

A provisional safeguard measure in the form of increased duties can be imposed before a safeguard investigation is concluded if a delay in imposing a remedy would cause damage that would be difficult to repair. A provisional measure is limited to a maximum of two hundred days, and the increased duties must be refunded if after the investigation safeguard remedies are not imposed.

## Compensation to Trading Partners

WTO members applying safeguards have an obligation to compensate trading partners adversely affected by providing a substantially equivalent concession (a tariff reduction for other imports or a tariff increase on exports). This is normally done through negotiation. If the parties cannot agree, the affected trading partners are free to retaliate by, for example, imposing increased tariffs on imports from the country applying safeguards. However, in situations where there is an absolute increase in imports, trading partners cannot retaliate during the first three years of safeguards.

*Special and Differential Treatment*

Developing-country WTO members are entitled to special and differential treatment regarding the safeguard measures imposed by other countries. A safeguard measure cannot be applied to imports from a developing country member if the imports do not exceed 3 percent of total imports as long, as developing country imports do not amount to more than 9 percent of total imports.

During the period October 2013 through October 2014, the following WTO members initiated safeguard cases:

| Country | Product |
|---|---|
| Australia | Canned tomatoes; certain processed fruit products |
| Chile | Frozen pork |
| Colombia | Steel wire rod; steel angles; bars of iron or nonalloy steel (rebars) and wire rods of iron or nonalloy steel; angles, shapes, and sections of iron or nonalloy steel |
| Costa Rica | Pounded rice |
| Dominican Republic | Certain sports and dress socks |
| Ecuador | Wood and bamboo flooring |
| Egypt | Steel rebar |

| | |
|---|---|
| India | Seamless pipes, tubes, and hollow profiles of iron or nonalloy steel. Sodium nitrate; sodium citrate; bare elastomeric filament yarn; saturated fatty alcohols; sodium dichromate; flexible slab-stock polyol; cold rolled flat products of stainless steel; PX-13; not-alloyed ingots of unwrought aluminum |
| Indonesia | Flat-rolled product of iron or nonalloy steel; wheat flour; coated paper and paperboard; kilowatt hour meters; sheath contraceptive; cotton yarn; I and H sections of other alloy steel; bars and rods; mackerel |
| Israel | Glass wool and rock wool |
| Jordan | Writing and printing paper size A4; bars and rods of iron or steel |
| Kyrgyz Republic | Wheat flour |
| Malaysia | Hot-rolled steel plate |
| Morocco | Bars and rods; cold-rolled sheets and plated or coated sheets |
| Philippines | Newsprint; galvanized iron and prepainted sheets and coils; test-liner board |
| Russian Federation | Harvesters and modules thereof |
| South Africa | Frozen potato chips |
| Chinese Taipei | HDPE and LLDPE |
| Thailand | Nonalloy hot rolled steel products |

| Tunisia | Fiberboard of wood (MDF); glass bottles |
| --- | --- |
| Turkey | Terephthalic acid; polyethylene terephthalate; printing, writing, and copying papers; spectacle frames; travel goods |
| Ukraine | Tableware and kitchenware of porcelain; motorcars; casing and pump compressor seamless steel pipes |

Source: WTO

The above table indicates that safeguard remedies are actively pursued by some developing countries following an industrial policy. Safeguards are generally not pursued by the developed economies such as the United States, the European Union, and Japan because of the necessity to give compensation to trading partners equivalent to the safeguard remedies imposed. The last global safeguards remedy imposed by the United States was on basic steel products in 2002.

## Antidumping and Countervailing Duties

In contrast to safeguards, WTO antidumping and countervailing duty measures[70] are responses to so-called "unfair trade practices." Remedies are in the form of increased duties designed to eliminate price discrimination (dumping) or subsidies (countervailing duty). Also in contrast to safeguards, these remedies are applied only against the individual exporters in the specific countries where an investigation

---

[70] GATT Article VI and the Agreement on Implementation of Article VI of GATT; GATT Article VI and the Agreement on Subsidies and Countervailing Measures.

has determined that dumping or subsidization and injury are taking place, not against nations.

Antidumping and countervailing duty measures have been used extensively by developed economies, such as the United States and European Union, and by some large advanced, developing countries, such as China and Brazil. However, their application requires substantial financial resources as well as considerable specialized expertise on the part of the investigating authority. Therefore, these trade remedies have been rarely, if ever, used by small LDCs.

Some economists and trade policy specialists have argued against the use of dumping and countervailing duty measures, pointing out that low price imports benefit consumers and, therefore, on balance, may benefit the national economy. Moreover, businesses frequently reduce prices for legitimate reasons, such as to dispose of obsolete inventories or to introduce a product in a new market and should not be penalized for this. Similarly, governments may provide subsidies for many legitimate reasons, such as encouraging economic development in an economically depressed area, improving infrastructure, or attracting new investment. On the other hand, in some instances, dumped and/or subsidized imports may seriously injure or even drive out of business local producers, which, in turn, may injure the long-term economic development of a country.

In the United States, certain import-sensitive industries, such as producers of basic steel products, have frequently used antidumping and countervailing duty proceedings to restrict imports from export-oriented economies, such as China, Taiwan, Korea, and Japan.

## Procedure

A petition from the affected domestic industry to the national investigating authority almost always initiates antidumping and countervailing duty investigations. Petitions must contain evidence establishing a rebuttable presumption that dumping or subsidization and injury exist, that they are causing injury to local producers, and that the petitioners represent local producers.

After a petition is accepted and an investigation is begun, the investigating authority sends questionnaires to all concerned parties, including foreign governments and foreign exporters. The questionnaire responses are then normally verified by visits of investigators to the foreign exporters concerned. In the event that the foreign exporters (or governments) do not cooperate, determinations may be made on best available information, which usually means the information contained in the petition. Needless to say, sending teams of investigators to the exporting countries is an expensive and time-consuming proposition for both the investigating governments and the parties under investigation.

Antidumping and countervailing duty investigations are divided into three stages: (1) review and acceptance of a petition and initiation of an investigation, (2) preliminary determinations regarding the existence of dumping or subsidization and injury, and (3) final determinations regarding dumping or subsidization and injury. Because of the necessity to conduct investigations in the exporting country and requirements to permit all interested parties to submit evidence and argument, these investigations are time consuming and may take a year or longer before concluding.

As is the case with safeguards, before a final determination, provisional measures may be applied in the form of cash deposits or bonds in the event the investigating authority determines that provisional measures are necessary to prevent injury. Both antidumping and countervailing duty investigations can be concluded without the imposition of dumping or countervailing duties upon the acceptance of satisfactory voluntary undertakings from the governments and/or exporters concerned that price increases or other measures will be taken to revise prices or eliminate subsidies.

Antidumping and countervailing duty measures automatically expire after five years unless a "sunset" review determines that in the absence of measures dumping and/or subsidization and injury will continue.

### Criteria for the Imposition of Antidumping Duties

Dumping: A product is "dumped" at less than its normal value when its export price is less than its price in the exporting country. When there are no sales in the ordinary course of trade in the domestic market of the exporting country or for other reasons, there cannot be a proper comparison, then the price comparison can be made to by a comparison to export prices in a third country. In cases where there is no export price or the export price is deemed unreliable, the home market price may be constructed based on the price when resold to an independent buyer or using accounting data.

Injury: An injury determination must be based upon an objective examination of the volume of dumped imports and the effect of dumped imports on the prices in the domestic market for like products and the consequent impact on domestic producers of the like product. The investigating authority must also determine that there has been significant price undercutting or that the effect of dumped imports is to depress prices or prevent price increases. When dumping is occurring from more than one country, the effects of imports may be cumulated (added together) in certain specified circumstances.

Causation: A causal relationship between dumping and injury must be demonstrated by examining all relevant evidence. The investigating authority must determine that there has been a significant increase in imports either in absolute terms or relevant to domestic production. Injury to the industry caused by other factors must not be attributed to dumping. Relevant factors include the volume and prices of imports not sold at dumped prices, contraction in demand, or changes in consumption patterns.

Threat: A determination of threat of injury must be based upon facts and not mere conjecture. Factors to consider include a significant rate of increase in dumped imports, increasing capacity of the exporter, price levels and inventories.

*Criteria for the Imposition of Countervailing Duties*

Subsidies: A subsidy is a financial contribution by a government or any public body conferring a benefit to the recipient. A subsidy must be specific to be subject to countervailing duties. This means that it must apply only to a single enterprise or group of enterprises. Prohibited subsidies are those that are contingent in law or in fact on export performance or those favoring the use of domestic rather than imported goods. Actionable subsidies are those that cause injury to the domestic industry of another WTO member, modify or impair benefits under WTO agreements, or otherwise seriously prejudice the interests of a WTO member.

Injury: Injury determinations are identical to injury determinations in antidumping proceedings.

Causation: Causation determinations are identical to those in antidumping proceedings.

Threat: The determination of a threat is based upon the same considerations as a threat determination in antidumping proceedings.

In the United States, the Import Administration, International Trade Administration (ITA) of the US Department of Commerce is responsible for determining whether imports have been sold at less than normal value or have been improperly subsidized, and the US International Trade Commission (USITC) is responsible for making injury determinations. Other WTO member countries use varying institutions to conduct and make antidumping and countervailing duty determinations. In the European Union, the EU Commission is responsible for conducting antidumping and countervailing duty proceedings. In Canada, the Canadian Border Services Agency determines whether imports are dumped or subsidized and the Canadian International Trade Tribunal is responsible for determining injury.

The following table lists some of the active injury investigations at the USITC in early 2015. Cases designated as 701 are countervailing duty cases, and those designated as 731 are antidumping cases.

| Investigation Title | Investigation | Start Date |
|---|---|---|
| 53-Foot Domestic Dry Containers from China | 701–TA-514 and 731–TA-1250 | 11/26/2014 |
| Barium Carbonate from China | 731–TA-1020 | 2/3/2014 |
| Calcium Hypochlorite from China | 703–TA-510 and 731–TA-1245 (Final) | 7/25/2014 |
| Carbon and Certain Alloy Steel Wire Rod from China | 701–TA-512 and 731–TA-1248 | 9/8/214 |
| Certain Crystalline Silicon Photovoltaic Products from China and Taiwan | 701–TA-511 and 731–TA-1246, 1247 (Final) | 8/25/2014 |
| Certain Passenger Vehicle and Light Truck Tires from China | 701–TA-522, 731–TA-1258 | 1/27/2015 |
| Certain Polyethylene Terephthalate Resin from Canada, China, India, and Oman | 701–TA-531–533, 731–TA-1270–1273 | 3/10/2015 |
| Certain Steel Nails from Korea, Malaysia, Oman, Taiwan, and Vietnam | 701–TA-516–519 and 521 and 731–TA-1252–1255 and 1257 (Final) | 12/29/2014 |
| Certain Uncoated Paper from Australia, Brazil, China, Indonesia, and Portugal | 701–TA-528–529, 731–TA-1264–1268 | 1/21/2015 |

Source: USITC

As you can see from the table above, a wide variety of basic manufactured products are the subject of trade proceedings. The trend is for domestic industries to file both antidumping and countervailing duty cases to obtain maximum protection. Antidumping and countervailing duty cases in the United States have grown increasingly complex and expensive over the years. Now legal and consulting fees for cases can run to seven figures, so unless the amount of trade involved is substantial, it is not likely that domestic producers will file a case. On the other hand, if you are an importer of a product that is the subject of an antidumping and/or countervailing duty investigation or finding, you may be priced out of the US market unless you actively oppose the imposition of dumping and countervailing duties. This also may involve a major expense in legal and consulting fees.

> ### Trade Remedies and Competition Laws
>
> In the United States, it is a violation of antitrust laws for competitors to meet for the purpose of restricting competition and increasing prices. Nonetheless, this is done routinely when producers and labor unions meet for the purpose of pursuing trade-remedy cases because an exception to antitrust laws permits petitions to the government seeking government action. However, if meetings about trade remedies involving competitors are not carefully monitored, discussions regarding prices, profit levels, geographic division of markets, and other matters may lead to illegal horizontal agreements, which are subject to criminal and civil prosecution.

If you are a small business located in the United States conducting international trade transactions of goods, you should be aware of the possibility of the imposition of antidumping and countervailing duties to your imports. And if you are exporting goods from the United States to foreign markets, you should be aware of the possibility of the imposition of antidumping and countervailing duties and safeguard remedies to your exports.

These trade remedies all require a demonstration of injury or "threat of injury," so periodically monitoring statistical data regarding trade volumes and production and sales trends in the relevant markets may give you an advance warning of any potential problems.

For more information on trade remedies in
the United States, consult the ITA and USITC
websites: http://trade.gov/enforcement/

http://www.usitc.gov

## c. Regulations Affecting the Exports of Goods

Governments regulate the exports of all goods by requiring the filing of export declarations with their customs administrations when goods over a specified value are exported from a nation or economy. This is done for statistical purposes and also to identify exports as to which specific restrictions may apply (and some countries impose duties and taxes on exports). In the United States, about 90 percent of exports are subject to no other regulations. However, the remaining 10 percent may require export licenses because they are armaments, military equipment, or dual-use items that may have military utility. In addition, the United States imposes export restrictions of various types based upon foreign policy considerations. Other nations impose similar export restrictions, and international agreements govern the application of these restrictions.

Nations generally try to encourage exports of goods and services on the part of their national enterprises. Some governmental encouragement, such as the information and trade promotion services of the US Commerce Department's International Trade Administration and its US and Foreign Commercial Service, is permissible. (These programs are discussed in chapter 2.) However, direct or indirect subsidization of exports is prohibited by WTO rules. Subsidized exports are subject to countervailing duty actions brought by domestic producers (discussed above) and may also be addressed by complaints from the importing nation under WTO dispute-resolution procedures.

Some nations tax exports for revenue reasons or to discourage the exports of certain minerals or agricultural products. As examples, Russia imposes a tax on exports of petroleum products; Indonesia and Malaysia impose export taxes on palm oil; China imposes export taxes on coal, primary aluminum, and iron ore; and Argentina imposes export taxes on soybeans. However, differential export taxes designed to benefit domestic producers by lower or no taxes on exported processed products may result in WTO complaints.

> ### *The Export Taxation Clause*
>
> The Export Taxation Clause of the US Constitution (Art. 1, Sec. 9) prohibiting any tax on exports of goods or services was added to protect Southern economic interests. The clause has been strictly interpreted. Supreme Court cases have struck down a federal excise tax on insurance premiums paid to insure goods against loss during exportation and the application of the Harbor Maintenance Tax to exports.

For the United States, however, duties, taxes, or fees on exports of goods or services are unlawful because of a specific provision in the US Constitution prohibiting such taxes

## International Rules Regarding Exports

As is the case with imports, international rules apply to the national regulation of exports. It is usually not necessary for small business exporters to know the specifics of these international rules; just be aware that most nations will have similar export regulations.

A number of WTO provisions apply to the exports of goods. Some of these provisions, such as the WTO rule that permits the refund of customs duties and taxes when goods are exported, are of direct benefit to small businesses. Other rules form the basis for national regulations of exports.

First, WTO rules permit countries to refund customs duties and other indirect taxes when goods are exported (see the WTO Agreement on Subsidies and Countervailing Measures). This is of particular economic significance in connection with the refund of VAT and other sales taxes when goods are exported. In addition, customs duties and other import taxes and fees may be rebated based upon drawback procedures. These procedures were discussed in the section above regarding import regulations.

Second, the MFN (GATT Art. I) and national treatment (GATT Art. III) principles apply to exports as well as imports. This means, as examples, that WTO member nations cannot require export arrangements that favor one nation over another (for example, exempt exports to one nation from taxes but apply them to other nations), nor can a WTO member nation apply certain export regulations only to exports by nonnational firms.

Third, rules regarding fees and formalities (GATT Art. VIII) and marks of origin (GATT Art. IX) apply to both imports and exports. This means that fees and charges on exports must be limited to the approximate cost of the services provided, and marking regulations on exports must be uniformly applied.

Fourth, GATT Art XI generally prohibits export restraints other than duties, taxes, or other charges. However, there are seven nonnational security exceptions to this. Nonnational security export restrictions are permitted under GATT Articles XI and XX

1.  to temporarily relieve critical shortages of foodstuffs or other essential products (GATT Art. XI:2 (a));

2.  when necessary to the application of standards or regulations relating to the classification, grading, or marketing of commodities in international trade (GATT Art. XI:2 (b));

3.  when necessary to protect human, animal, or plant life or health (GATT Art. XX (b));

4.  to restrict the exportation of gold or silver (GATT Art. XX (c));

5.  to protect national treasurers of artistic, historic or archaeological value (GATT Art. XX (f));

6.  to conserve exhaustible natural resources if such measures are taken in conjunction with restrictions on domestic production and consumption (GATT Art. XX (g)); and

7.  to comply with obligations under any inter-governmental commodity agreement (GATT Art. XX (h)).

In addition to these restrictions, export duties, taxes, and other fees cannot be set at such a high level as to constitute an export ban.

Fifth, national security exceptions to WTO principles are contained in GATT Art. XXI. Article XXI provides in pertinent part that nothing in GATT prevents a contracting party from taking action that it considers necessary for the protection of its essential security interests. This includes actions relating to:

- fissionable materials or the materials from which they are derived;

- traffic in arms, ammunition, and implements of war and to such traffic in other goods and materials as is carried on directly or indirectly for the supplying a military establishment;

- time of war or other emergency in international relations; or

- pursuance of a member's obligations under the United Nations Charter for the maintenance of international peace and security.

GATT Article XXI provides the legal basis in the WTO system for export controls imposed by the United States and other nations for national security reasons.

Sixth, the WTO's Agreement on Subsidies and Countervailing Measures prohibits government subsidies of exports that are contingent on export performance or on the use of domestic over imported goods. In addition, other subsidies affecting trade may be "actionable" under the Agreement.

> **Dual Use**
>
> Dual-use goods and technologies can be used for both nonmilitary and military purposes.

In addition to WTO disciplines, international agreements also limit the export of munitions and dual-use goods and technologies. The Wassenaar Agreement is a multilateral export control regime designed to restrict the transfer of conventional arms and dual-use technologies. Controlled items are divided into two parts—the munitions list and list of dual-use materials and technologies. In order for an item to be placed on the list, four factors are taken into account: (1) availability outside participating states, (2) the ability to effectively control exports, (3) the ability to make clear and objective specifications, and (4) whether the item or technology is controlled by another international regime. Members must be producers of arms or sensitive industrial equipment and maintain nonproliferation policies and fully effective export controls. As of early 2015, forty-one nations, including the United States, were members, and several other significant arms suppliers, including China and Israel, have aligned their export control regimes with Wassenaar. Even a small country like Armenia had conformed its export control regulations to Wassenaar when I worked there recently.

Other international agreements and groups limiting the export of nuclear, chemical, and biological weapons include the Australia Group, the Nuclear Suppliers Group, the Zangger Committee, the Missile Technology Control Regime, the Biological Weapons Convention, the Nuclear Nonproliferation Treaty, and the Chemical Weapons Convention.

## Export Declarations

When goods are exported, customs administrations require export declarations to be submitted identifying and describing the exporter and ultimate consignee, the goods shipped and their value, their classification for export control purposes, the date of exportation, and the method of transportation used. These declarations are used for statistical purposes and also to apply export controls, if any are applicable. Many export declarations are now submitted in electronic format, with the information contained then disseminated to the various government agencies with regulatory responsibilities.

In the United States, information regarding export shipments valued above $2500 must be submitted electronically prior to exportations using the Automated Export System (AES). Goods are coded based upon the approximately eight thousand classifications in the US Census' "Schedule B," which parallels the HS tariff nomenclature. The export license number and export control classification number designations must also be provided when required. The submission time required in advance of exportation depends upon the mode of transport. AES has been incorporated into CBP's Automated Commercial Environment (ACE) trade processing system. More information about AES can be obtained from the US Census' AES website: https://aesdirect.census.gov.

## US Export Controls

The United States has a comparative advantage in international trade in high-technology goods and military equipment. However, the export controls applied by the United States on these goods and services are complex and can present compliance challenges for small business exporters. Five agencies have primary responsibility for the application of export controls. These are the Department of Commerce's Bureau of Industry and Security (BIS), the Department of State's Directorate of Defense Trade Controls (DDTC), the Department of Treasury's Office of Foreign Assets Controls (OFAC), the Department of Energy's Nuclear Regulatory Commission (NRC) and Office of Fossil Energy, and the Department of Homeland Security's Customs and Border Protection (CBP), and Immigration and Customs Enforcement (ICE).

## BIS

Commerce's BIS regulates the exports of dual-use goods through the application of the Export Administration Regulations (EARs) and the Commerce Control List (CCL). Goods regulated are given export control classification numbers or "ECCNs." Those goods that are identified as dual use or are subject to embargoes or sanctions must be licensed prior to export. If you are not certain about whether a product in covered by the ECCN, you should contact the manufacturer to obtain the ECCN or submit an online requires to BIS for a classification. Goods not covered by the CCL are classified as EAR99 and may be shipped with no license required (NLR) unless they are shipped to a country subject to an embargo or sanction, or to a prohibited end user or for a prohibited end use. Exporters must exercise due diligence in complying with the EARs; violations may be subject to significant penalties. Information about BIS regulations and licenses can be obtained at www.bis.doc.gov.

> ### BIS and Dual-Use Goods
>
> In FY 2014, BIS processed 23,229 export license applications worth approximately $204.1 billion – $113.6 billion of which were licenses for crude oil exports. It denied less than 1 percent of license applications although some licenses were approved with conditions.
>
> —The US Export Control System and the President's Reform Initiative (Congressional Research Service (January 2014), p. 3.

## DDTC

State's DDTC regulates the export of military equipment, services, and related technologies using a similar approach to BIS's. DDTC administers the Arms Export Control Act and the International Traffic in Arms Regulations (ITAR). It publishes a US Munitions List (USML), and goods on the list must be licensed prior to export. Items designated as significant military equipment require special controls. Special guidelines also apply to the transfer of software. Exporters uncertain whether their goods are covered should submit a commodity jurisdiction request to DDTC. If your proposed exports are covered, you must first register with DDTC and then request a specific license. Information about DDTC regulations and licenses can be obtained at https://www.pmddtc.state.gov.

*OFAC*

Treasury's OFAC is responsible for the administration of sanctions on exports to certain countries and to certain prohibited parties. As of early 2015, OFAC was operating sanctions programs against Iran, Ukraine-Russia, Syria, Somalia, Sudan, Venezuela, North Korea, Libya, and a number of other countries, regions, and individuals. Sanctions are imposed or removed depending on changes in the international political situation. Licenses are normally issued for agricultural goods, medicines, and other humanitarian supplies to sanctioned countries. OFAC's Specially Designated Nationals list (SDN list) is one of the lists that names parties excluded by law. Others are the denied persons list (maintained by BIS), the Entities list (maintained by BIS), and the debarred parties list (maintained by the State Department). A consolidated list is now published by BIS. http://export.gov/ecr/eg_main_023148.asp. There is, at times, overlap between OFAC and BIS regulations requiring a license from both agencies. OFAC information can be obtained at http://www.treasury.gov/resource-center/sanctions/Pages/default.aspx.

*"The US export control system is a 'byzantine amulgam of authorities, roles, and missions scattered around different parts of the federal government.'"*

—Secretary of Defense Robert Gates, April 20, 2010

## NRC and Others

NRC licenses nuclear technology and materials for export. The Department of Energy Office of Fossil Energy also licenses the exports of electrical power and natural gas (including LNG). CBP is the agency present on the border responsible for enforcing export controls along with ICE. Exports violating export regulations are subject to seizure by CBP and ICE officers and the imposition of penalties.

The complexity of the export regulatory regime has led to efforts to simplify and consolidate the regulations dating back at least to the Reagan Administration. The Obama Administration is attempting to consolidate regulations into one control list administered by a single licensing agency. This reform also includes the development of a single enforcement structure and a single information-technology system.[71] Reforms leading to a single control list involve an attempt to turn the CCL and the USML into positive lists that impose controls based upon objective criteria rather than subjective, intent-based criteria that produces ambiguities and to create tiers based upon the degree

> ### Exports of Technical Data and Higher Education
>
> The dissemination of technical data is controlled by ITAR. This includes information that provides meaningful insights into the design or production of military equipment. The disclosure of technical data to a foreign person *inside* the United States is deemed to be an export to that person's home country. This presents special challenges to universities that include foreign nationals in their education and research programs, and many of them have established export-control education and compliance programs.

---

[71] See The US Export Control System and the President's Reform Initiative (Congressional Research Service, January 2014).

of sensitivity of the technologies. Consolidation to provide a single enforcement structure may result in the transfer of BIS enforcement functions to ICE. The USEXPORTS database, currently used by the Department of Defense to track license applications referred to it, is being expanded to include the State and Commerce departments. It could ultimately become a government wide IT platform for export controls. However, it remains to be seen whether these initiatives will be successful.

Because of the substantial penalties involved and the potential loss of government business in the event export control regulations are violated, businesses and educational institutions that are exporting controlled goods and technologies must be vigilant in exercising due diligence to assure compliance with these regulations. BIS, DDTC, and OFAC provide online and telephone advisory assistance, but it may be necessary for small businesses to also use the services of lawyers and other export control specialists to establish a compliance program.

### Cargo Security and Authorized Economic Operators (AEOs)

Increased cargo security measures are affecting small businesses engaged in the export and import of goods. However, new technologies and procedures are resulting in both improved cargo security *and* improvements in trade facilitation.

In recent years, border controls have expanded to include a much more rigorous supervision of the supply chains for exported goods. This has been accomplished, in part, through the use of new methods and technologies: the application of risk management, new IT systems, including mobile computing, electronic tracking, x-ray and radiation scanning, and other logistics innovations. Equally important to improved supply-chain security have been the development of public-private partnerships between customs administrations and the business community that facilitate the trade of participating businesses if businesses adopt and implement required supply chain security measures. The goals of these measures are to increase supply-chain security, while simultaneously improving trade facilitation. An additional development improving supply chain-security has been greatly increased cooperation, including electronic data sharing, between national customs administrations.

After the terrorist attack of 9/11 in the United States and similar terrorist attacks elsewhere in the world, governments and the trading community took steps to protect international trade in goods from exploitation by terrorists. Customs administrations are on the front line of protective efforts because of their border inspection responsibilities and supervision of trade in goods, so much of this work took place at the World Customs Organization. WCO efforts resulted in the development of an international agreement and program called the SAFE Framework of Standards (SAFE), designed to both secure and facilitate the international movement of goods on a worldwide basis.

As of March 2014, 168 WCO members committed to implementing the provisions of SAFE. Key elements of SAFE, such as advance electronic information, AEO procedures, and cooperation between customs administrations, were also included in the WTO's Trade Facilitation Agreement. This should aid implementation by LDCs because a key component of the Trade Facilitation Agreement is the provision of technical assistance to developing country members.

The SAFE framework consists of four core elements:

- It requires harmonization of advance electronic cargo information requirements for inbound, outbound, and transit shipments of goods.

- Each national member agrees to employ a consistent risk management approach to detect security threats.

- It requires that at the request of a nation receiving a shipment scheduled to be exported, the exporting nation's customs administration will perform an outbound inspection of high-risk cargo and transport conveyances. Inspections should employ nonintrusive detection equipment such as X-rays and radiation detectors when possible.

- Businesses that meet supply-chain security standards and best practices will receive preferential treatment for their shipments.

SAFE requires a shift from the supervision and inspection of cargo and transport conveyances after they arrive for importation at a destination to performing screening and inspections *prior to* the arrival of goods and conveyances. This is made possible through the use of advance electronic information to identify high-risk cargo and conveyances. These are identified as early as possible in the supply chain, at or before the point of departure. When cargo and conveyances are targeted for inspection, customs administrations are then required to use modern technologies, such as large-scale x-ray equipment and gamma-ray machines as well as radiation-detection devices. Customs tamperproof seals are then affixed after inspections. This maintains cargo and container integrity and facilitates trade.

An important part of these new procedures is the submission of advance electronic goods declarations and an adequate period of time prior to exportation of the goods. For imports, the importer must also submit an advance electronic import goods declaration to customs prior to the arrival of the conveyance at the first customs office in the importing country or, for maritime container shipments, prior to loading for export.

Authorized economic operators, or AEOs, are traders and other businesses in the supply chain that comply with the security requirements of SAFE and as a consequence receive authorization as an AEO and expedited treatment of their goods shipments and other preferences. AEO programs should permit customization of security plans based upon the AEO's business model. AEO implementation plans jointly produced by the AEO and Customs should have verifiable processes to assure compliance with the security standards in the SAFE Framework.

> ### Authorized Economic Operators (AEOs)
>
> AEOs are organizations involved with the international movement of goods that comply with supply-chain security and trade-facilitation standards. They can include manufacturers, importers, exporters, freight forwarders, brokers, carriers, ports, airports, warehouses, and others involved in trade transactions.

AEOs must incorporate cargo security "best practices." These include secure access to their facilities, use of advanced electronic sealing and tracking technologies, background investigations and clearances of all employees, protection of trade-sensitive data against loss or errors, and training of employees to recognize and react to security threats. In addition, to qualify for and retain AEO status, AEOs must be subject to audits by customs of their records and procedures.

In the United States, the SAFE Framework of Standards AEO program for the business community is known as the Customs-Trade Partnership against Terrorism, or "C-TPAT." C-TPAT is a voluntary public-private sector partnership program designed to increase the level of cargo security. By 2014, more than ten thousand businesses accounting for more than 54 percent of all imports were participating in C-TPAT. Benefits to C-TPAT participants include the following:[72]

- Reduced examination rates (depending on "tier status"). Non-C-TPAT businesses are three times more likely to undergo a security-based inspection than a Tier II business and nine times more likely to undergo a security-based inspection than a Tier III business.

- Access to free and secure trade (FAST) lanes at border. Expedited border crossing privileges are granted to C-TPAT carriers.

- Stratified exam benefit for importer partners. (When imports consist of multiple containers, when only one container is targeted for examination, the other containers may be removed to the trader's premises.)

- Front-of-the-line-processing. When shipments are subject to examination, C-TPAT shipments are given priority over non C-TPAT shipments.

---

[72] US Customs and Border Protection. "C-TPAT Program Benefits Reference Guide." January 2014.

- Business resumption. In the event of a significant delay or disruption in CBP cargo processing, CBP maintains communication with C-TPAT partners to accelerate the resumption of processing.

- Expedited trade processing. C-TPAT partner trade compliance issues are given priority by CBP's Centers of Excellence and Expertise.

- Access to a C-TPAT supply chain security specialist. Each C-TPAT partner is assigned a specialist (account executive) who manages the relationship with CBP.

- Access to C-TPAT secure portal system. Through the automated secure portal system C-TPAT partners are able to communicate with CBP and access information about the C-TPAT program.

- Eligibility to attend C-TPAT's annual conference and other training programs. This allows C-TPAT partners to participate in relevant training and network with government and private sector supply-chain experts.

- Eligibility to participate in the importer self-assessment program (ISA). ISA is a voluntary program where participants are responsible for self-assessing compliance with regulatory requirements. Benefits include exemption from compliance audits and reduced inspections and delays.

- Penalty mitigation. Reduced penalties are applied to C-TPAT sea carriers for late submission of importer security filing data.

- Eligibility for other programs. C-TPAT partners may be eligible for other government programs facilitating trade.

If you are a small business exporting or importing goods, participation in C-TPAT or a similar AEO program may give you a significant commercial advantage over competitors that do not participate.

As might be expected, the implementation of SAFE procedures and AEO programs vary from nation to nation, depending on the degree of economic development, available financial resources, and reliance on trade by the implementing nation. Advanced economies have, by and large, implemented SAFE procedures and adopted AEO programs. In addition to the United States, these include the member countries of the European Union, Canada, Mexico, Japan, Singapore, Taiwan, Korea, Australia, New Zealand, Israel, Turkey, and Switzerland.[73] A number of developing nations, most notably China and India, have also adopted AEO programs, and more are scheduled to do so in the future.

The AEO program is particularly valuable for exporters in nations like Jordan, which are located in high-risk regions. In Jordan, the AEO program is called "the golden list." Recently, I had the opportunity to discuss the benefits of the golden list with executives of Petra Engineering, a manufacturer of air-conditioning equipment located in Jordan. Petra exports its products to the United States and more than forty-five other countries. It is competitive in export markets based in part on delivery time. It was the first company in Jordan to start using golden-list procedures for its exports. Every container

---

[73] See WCO. "Compendium of Authorized Economic Operator Programs." 2014.

destined for the United States is scanned, which creates some delays. However, C–TPAT and the golden list have mutual recognition. The golden list allows Petra to be competitive with other exporters in the United States, and other countries that have adopted AEO procedures.

## 2. Trade In Services

Most small businesses in the United States and other developed economies are service providers, so if you are thinking about entering international markets, you are most likely concerned about the regulations and restrictions applicable to your service products. A WTO agreement as well as bilateral and regional trade pacts establish some basic principles for trade in services. However, generally speaking, international disciplines on trade in services are limited and available services trade data is also limited. As a result, you will have to research thoroughly the regulations applied by the particular country or economy where you plan to do business.

I have provided international trade consulting services in more than fifty countries around the world. However, many of my clients have been international organizations, such as the World Bank, or national government organizations, such as the US Agency for International Development. The political reach of these clients has eased the way for me to obtain visas to enter foreign countries and to deal with other local regulations applicable to consultants. National entry and presence restrictions have, at times, proven to be more difficult when private clients have engaged me.

If you are a US citizen, you can visit most countries or territories without a visa or by purchasing a visa online or on arrival (some countries use the purchase of visas as fees to finance airport, embassy, and other government expenses). However, some important trading countries, such as Brazil, China, India, Russia, Saudi Arabia, and Nigeria, require a business visa for entry, and this may entail providing detailed contact information about your local business connections and planned residence when in the country. And if the services project is of lengthier duration, a work permit may be required. Work permits may not be easy to obtain because of concerns that foreign workers may displace domestic workers also qualified for a job. This is the case in the United States.

In addition to visa and work-permit requirements, some countries closely monitor the movements of foreign business people for national security reasons. For example, Kazakhstan requires most business visitors to register with the local police within five days of arrival. Jordan has a similar requirement after presence in the country for thirty days. Russia requires registration of foreigners.

Services are intangible products (for example, information) provided by a service provider and consumed by a service consumer. They currently account for about two-thirds of global output, but only about 20 percent of world trade. Services are frequently included with, or "bundled," with the sale of goods. As an example, the small-business equipment manufacturer located in California that was discussed in chapters 1 and 2 routinely provides technical assistance for assembling and maintaining its equipment when its equipment is delivered to foreign purchasers.

It is important to note that not all services are tradable services (services that are traded internationally). For example, nonbusiness sector services provided by governments, primary schools, and charitable and religious institutions are normally not tradable. Similarly, business-sector services, such as small retailers, taxi driving, hairdressing, physical therapy, home construction, cleaning, catering, and similar essentially local services, rarely involve crossing national boundaries.

On the other hand, services such as air and sea transport, telecommunications, banking and insurance, tourism, information technology, Internet, engineering and architecture, health, education, royalties and license fees, and business consulting, are tradable internationally. When more service providers are located in a particular location than consumers of that service, this may indicate the "tradability" of that service.[74] Examples of this are the location of many software and IT providers in Silicon Valley and Seattle and the location of many movie production firms in Hollywood.

> "Anything sold in trade that could not be dropped on your foot is a service."
>
> —Business Guide to the World Trading System (International Trade Centre 2d ed. 1999), p. 192

There are two types of regulations or restrictions imposed on exports of services—regulations imposed by the exporting country and regulations imposed by the importing country.

### Regulations Imposed on Exports of Services

For the United States and other developed economies, the regulations imposed on exports of services are, for the most part, the same national-security and foreign-policy restrictions as the controls imposed on the exports of goods previously discussed in this chapter. For example, for exports of services

---

[74] See Jensen, J. Bradford. "Overlooked Opportunity: Tradable Business Services, Developing Asia and Growth." *Asian Development Bank* January 2013.

from the United States, BIS licenses dual-use services, DDTC licenses the export of services related to military equipment, NRC licenses services relating to the export of nuclear materials, and OFAC licenses exports of services to sanctioned regimes and individuals. This means that providers of any service that may have dual use, military or nuclear energy applications, or may be provided in a nation or to individuals subject to sanctions must obtain a license prior to providing the service. Special challenges exist for research institutions that include foreign nationals in their research or teaching programs that may relate to dual-use, military, or nuclear technologies.

In addition, as previously mentioned in this chapter, some nations may impose taxes and fees on the exports of services, but not the United States (the US Constitution prohibits duties, taxes, or fees on exports).

*Regulations Imposed on Imports of Services*

Regulations imposed by the importing country on services are quite different from the regulations imposed on imports of goods. Except for immigration restrictions, border controls are usually not an issue, and there are no import tariffs. Instead, trade in services are subject to sector-specific domestic regulations. Competency standards (education and licensing requirements) may be imposed on doctors, lawyers, architects, accountants, and other professionals. Telecommunications providers may be restricted to state monopolies or only a few selected

> ### Compliance Programs
>
> In order to assure compliance with export control requirements, many businesses and educational institutions have established compliance programs to educate their employees regarding the need to obtain licenses to share information with foreign nationals in the United States as well as when information is transferred to a foreign country.

commercial providers. Services by foreign consultants may be restricted based upon requirements designed to protect local workers.

A recent World Bank survey looked at the restrictions imposed by services importing countries in five sectors: financial, telecommunications, retail, transportation, and professional services.[75] The survey found the following:

- Banking and insurance were relatively free of specific restrictions. Only a few countries, including Iran, Ethiopia, and Qatar, imposed significant restrictions or outright prohibitions.

- The telecommunications sector had also been liberalized for FDI, and only 10 of the 103 countries sampled were closed or virtually closed to foreign firms.

- Of the countries surveyed, 60 of the 103 were open to FDI in the retail sector. However, openness to FDI can be deceptive because of various behind-the-border restrictions.

- In the transportation sector, there were still many measures applied to protect national flag carriers and domestic carriers from foreign competition. A few countries have completely closed foreign transportation subsectors to foreign competition.

- Many nations have restrictive policies regarding professional services provided by nonnationals. The

[75] Borchert, I., G. Gootiiz and A. Mattoo, "Policy Barriers to International Trade in Services." Policy Research Working Paper 6109, World Bank, June 2012.

practice of accounting and foreign law tends to be more open than that of auditing or the practice of domestic law.

## International Standards

Trade in services are regulated internationally by the provisions of the WTO's General Agreement on Trade in Services (GATS) and by regional trade agreements. The WTO's General Agreement on Trade in Services identifies four modes of trade in services:

- Mode 1: Cross-border services where both the provider and consumer remain in their home territory. Internet and telecommunication services are examples.

- Mode 2: Services provided to a consumer who travels to the territory of the provider. Examples include tourism and medical treatment.

- Mode 3: Services provided when the provider establishes a commercial presence in the territory of the user. Examples include bank branches, consultancy firms, franchises, and insurance agencies that establish foreign offices.

- Mode 4: Services provided when a natural-person provider temporarily resides in the territory of the consumer. Examples include teachers and IT consultants who travel to a foreign territory to provide their services on a short-term basis.

GATS is divided into parts that provide for general obligations and disciplines; specific commitments, such as market access; continual liberalization through negotiations; and institutional arrangements. The liberalization commitments made are listed in each WTO member's schedule of commitments. For the purpose of structuring commitments, the WTO uses a 12-core service sector classification system, divided into 160 subsectors.

MFN treatment is a key GATS principle. However, WTO members can maintain measures inconsistent with MFN treatment for national security and a few other reasons and if the measure is listed in the annex on exemptions. Currently, around ninety members maintain exemptions.[76]

National treatment is also a key GATS principle. National treatment prevents the imposition of higher taxes or more stringent regulations on foreign service providers. However, national treatment is limited to the service sectors actually listed in an individual WTO member's Schedule of Specific Commitments, and even these can be qualified. But for those sectors listed, WTO members cannot limit (1) the number of foreign service suppliers, (2) the value of transactions, (3) the total quantity of service outputs, (4) the number of natural persons that can be employed, (5) the type of legal entity that can be used, or (6) participation of foreign capital or investment.

Other general GATS obligations include transparency measures (which involves maintaining inquiry points), mutual recognition agreements regarding licensing and certification, and limitations on monopolies and anticompetitive practices.

The liberalization of trade in services by GATS depends on both the general obligations and the sector-specific commitments

---

[76] As of January 2013.

made. However, when GATS entered into force, sector-specific negotiations had not been completed for financial services, telecommunications, and maritime transport. Agreements for financial services and telecommunications were subsequently completed, but an agreement on maritime transport has been deferred until new WTO services negotiations.

GATS provides for progressive liberalization of services trade through future negotiations. However, service-trade negotiations have stalled in the Doha Development Round negotiations. The best prospects for more ambitious agreements now appear to be a possible WTO plurilateral agreement and the inclusion of services trade disciplines in new regional trade agreements, such as the Trans-Pacific Partnership Agreement.

In addition to GATS, some regional and bilateral trade agreements include services provisions. Of these, the Korea-US FTA may be the most extensive. The Korea-US FTA grants national and MFN treatment to all service sectors and allows market access without meeting local presence requirements. In addition, the FTA includes "GATS plus" commitments regarding business services, banking and insurance, telecommunications, tourism, and additional services. The North American Free Trade Agreement (NAFTA) contains provisions regarding national and MFN treatment for cross-border trade in services and the abolishment of local presence requirements (NAFTA, Arts. 12, 14).

In 2015, the United States had bilateral or regional trade agreements in effect with twenty countries and all of these agreements contained provisions regarding trade in services. The European Union has also concluded a number of RTAs that include trade in services provisions. The Association of

Southeast Asian Nations (ASEAN) is in the process of attempting to eliminate restrictions to trade in services between ASEAN members, and Japan and China have also entered into regional agreements that include trade in services provisions.[77]

As you might guess, the international agreements negotiated regarding services are primarily designed to protect the interests of major multinational enterprises engaged in finance and insurance, telecommunications, transport and logistics, retail and franchising, and IT and business services, with an emphasis on establishing a commercial presence in a foreign country (mode 3). If you are a small business providing computer software, architectural, or accounting or legal services, the provisions of international agreements may be of little assistance.

How does this complex regulatory picture regarding the exports of services affect your exports? It is mainly the provision of mode-3 services that are restricted. If you are providing a mode-1 service (the transfer of your services electronically or otherwise to a customer or client without physical presence), it is not likely that you will encounter any restrictions. If you are providing a mode-2 service (for example, the consumer travels to your business establishment, as in the case of tourism or medical treatment), the traveler may be required to obtain a visa, but this should not be a significant impediment. If you are providing a mode-4 service (for example, a consultant or lawyer traveling to a foreign country), visa and local professional and employment regulations may be applicable. However, if you are providing a mode-3 service (for example, a financial institution or franchiser establishing a commercial presence

---

[77] See VanGrasstek, Craig. "The Political Economy of Services in Regional Trade Agreements." OECD 2011.

in a foreign country), many local restrictions could apply, and thorough research regarding international agreements and local regulations should be undertaken before completing any business arrangements.

GATS' transparency provisions require WTO members to maintain inquiry centers providing information on their services restrictions and members' services obligations under GATS are also available on the WTO's website, www.wto.org.

### 3. Additional Government Regulations Affecting International Trade Transactions

In addition to regulations applicable to the imports and exports of goods and services, several other important government regulations affect international trade transactions. These include income taxes on foreign income and penalties on illegal conduct, including bribery, boycotts, anticompetitive actions, and money laundering.

### Taxes on Foreign-Source Income

The taxes applied to foreign-source income derived from international trade transactions are complex and vary from country to country. The following description is a very simplified overview. For specific tax information, you should consult a tax specialist.

For individuals and businesses that conduct international trade transactions and receive taxable income in a foreign country, a major concern is the potential for double taxation—taxation of income received by the foreign country where the individual worked or the business received income and then taxation on the same income by the individual's or business's home country.

National tax authorities use two methods to reduce or eliminate this double-taxation problem—the worldwide method and the territorial method. Under the wordwide method, income earned in a foreign country by individuals and businesses located in the foreign country is subject to tax in the home country, with a credit for taxes paid to the foreign government. The United States and a few other countries follow this approach. Under the territorial method, income earned in a foreign country by individuals and businesses is wholly or partially exempt from home-country taxes. No credits are given for taxes paid to the foreign country. Most countries follow the territorial approach.

Under the territorial approach, a business's foreign subsidiary earnings may be repatriated with no or a minimal tax. However, under the worldwide system, repatriated income is normally subject to additional tax if the foreign tax rate is below the home tax rate. This is the case for businesses located in the United States, which has one of the highest corporate tax rates in the world.

Bilateral and multilateral tax treaties are also used to eliminate or mitigate the problem of double taxation. The benefits of these treaties are available to natural persons or business organizations that are resident in one of the treaty countries. This may be based upon the primary place of abode, which may be defined as spending more than a fixed number of days as a resident of a treaty country. Tax treaties also typically include provisions for the exchange of information and enforcement assistance. The United States is party to more than sixty-five tax treaties.[78]

---

[78] http://www.irs.gov/Businesses/International-Businesses/United-States-Income-Tax-Treaties---A-to-Z

Although foreign-source income realized by the foreign subsidiaries of US businesses is subject to taxation at the higher US corporate tax rate after any credits for foreign taxes paid, a US tax provision currently permits the deferral of profits that are realized by foreign subsidiaries. Taxation is only triggered if the parent company repatriates the foreign subsidiary's profits, including them on the parent firm's balance sheet. This gives US multinationals an incentive to shift profits onto the balance sheets of their foreign subsidiaries. As of 2014, an estimated $2 trillion in profits untaxed by the United States (but potentially subject to taxation in the country where the foreign subsidiary is located) had been recorded as offshore income by US businesses.

US citizens and resident aliens must report income received from all sources, including sources outside the United States. The rules for filing tax returns and paying estimated taxes are generally the same whether the person is living in the United States or in a foreign country. Individuals living outside of the United States for a specified period of time each year may qualify for foreign-earned income exclusion as well as foreign housing exclusions and deductions. For 2015, the income that could be excluded was limited to $100,800.

Many countries encourage the exports of goods and services through favorable tax provisions. However, these

> ### The Tax-Free Consultants
>
> While working in foreign countries as an international consultant residing primarily in the United States, I received no tax breaks. However, many of my colleagues, both US and foreign nationals, established residence in low- or no-tax countries and were then able to work as consultants essentially tax free. For US citizens, this was possible because of income tax exclusions and deductions, and for citizens of "territorial tax countries," such as Canada, this was possible because their home government tax authorities waived all claims to income received.

"tax breaks" can run afoul of the WTO's disciplines prohibiting export subsidization if they are not carefully designed. In the past, the United States has had several tax export promotion programs found to be illegal by GATT/WTO.

In 2015, US exporters realizing profits on their sales of products originating in the United States could qualify for tax reduction by using an Interest Charge Domestic International Sales Corporation ("IC-DISC"). The owner or owners of an IC-DISC pay interest to IRS on the deferred tax on undistributed earnings. An IC–DISC is not subject to corporate income tax; thus, commissions paid to the IC-DISC by the exporter are not taxable, and commissions paid are deductible expenses for the exporter. And when the IC-DISC distributes income, the income is distributed as dividends and taxable at the qualified dividend rate, rather than normal corporate income rate. This also can provide a significant tax savings.

## Foreign Government Contracts

Government procurement averages between 15 percent to 20 percent of GDP in both developed and developing countries. The percentage is much higher in the few remaining countries with a centrally planned economy, such as Cuba and North Korea. Thus, government procurements offer significant opportunities for exporters of goods and services, assuming procurements are open to foreign suppliers.

Many nations use government procurement to achieve domestic and national security policy goals, and this can result in discrimination against foreign suppliers. Both GATT and GATS exclude government procurements from the application of MFN and national treatment. However, the WTO's plurilateral Agreement on Government Procurement (GPA) opens government procurements to the foreign suppliers of participating WTO GPA members. As of early 2015, forty-three states (including the twenty-eight current members of the European Union) are participating members, and a number of other WTO countries, most notably China and Russia, are in the process of accession. The revised GPA entered into force in April 2014.

The GPA encompasses three basic principles: nondiscrimination (national and MFN treatment), transparency, and procedural fairness. Each member's coverage is defined in annexes to the GPA. Contracts directly involving national security and defense are excluded. The annexes specify which national organizations at the central and subcentral levels of government are eligible, the monetary thresholds below which the GPA's provisions do not apply, the categories of services covered by the GPA, and specified exclusions.

The GPA does not cover small-value procurements. The United States and most other signatories adhere to thresholds of 130,000 Special Drawing Rights (SDRs)[79] for goods and services procured at the central government level and 5 million

> ### *GPA Annexes*
>
> - Annex 1–central government entities whose procurement is covered
>
> - Annex 2–subcentral government entities whose procurement is covered
>
> - Annex 3–all other entities whose procurement is covered
>
> - Annex 4–the goods covered
>
> - Annex 5–services (other than construction services) covered
>
> - Annex 6–construction services covered
>
> - Annex 7–general notes

---

[79] SDRs are determined daily by the IMF when the IMF is open for business. In March 2015, 1 SDR = US $1.39.

SDRs for construction permits. The recent revision of the GPA specifically incorporates electronic procurement processes and prohibits conflicts of interest and corrupt practices. In addition, it includes provisions intended to better accommodate the needs of developing countries. Disputes are resolved by the WTO's dispute resolution process.

For covered procurements, the GPA requires that a procuring entity must normally publish a notice of intended procurement in the appropriate paper or electronic medium listed in Appendix III to the GPA. The parties are also encouraged to publish planned procurements.

Additional information about the GPA
can be obtained at www.wto.org.

Some bilateral and regional trade agreements also contain provisions regarding government procurements. For example, the US-Korea Free Trade Agreement, the US-Dominican Republic Central America Free Trade Agreement, and NAFTA all have government procurement provisions.

Small businesses in the United States interested in participating in government procurements in a foreign country should consult with that country's desk officer at Commerce's International Trade Administration and, if the country is a GPA member, also review GPA's Appendix III, which lists where intended procurements will be published.

## Three Traps: Bribery, Anticompetitive Conduct and Boycotts, and Money Laundering

Small businesses involved in international trade transactions should be vigilant against three traps that can affect their business and result in serious legal penalties. These are laws prohibiting bribery, anticompetitive behavior and boycotts, and money laundering.

## Bribery

Bribery involves the soliciting or receiving of anything of value to influence the actions of a government official or anyone else responsible for a public or legal duty. Bribery of government officials constitutes a crime in almost all nations, and both the giver of a bribe and the recipient may be prosecuted. Unfortunately, bribery of government officials is relatively common in some societies, and prosecution may be nonexistent or selective.

Transparency International, a global NGO devoted to fighting government corruption, conducts an annual survey of perceived corruption in 175 countries and territories.[80] Its survey is called the Corruption Perceptions Index. Countries and territories are ranked on a scale of zero to one hundred, with one hundred indicating the least corruption. In the 2014 survey, Denmark ranked highest with a score of ninety-two out of one hundred. Other high-scoring countries included Finland, Sweden, Norway, Switzerland, and Singapore. The United States was tied for seventeenth with Barbados, Hong Kong, and Ireland with a score of seventy-four. Important trading countries that ranked relatively low on the index included China (100th, tied with two other countries), Mexico (103rd, tied with several other countries), and Nigeria and Russia (tied for 136th with several other countries). The lowest ranked countries included Iraq (170th) and Afghanistan (172nd).

---

[80] www.transparency.org/

The Organization of Economic Cooperation and Development (OECD), a group of developed and advanced-developing countries, has developed an international agreement designed to combat bribery. It is known as the Convention of Combating Bribery of Foreign Public Officials in International Business Transactions (OECD Bribery Convention). Forty-one countries are currently signatories. The convention requires signatories to enact legislation that makes bribery a criminal offense and to also specifically disallow the tax deductibility of bribes to foreign public officials. However, a recent Transparency International Report states, "Fifteen years after the Convention entered into force, there are still 22 countries with Little or No Enforcement and eight countries with only Limited Enforcement. As a result, the Convention's fundamental goal of creating a corruption-free level playing field for global trade is still far from being achieved."[81]

Other international antibribery conventions include the United Nations Convention Against Corruption and the Inter-American Convention Against Corruption.

In the United States, the Foreign Corrupt Practices Act (FCPA) applies the provisions of the OECD Bribery Convention. The FCPA prohibits individuals and businesses from bribing foreign government officials to obtain or maintain business, and for public companies (companies whose stock is traded on exchanges or over-the-counter) the FCPA imposes certain recordkeeping and internal controls requirements. Violations of the FCPA can result in criminal and civil penalties and imprisonment. Recent prosecutions are listed on the US Securities and Exchange Commission's website, www.sec.gov.

[81] Transparency International. "Exporting Corruption: Progress Report 2014: Assessing Enforcement of the OECD Convention on Combating Foreign Bribery."

The FCPA contains a narrow exception for "facilitating payments"—these are payments to expedite routine government actions such as the issuance of a visa, supplying utilities, or to expedite customs clearance of goods. These are actions that involve no discretion on the part of the official; the only issue is when the action will be taken. However, facilitating payments do not include actions that are within a government official's discretion, such as deciding whether goods should be subject to a border inspection.

> **Paying Bribes to Customs Officials**
>
> In 2010, a global express company and six of its clients settled charges under the FCPA that it had bribed foreign customs officials to evade customs duties to improperly expedite the importation of goods and equipment and to obtain false documents and lower tax assessments. The improper payments involved both retaining existing business and obtaining new business. The seven companies paid more than $235 million in criminal and civil penalties and disgorgement.
>
> —A Resource Guide to the Foreign Corrupt Practices Act (Criminal Division, US Justice Department and Enforcement Division, SEC (November 2012), p. 13.

Potential liability for bribery under US and foreign law should be taken seriously by businesses engaged in international trade transactions. Legal counsel should be promptly consulted if questionable circumstances arise and their advice followed. In addition, those doing business in high-risk environments should adopt compliance programs involving training and reporting systems.

## Anticompetitive Conduct and Boycotts

Competition laws are laws designed to promote free market competition by penalizing anticompetitive conduct by business firms. Anticompetitive conduct can include price fixing, allocation of customers and markets, boycotts, monopolization, and other restrictions on market competition. The United States and many other nations have adopted competition laws. These laws are generally national in scope (the European Union maintains EU-wide competition law provisions) but in some cases may be applied internationally based upon the "effects doctrine."

*Antitrust Violations*

The US antitrust laws, such as the Sherman Act's prohibition on agreements among competitors that restrict trade, apply to international trade transactions. and the US Justice Department's Antitrust Division aggressively prosecutes violations. A typical recent case involved an ocean-shipping executive of a Japan-based company, convicted of conspiracy to fix prices, allocate customers, and rig bids for international shipping services for roll-on-roll-off cargo, such as cars and trucks.

> According to the one-count felony charge filed in US District Court for the District of Maryland in Baltimore on January 16, 2015, Susumu Tanaka, who was a manager, deputy general manager, and general manager in NYK's car carrier division, conspired to allocate customers and routes, rig bids, and fix prices for the sale of international ocean shipments of roll-on-roll-off cargo to and from the United States and elsewhere, including the Port of Baltimore. Tanaka participated in the conspiracy from at least as early as April 2004 until at least September 2012...[Tanaka pled guilty and was sentenced to a fifteen-month prison term and a fine of twenty thousand dollars.]

> Three corporations have agreed to plead guilty and to pay criminal fines totaling more than $136 million...
>
> —Third Shipping Executive Pleads Guilty to Price Fixing on Ocean Shipping Services for Cars and Trucks (US Justice Department Press Release, March 10, 2015)

As the above case illustrates, antitrust violations may involve very significant penalties. Small businesses are not immune; many prosecutions have targeted small businesses and their executives. Moreover, in the United States a criminal conviction frequently leads to subsequent civil antitrust claims, for treble damages and attorneys' fees.

Boycotts may be one form of anticompetitive behavior. In a business context, a boycott is a refusal to deal with a person or business for competitive or political reasons. In the United States, group boycotts, or agreements among competitors not to do business with specific individuals or businesses, may violate antitrust laws. One example is a group boycott used to enforce an illegal price-fixing agreement.

During my career as a lawyer, I have represented a number of businesses and individuals that have been involved in antitrust investigations and prosecutions. Even if the ultimate outcome is favorable, the time and expense involved with these cases is a major burden. The best business practice is to stay clear of any situation or conduct that might be considered to be a violation of competition laws.

## Office of Antiboycott Compliance

Participation in a political boycott, such as the refusal to do business in a particular country or with that country's business enterprises, may also violate US law. The Office of Antiboycott Compliance of BIS is responsible for enforcing reporting requirements and prohibitions against participation by US businesses in other nations' economic boycotts or embargoes. The boycott of Israel by certain Middle Eastern countries is the principal boycott of concern to BIS.

Doing business with Arab country businesses maintaining the Arab boycott of Israel can be a real trap for small businesses operating under the jurisdiction of US laws. An example of a prohibited boycott condition in a contract follows:

> *The Contractor shall comply in all respects with the requirements of the laws of the State of Bahrain relating to the boycott of Israel. Goods manufactured by companies blacklisted by the Arab Boycott of Israel Office may not be imported into the State of Bahrain and must not be supplied against this Contract. For information concerning the Boycott List, the Contractor can approach the nearest Arab Consulate.*

—BIS, examples of boycott requests

Boycott requests must be reported to the Office of Antiboycott Compliance. Penalties for each knowing violation can include a penalty of fifty thousand dollars or five times the value of the exports involved, whichever is greater, and imprisonment up to five years.

Compliance with antitrust and other competition laws and antiboycott regulations should be taken seriously by businesses engaged in international trade transactions. Legal counsel should be promptly consulted if questionable circumstances arise and their advice followed.

## Trade-Based Money Laundering

Money laundering involves transferring the proceeds of criminal activity into supposedly legitimate funds or assets. Trade-based money laundering is an attempt to disguise criminal proceeds by using trade transactions. The basic techniques include

- over- and under invoicing of goods and services;

- multiple invoicing of the same goods and services;

- over- and under shipments of goods and services; and

- falsely describing and concealing the nature of goods and services.

By invoicing goods or services at prices *below* the real market price, the exporter is able to transfer money to the importer. Conversely, by invoicing goods or services at prices *above* the real market price, the importer is able to transfer money to the exporter. Needless to say, customs administrations scrutinize the value of trade transactions in goods for the purpose of assessing duties and taxes, and they may detect under invoicing. However, they have little reason to detect over invoicing unless the parties have been targeted as possible participates in money laundering.

Money launderers may also be able to transfer funds without detection by making multiple payments for the same goods and services. The value, quantity, and the nature of the goods are accurately represented, so multiple invoicing of goods may not be detected by customs administrations. Several financial institutions may be used to disguise the duplicate payments, and if multiple invoicing is detected, explanations such as the amendment of payment terms or payment of late fees may be used to explain the multiple payments.

Another money laundering technique is the over- and undersupply of goods. The quantity of goods may be overstated or understated, resulting in the transfer of money to the exporter if the quantity is overstated or to the importer if the quantity is understated. However, this technique is subject to checks by both logistics providers and customs administrations. The undersupply (and over invoicing) of services allows the transfer of money to the service supplier. However, the oversupply (and under invoicing) of services is not an effective money-laundering technique unless the services are then reinvoiced to a third party at their real value.

Lastly, a money launderer may misrepresent the type or quality of goods or services. Inexpensive goods may be invoiced as more expensive goods to shift money from the importer to the exporter. Conversely, expensive goods may be invoiced as inexpensive goods to shift money from the exporter to the importer. This method can also be used with services: money may be transferred by paying for nonexistent services.

Many nations have established Financial Intelligence Units (FIUs) to combat money laundering and terrorism financing. The US FIU is the Financial Crimes Enforcement Network (FinCEN), a bureau of the US Treasury Department. FinCEN works with banks and other financial institutions and law enforcement agencies to combat money laundering.

---

### Money Laundering by a Colombian Drug Cartel

US law enforcement authorities uncovered the following trade-based money laundering scheme:

A Colombia cartel smuggled illegal drugs into the United States and sold them for cash.

The cash was deposited in US banks in small amounts and in multiple accounts to avoid detection. This is known as "smurfing."

The cash is then used to purchase gold bullion exported by the cartel from Colombia.

Cooperating jewelers melted the gold bullion and recast it into hardware items, such as nuts, bolts, and household tools. The gold was enameled to make the shapes look like ordinary, low-value hardware.

The hardware items were exported to Colombia, where they were melted and recast as gold bullion.

The cycle begins again.

Source: US Treasury Department

---

You should be alert to the possibility of trade-based money laundering if a trading partner suggests that you engage in a scheme to move money between countries using trade transactions and report suspicious circumstances to the appropriate law-enforcement authorities.

## Takeaways for Chapter 6

- Know, in general, how customs duties and other border assessments are determined as well as the border procedures, restrictions, and prohibitions that may be applicable and how international trade is regulated. In particular, understand the methods used to classify and value goods and determine country of origin.

- Be aware of the possibility of obtaining advance rulings determining the classification, valuation, and origin of goods.

- Understand useful customs procedures, such as bonded warehouses, foreign-trade zones, transit, and drawback and how they can be applied to your trade transactions.

- Be aware of the WTO's three trade remedies, antidumping and countervailing duty proceedings and safeguards, and how they may affect your trade transactions.

- Understand the application of export controls to dual use and military goods and services and make certain that your exports of goods and services comply with all licensing requirements.

- Know the four modes of trade in services and the national restrictions that may be applicable, particularly to mode-three services.

- Be aware of the legal sanctions relating to bribery, anticompetitive conduct, boycotts, and money laundering. Conduct your business to avoid those problems.

# Chapter 7

# Why Is Social Responsibility Important to Your Bottom Line?

Be the change that you wish to see in the world.

—Mahatma Gandhi

International trade transactions do not take place in a vacuum. Rather, trade transactions may affect many stakeholders beyond the immediate parties. In addition to customers and suppliers, affected stakeholders may include employees, investors, communities, environmental and labor interests, local and foreign governments, and others.

Small businesses contribute to their own financial wellbeing and the wellbeing of others by carefully considering the impact that they have on *all* their stakeholders when they make business decisions. In the words of management expert Michael Porter, "[E]very activity in a firm's value chain overlaps in some way with social factors—everything from how you buy or procure to how you do your research ... The goal is to leverage your company's unique capabilities in supporting social causes, and improve your competitive context at the same time."[82]

Four problems illustrate the wide range of social-responsibility issues facing small businesses engaged in international trade transactions. These are problems in the garment manufacturing, seafood and agricultural sectors, and the impact of offshoring on small communities.

*The Garment Industry and Work Conditions*

The garment industry has frequently been a poster child for lack of social responsibility. The garment industry in the United States is comprised of both small and large businesses that source most of their products overseas in China, Vietnam, Indonesia, and Bangladesh—countries where the working conditions and labor standards of individual factories may not meet international norms. Importers may attempt to shield themselves from scrutiny regarding their responsibility for worker conditions by contracting through middlemen and then claiming ignorance of local labor, safety, and environmental conditions. However, in the United States, all garments must be labeled with the country of origin and publicity about poor working conditions in particular countries may affect consumers' purchase decisions.

Problems in garment factories in the Far East are legion. For example, a recent study of working conditions at certain production facilities in Guangdong Province, China, revealed that workers are forced to work overtime, including weekend time, in order to receive a living wage, and their overtime work is not electronically recorded in order to evade legal

---

[82] Michael Porter, Professor, Harvard Business School, at the April 2005 Business and Society Conference on Corporate Citizenship.

requirements.[83] In addition, high shop-floor temperature, sewage flowing on the shop floor, poor ventilation with high cotton-dust levels in the air, and electrical leakage pose serious risks to workers' health and safety.[84]

In Bangladesh, on April 24, 2013, the Rana Plaza, an eight-story building housing garment factories collapsed, killing more than 1,100 workers after they were forced to return to an unsafe building. The factories had manufactured clothing for a number of garment importers in North America and Europe. Despite efforts to improve working conditions, serious safety violations continue to be uncovered in Bangladesh garment factories by international inspectors.

In 2012, the US Department of Labor designated Vietnam as one of seven countries using forced and child labor in the production of garments.[85] Workers face serious safety and health hazards on the job. The most frequent cause of injury was the lack or inadequacy of safety gear. Wage levels in the apparel-export sector are insufficient to assure minimum living standards for employees and their families.

Similar problems exist for garment workers in Indonesia. In June 2014, a tribunal found systematic violations of workers' rights, including the "suspension of minimum wage payments, illegal compulsory overtime, inhuman productivity measures, systematic denial of social security payments, gender

---

[83] Chan, Alexandra. "Investigative Report on the Working Conditions of UNIQULO's China Suppliers." Students and Scholars Against Corporate Misbehavior. January 2015.
[84] Ibid.
[85] Made in Vietnam: Labor Rights Violations in Vietnam's Export Manufacturing Sector (Worker Rights Consortium May 2013).

discrimination, and active suppression of the right to freedom of association in the industry."[86]

*Seafood Production, Food Safety, and Sustainable Ocean Harvests*

Another sector with chronic social responsibility problems is seafood production. Shrimp has become the most consumed seafood in the United States, exceeding canned tuna and salmon. However, more than 90 percent of shrimp is imported, and most of this is farm raised. In many instances, shrimp farmworkers have poor labor conditions. Shrimp are grown in large ponds that can damage local ecosystems. Polluted water from the shrimp farms is released into the surrounding environment, causing damage. Chemicals used in the farm operations may, in some cases, be dangerous to human health.

A major problem with commercial fishing is "bycatch." Bycatch is fish or other sea creatures caught accidentally by fishermen and then thrown back into the water dead or dying. The highest rates of this are reported to result from tropical shrimp trawling. Shrimp trawlers can produce bycatch ratios as high as 15:1. Another example of bycatch is dolphins caught in tuna nets. Dolphins are mammals and do not have gills, so they may drown when caught in nets and held under water. Other cetaceans, whales, and porpoises can also be seriously injured by entanglement in fishing nets.

Another serious problem is overfishing. Overfishing occurs when fish are harvested at a greater rate than they can reproduce. Today, giant factory ships roam the oceans, catching and processing large amounts of fish using modern technologies, such as sonar and GPS. The ships use huge nets

---

[86] Indonesian wage trial: human rights violations 'systemic,' Clean Clothes Campaign (June 24, 2014).

with the capacity to pull extremely heavy loads. They also incorporate facilities for processing, packing, and freezing fish. Since 1988, the amount of fish caught worldwide has been shrinking. Five out of the eight tuna species are threatened with extinction. Shark populations have been seriously depleted because sharks are caught as bycatch and for their fins. More than one-third of freshwater fish are facing extinction.

*Coffee Production, Worker Conditions, and Environmental Degradation*

The treatment of workers producing coffee in developing countries is frequently a problem. After petroleum, coffee is the world's second-most-valuable traded commodity. There are more than twenty-five million farmers and workers in more than fifty countries that produce coffee. The global supply chain involves producers, middlemen, exporters, importers, logistics companies, roasters, wholesalers, and retailers before coffee reaches the consumer.

Smaller farmers, typically relying on their family's labor, may sell to exporters who may pay them well below market prices, whereas large farmers relying on hired labor frequently process and export their own harvests, obtaining better prices. However, low wages and poor working conditions for farmworkers are typical of most coffee farm jobs. Many coffee workers are denied the right to organize and work below minimum wage.

Coffee farming has also resulted in environmental problems. Traditional coffee farming in Africa took place under shade trades. However, shade-growing techniques have been replaced in many locations with sun-growing techniques in order to increase yields. This has resulted in the destruction of forests, accelerating global warming, pesticide pollution, contaminated water, and the threatened extinction of species such as songbirds.

Similar labor and environmental problems exist in connection with the growing and harvesting of cocoa, sugar cane, corn, rice, cut flowers, and other agricultural crops produced in developing economies.

*International Trade's Impact on Small Communities*

International trade transactions may adversely affect communities both in a foreign country where goods and services are sourced or sold and in the country where the business is headquartered. One example of effects in foreign countries is "Maquiladora" manufacturing operations in Mexico. Maquiladoras are a form of free zone, with duty and other tax exemptions designed to stimulate manufacturing and assembly operations in Mexico through the use of inexpensive labor. They are generally located in small communities near the US border. Workers, mostly women, are poorly paid and receive minimal social benefits. Many employees live in the vicinity of the factories where the air and water is polluted with harmful emissions. Local communities frequently use water from shallow wells polluted by human waste and toxins.

Another example is the impact of "offshoring" on small communities in the United States. Call centers have economically benefitted many small communities, but in recent years, they have been offshored to India, the Philippines, and other countries.

In the past few years, the call center and back-office industry, once seen as a key economic generator for the hundreds of jobs it brought to the Yakima Valley, has dwindled amid layoffs and closures, including the April 12 [2011] closure of the Whirlpool call center in downtown Yakima, leaving 160 people jobless. In 2009, Yakima County had an annual average of 1,487 jobs in the administrative and support-service sector, well below the 2,009 jobs the county had in 2007 and the 2,093 jobs in 2004, according to the latest data available from the state Employment Security Department. A lion's share of the loss was from the call center and back- office industry, said Don Meseck, regional economist for state Employment Security.

—Yakima Herald-Republic, 4/25/11[87]

The recent offshoring of service industries, such as call centers, follows on the heels of a long-term offshoring trend for manufactured goods. Businesses are free to move their operations to low-cost production sites. In fact, their failure to do this may jeopardize their continued profitability. However, offshoring may lead to social problems for both the communities losing businesses and the communities gaining businesses. The failure of businesses to consider social-responsibility issues when offshoring may adversely affect their long-term profitability.

---

[87] Quoted in "Why Shipping Call Center Jobs Overseas Hurts Us Back Home," Communication Workers of America. December 2011.

## Should Businesses Be Responsible for Social and Environmental Problems Resulting from Their Trade Transactions?

Some argue that a business's only obligation is to operate in the most efficient manner to return profit on investment. Their view is that national and local governments have full responsibility for social and environmental problems and that a business's only "social" obligation is to comply with applicable laws (even if those laws are inadequate or are not enforced). Businesses should not sacrifice profits for social interests. The economist Milton Friedman eloquently stated this view:

> What does it mean to say that the corporate executive has a 'social responsibility' in his capacity as businessman? If this statement is not pure rhetoric, it must mean that he is to act in some way that is not in the interest of his employers ...

> —Milton Friedman, "The Social Responsibility of Business is to Increase Profits" (New York Times Magazine, September 13, 1970).

However, Friedman's view oversimplifies the issue. Although charitable foundations and individuals ranging from Bill Gates and Warren Buffet to the owners of the smallest businesses may make significant financial contributions to charities working for the public good, there is little evidence that businesses themselves actually sacrifice profits in the social interest.[88]

---

[88] Reinhardt, Forest, Robert Stavins and Richard Vietor, "Corporate Social Responsibility Through an Economic Lens." NBER May 2008.

On the other hand, there are many socially responsible actions that *also* contribute to a business's financial goals. It is this area of overlap between profit seeking and socially responsible goals that is discussed in this chapter.

### Business Social Responsibility Defined

**Business social responsibility (BSR)** is the responsibility of a business for the effects of its activities and decisions on its stakeholders. Socially responsible businesses conduct their activities and decisions in a transparent and ethical manner that is consistent with applicable law and international norms of behavior. BSR includes

- commitments to health and safety;

- environmental stewardship;

- protection of labor rights and other human rights;

- assuring good conditions of work (including safety and health, hours of work, and wages);

- community involvement and other philanthropy; and

- adherence to principles of fair competition.

The economic case for business social responsibility varies depending on the size of the business, its products, activities, location, suppliers, and long-term business strategy. However, there is a strong correlation between adopting BSR policies and long-term organizational success.

We believe in [BSR] because it is a proposition aligned with our values, but also because it makes business sense. Our commercial partners expect from us sound environmental and social practices. We get and understand the message and are actively promoting [BSR] among associates. We want to be recognized as a responsible industry, adding value to our products.

—Ronald Brown, president of Chilean Fruit Exporters Association, October 2006

> ### Corporate Social Responsibility vs. Business Social Responsibility
>
> Corporate social responsibility is more or less synonymous with business social responsibility. However, corporate social responsibility specifically relates to corporations, which excludes the many small business organizations that are sole proprietorships and partnerships and focuses on major multinational enterprises. Business social responsibility is a more inclusive term.

Specific benefits to small businesses from adopting BSR polices can include

• better management of business risk by considering the interests of all stakeholders;

• improving relationships with suppliers, customers, communities, and government regulators;

• increasing the value of product brands and business assets;

• enhancing the ability to recruit and retain employees;

- improving competitiveness and realizing cost savings through consideration of feedback from employees, customers, and other stakeholders;

- enhancing ability to build effective supply-chain relationships;

- greater agility to anticipate market and technological changes; and

- improving access to capital.

There is no standard template for a small business BSR program. Each business has unique characteristics and circumstances that will determine its BSR program. However, implementation of BSR will usually involve the following tasks and activities, even for the smallest business enterprise.

## BSR Implementation Program

| Task | Activity |
|------|----------|
| Conduct BSR assessment | <ul><li>Assemble team</li><li>Identify legal requirements</li><li>Identify and engage key stakeholders</li><li>Assess current situation</li></ul> |
| Develop a BSR strategy | <ul><li>Research what similar businesses are doing</li><li>Prepare a list of proposed activities</li><li>Analyze business case for each proposal (costs and benefits)</li><li>Select proposals for possible implementation</li></ul> |

| Develop BSR commitments | <ul><li>Discuss proposals with stakeholders</li><li>Refine proposals based upon comments</li><li>Obtain agreement from stakeholders</li></ul> |
|---|---|
| Implement BSR program | <ul><li>Establish performance measurements and measurable targets</li><li>Design and conduct employee training, as appropriate</li><li>Develop communications plan</li><li>Make BSR commitments public</li></ul> |
| Monitor and report on progress | <ul><li>Measure performance</li><li>Report on program achievements</li><li>Publicize through website and media</li></ul> |
| Evaluate and revise, as appropriate | <ul><li>Obtain stakeholder feedback regarding program</li><li>Develop and implement improvements</li></ul> |

## Case Histories of Successful BSR Programs

Many consumer-oriented businesses have augmented their profitability and investor value by incorporating BSR goals in their business operations and product design. Leading examples are Ben and Jerry's Ice Cream, Apple, Whole Foods Markets, Etsy, and Starbucks.

*Ben and Jerry's Ice Cream and Social Responsibility Branding*

Ben and Jerry's Ice Cream is an example of a small business that adopted a robust BSR program and then both maintained its program and influenced the BSR of its parent after the business grew substantially and was sold to a major multinational enterprise.[89]

In 1978, Ben Cohen and Jerry Greenfield opened an ice cream parlor in a renovated gas station in Burlington, Vermont. Two years later, they started packing their ice cream in pints to sell to grocery stores. By 1984, sales had increased to more than $4 million. In 1985, the B&J Foundation was established by the owners and was funded with 7.5 percent of pretax profits. In 1988, more than 80 "scoop shops" were started, and the owners were named small business persons of the year by President Reagan. In 1989, the owners received Columbia University's Lawrence A. Wein prize for social responsibility.

The business's BSR concerns are also evident in some of its products. One product was the "Peace Pop," an ice cream bar from which one percent of profits were used to build awareness of and raise funds for peace. Rainforest nuts were purchased for some of its products, and proceeds from sales of "Rainforest Crunch" were devoted to rainforest preservation. The company adopted an "Eco-Pint," an unbleached paperboard container that is more environmentally friendly.

The business also adopted a compensation ratio, limiting the salaries of top executives to give all employees the sense of working as a collaborative team. Growth was controlled so that the company's values would not be lost. Employee benefits

---

[89] See Managing Social Responsibility and Growth at Ben and Jerry's, Daniels Fund Ethics Initiative, University of New Mexico.

included free ice cream, free health club memberships, and a partially subsidized child-care center. All production continued at the firm's facility in rural Vermont.

The biggest challenge to the firm's BSR philosophy was when Unilever, a major multinational, purchased the business in April 2000. Ben and Jerry's ice cream is now sold around the world. However, under the terms of the acquisition, Ben and Jerry's retained an independent board of directors for the purpose of maintaining its BSR programs. The agreement also provided an opportunity for Ben and Jerry's to influence Unilever's worldwide BSR program.

In the decade and a half since the acquisition, Ben and Jerry's has continued its commitment to BSR. As one example, it established the "Caring Dairy TM" program that helps dairy farmers in Vermont and the Netherlands develop more sustainable farming practices. As another example, the Ben & Jerry's Foundation supports many nonprofit organizations.

*Apple Inc. and its Supplier Responsibility Progress Report*

Apple started as the smallest of businesses, operating out of the garage of founder Steve Job's parents. In 2015, based upon market capitalization, it was the most valuable business in the world. Apple incorporates BSR principles in its product designs and operations to increase product acceptance and profitability. According to Apple, its computer operating systems are designed to maximize energy savings. In addition, harmful toxins, such as mercury, lead, arsenic, and PVCs, have been eliminated from Apple products. Many of its offices and other facilities are powered by renewable energy.

Based in Cupertino, California, Apple currently outsources the production of its products to hundreds of suppliers located around the world. In order to do business with Apple, every supplier must agree to comply with the standards in Apple's Supplier Code of Conduct and Supplier Responsibility Standards.[90] These standards include requirements regarding labor and human rights; health and safety; environment; management systems; and ethics that frequently exceed requirements imposed by local law. In 2014, Apple assured compliance by conducting 633 supplier audits. These audits resulted in millions of dollars repaid to foreign contract workers because of excessive recruitment fees charged by labor brokers, payments to workers because of unpaid overtime, underage workers sent back to school with full tuition and salary, and a doubling of mineral smelters certified as conflict free. Apple has also supported worker empowerment through education, investing millions of dollars to operate its Supplier Development and Education Program (SEED).

Apple's Supplier Responsibility 2015 Progress Report lists the result of audits of suppliers monitoring education, labor and human rights, eliminating conflict materials from the supply chain, health and safety, environment, ethics, and management systems. The audit revealed supplier compliance ranging from 70 percent for health and safety to 93 percent for ethics.

*Whole Foods Market and Socially Responsible Food Products*

Whole Foods Market was a small business founded in Austin, Texas, in 1980 when four local businesspeople decided that a supermarket format was appropriate for the sale of organic foods. The company expanded quickly through the acquisition

---

[90] Apple's Supplier Responsibility 2015 Progress Report.

of other businesses, and today, it is one of the largest food retailers in the United States. Many of its products are purchased from foreign suppliers.

Social responsibility regarding the food products that it purchases and sells is a key component of Whole Foods' business plan. Its organic food products are grown using renewable resources and conservation of soil. The use of genetically engineered seeds is prohibited, as are long-lasting pesticides, herbicides, and fungicides. Livestock management practices emphasize humanely treated animals and no antibiotics or added growth hormones. Food processing protects the organic nature of the products. Whole Foods cooperates with the Marine Stewardship Council to help assure the sustainability of wild-caught seafood. Whole Foods also emphasizes supporting local communities where stores are located as well as fighting global poverty through microlending and partnerships with small suppliers.

*Etsy Goes Public*

Etsy, an e-commerce firm founded as a small business in 2005 to market artists' wares, also emphasizes social responsibility as a corporate value. When the firm announced its initial public offering in March 2015, Etsy said that it was dedicated to business social responsibility and that it could choose environmentally friendly actions, such as investing in cleaner shipping methods or building low-impact data centers, even if they hurt the firm's profitability.[91]

---

[91] Harwell, Drew. "IPO delivers $300 million–in values." The Washington Post April 17, 2015.

*Starbucks and College Education for Its Employees*

In 2014, the CEO of Starbucks announced that the company would team with Arizona State University to help Starbucks employees complete a college education. All of the company's 135,000 employees were eligible for the program as long as they worked 20 hours or more per week. Those with at least two years of college credits would be fully reimbursed for the tuition to complete their education.[92]

## Small Businesses and BSR

For some small businesses engaged in international trade transactions, incorporating BSR in the products or services that they offer may be a marketing strategy. For example, consulting firms whose business it is to provide services assisting developing country governments and civil society to implement environmental protection and labor rights standards are incorporating BSR. Similarly, small businesses importing and selling specialty food products that are only obtained from certified fair-trade suppliers are using BSR for product differentiation.

B Lab, a charitable organization started in the US in 2006,

> ### Fair Trade
>
> Fair trade is a social movement organized to help producers in developing countries to achieve better trading conditions, promote economic development, and protect the environment. There are several fair-trade certifiers. Packers pay a fee to use the fair-trade brand and logo. Products such as coffee are produced by fair-trade cooperatives that are paid above-world prices plus a premium for community-development projects. To become a certified producer, growers and cooperatives must meet standards imposed by the certifiers.

[92] Ripley, Amanda. "How to Graduate from Starbucks." *The Atlantic* May 2015.

is dedicated to helping entrepreneurs to be socially and environmentally proactive in their business operations.[93] B Lab has developed a certification program, called B Corp, that recognizes businesses that meet rigorous standards of social and environmental performance. By the end of 2014, B Lab had certified more than 950 businesses in more than 30 countries.

Small businesses that are suppliers to large multinationals such as Wal-Mart may be required to adopt a BSR program as a condition to being a supplier to the multinational. The multinational may require annual BSR inspections of the business' foreign production operations and implementation of changes when deficiencies in labor or environmental conditions are uncovered. The multinational may even charge the small business supplier for all costs related to an annual audit.

For small businesses that are involved in international trade and that sell products or services that do not easily lend themselves to product differentiation based upon BSR, a logical place to start implementing BSR initiatives is in the local communities where they do business. Small businesses are generally more socially and economically identified with the communities in which they operate than large multinationals. Frequently, their owners and executives have strong roots in the local communities, and their businesses were started there. The local business and social networks to which they belong, such as local chambers of commerce and other business clubs, likely influence their BSR activities. Examples of BSR programs funded by local businesses are "Hire a Vet" or "Train Long-Term Unemployed" programs. These and similar programs can be a

---

[93] https://www.bcorporation.net/what-are-b-corps/
the-non-profit-behind-b-corps

valuable source for employment recruitment and also generate new business from socially concerned customers and clients.

For small businesses that are delivering services or obtaining goods in communities in foreign countries, an active BSR program can also help them achieve their business objectives. Business people in many societies are reluctant to deal with foreigners until they prove themselves as reliable and ethical business partners. Funding charitable programs in local communities and insisting on best practices regarding labor and environmental standards may be a much more effective business expenditure to build relationships than endless social engagements and golf outings.

Crowe & Co. is a small business that is an example of the business benefits derived from community work. Crowe, located in South Carolina, makes explosion-detection kits, or EDKs. The technology for its kits is licensed from the Indian Defense Ministry but has been further developed by the company. In addition to the EDKs, Crowe provides training and technical support for its use. Its customers are foreign governments and other organizations in conflict zones. Faye Crowe, the company's chief executive, says:

> No matter how small you are, support for local communities is extremely important for business success. It is particularly important for American firms because of the perception in many developing countries that all American businesses are large, wealthy enterprises that are uncaring about the people and communities where they do business.

## *Takeaways from Chapter 7*

- Adopting an active BSR program may benefit businesses in many ways, including increasing the value of their products and services; improving relationships with customers, suppliers, local communities, and governments; and enhancing their ability to attract and retain employees.

- There is no standard template for adoption of a BSR program, but every business involved in international trade should systematically consider adopting a BSR program tailored to its products or services and supporting the communities where they do business.

# Chapter 8

## The Future of International Trade Transactions—Five Predictions

Study the past if you would define the future.

—Confucius

In the first seven chapters, we first took a quick tour of the history of international trade and observed the inverse relationship between the volume of international trade and trade-transaction costs. We then reviewed principles applicable to obtaining and retaining international customers, getting paid, protecting intellectual property rights, and supply-chain management. Finally, we examined government regulations applicable to international trade transactions and the importance of business social responsibility to profitability.

In this chapter, I make five predictions about the evolution of international trade transactions over the next few years. These predictions are extrapolations of current trends, and it always is possible that unforeseen events, such as war or a major political or economic disturbance, will temporarily disrupt long-term trends. This, of course, happened during the period 1914–1945, and recently as a result of the international financial collapse of 2008–2009. While I believe that all of the five developments will be important, prediction 1, the rapid increase in cross-border e-commerce, may be the most significant.

The five predictions are presented below in what is, in my opinion, the reverse order of their importance, from least significant to most significant. However, the predictions are interrelated. Increases in cross-border e-commerce—the development I believe will be the most significant—will be dependent upon continued rapid economic development in new markets such as China and India, improvements in global supply chains, new trade agreements reducing and eliminating tariff and nontariff barriers to trade (including e-commerce), and new technologies.

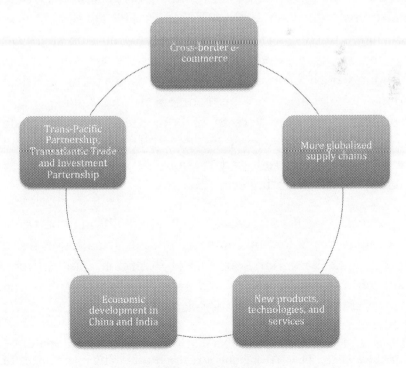

10, 5 predictions

## Prediction 5: New Regional Trade Agreements Lower Trade-Transaction Costs, Resulting in Increased Trade

Because of the number of WTO members[94] and their diverse economies and interests, with the exception of the Agreement on Trade Facilitation completed at the end of 2013, it has not been possible in recent years to conclude significant new multilateral trade agreements.[95] As a consequence, the focus on the part of developed economies, such as the United States and the European Union, to further reduce tariff and nontariff barriers through trade pacts has shifted to the negotiation of regional trade agreements.

Two significant regional trade agreements were under consideration when this book was written—the Trans-Pacific Partnership Agreement (TPP) and the Transatlantic Trade and Investment Partnership (T-TIP). A TPP agreement was concluded in early October 2015 and must now be approved by the US Congress and the governments of other TPP parties. Although both proposed agreements face strong political opposition from labor, environmental, and farm groups, I predict that some version of both these regional trade agreements will be adopted by 2017 - 2018 and that they will result in reduced trade-transaction costs, increasing trade among the participating economies.

A potential negative aspect of TPP and T-TIP may be trade diversion—trade lost by countries not participating in these agreements. Potential examples of diversion could include reduced exports of textiles and garments from China to the United States as a result of increased access to the US market

---

[94] By November 2015 WTO membership had grown to 162 economies.

[95] In July 2015, 54 WTO members reached a tentative agreement to eliminate tariffs on over 200 information technology products.

on the part of TPP members, such as Vietnam and Indonesia, and reduced exports of agricultural products from Brazil and Argentina to the European Union as a result of increased access to the EU market for agricultural products on the part of T-TIP member the United States.

## TPP

The TPP is a proposed regional free trade agreement between twelve Asia-Pacific countries: the United States, Australia, Brunei, Canada, Chile, Japan, Malaysia, Mexico, New Zealand, Peru, Singapore, and Vietnam. The United States and Japan are the two largest economies among this group. TPP countries account for slightly more than 40 percent of all US trade (Canada, Mexico, and Japan are the largest contributors).

TPP's objective is to further eliminate tariff and nontariff barriers to trade and to harmonize existing free-trade agreements between the parties (for example, the United States already has FTAs with six of its eleven TPP partners with differing provisions in each FTA). Negotiations covered the usual topics of regional trade agreements—market access for goods, services and agriculture, and, in addition, negotiations are addressing disciplines on intellectual property rights, services, government procurement, investment, rules of origin, competition, labor, the environment, trade facilitation, and other issues. The overall objective was to conclude a high-quality FTA that goes well beyond WTO agreements in removing tariff and nontariff barriers to trade.

The economic significance of the TPP will, of course, depend upon the extent of trade liberalization achieved. However, Japan's participation greatly increases the potential economic significance of an agreement. Economic models project modest overall welfare gains for the US economy as a result of TPP implementation,[96] but the services sector is projected to see significant gains.[97] Increased trade in goods could be significant for developing countries such as Vietnam and Malaysia, whose exports would become more competitive with exports from China as a result of reduced or eliminated tariffs. Some suggest that if the TPP is successful, China may eventually join the agreement. If this happens, the economic significant of TPP will greatly increase.

## T-TIP

T-TIP is a proposed trade agreement between the United States and the European Union. The United States and European Union currently account for almost half of the world's gross domestic product and approximately 30 percent of global exports. Issues under negotiation include improved market access in goods, services, and agriculture; regulatory issues, such as the treatment of genetically engineered foods as well as different standards and testing requirements; trade-related rules regarding investment, IPR,

---

### Differing Regulatory Schemes Can Impede Trade

The manufacturing and distribution of motor vehicles is international, and, more or less, identical models are sold in the European Union and United States. However, a US-based manufacturer of light trucks found that in order to sell a popular model in Europe it had to incur substantial design, development, and testing expenses to meet EU regulatory requirements even though the required changes resulted in no performance differences regarding safety or emissions. (See Proposed Transatlantic Trade and Investment Partnership in Brief, Congressional Research Service, June 11, 2014, p. 8.) This is also true for imports of vehicles from the European Union to the United States, where NHTSA regulations require significant vehicle modifications to meet safety standards.

---

[96] See Ferguson, Ian F., William H. Cooper, Remy Jurenas and Brock R. Williams. "The Trans-Pacific Partnership (TPP) Negotiations and Issues for Congress." *Congressional Research Service* March 20, 2015, p. 12.
[97] Ibid.

labor, the environment, and state-owned enterprises; investor-state dispute settlement; and digital trade.

It is difficult to assess the potential economic impact of T-TIP because much of the proposed agreement relates to regulatory reform and harmonization, not easily subject to economic modeling, and the agreement's terms have yet to be concluded. However, a study by the Centre for Economic Policy Research projected that by 2027 an ambitious T-TIP could result in gains of about $164 billion for the European Union and $131 billion for the United States.[98]

### Prediction 4: China and India Continue Rapid Growth, Stimulating Trade

The two fastest growing major-developing country markets are China and India. According to World Bank data, China's growth rate for the period 2010–2014 was 7.7 percent, and India's was 6.9 percent.[99] China's population is estimated at 1.4 billion, and India's at 1.3 billion. Per capita income in 2014 was estimated by the World Bank at $6,800 for China and $1,500 for India.[100] Continued rapid growth is projected for both these economies, and they will become increasingly significant in global trade in the near future. The other two BRIC-developing economies, Brazil and Russia, do not appear to be as fortunate. Russia's economy is resource dependent, and the recent decline in petroleum prices combined with its adventurist foreign policy have resulted in a negative growth rate. Brazil's growth rate in 2014 was only 2.5 percent, and its exports are

---

[98] Centre for Economic Policy Research. "Reducing Transatlantic Barriers to Trade and Investment, Final Project Report." March 2013, p. 47.
[99] http://data.worldbank.org/indicator/NY.GDP.MKTP.KD.ZG
[100] http://data.worldbank.org/indicator/NY.GDP.PCAP.CD

predominately agricultural and mineral products; thus, like Russia, its economic growth is tied to world commodity prices.

About 22 percent of trade transactions in 2015 took place in Chinese currency, the RMB, and some project that this will increase to around 50 percent by 2020. There are predictions that China's GDP will overtake and surpass the economies of the European Union and the United States within the next decade. However, this remains to be seen. Some observers argue that China's GDP numbers have been greatly inflated by provincial and national authorities for political reasons.[101] By early 2016, China's growth had slowed to below 7 percent per annum with further declines projected, and China's stock market was showing signs of severe instability. Economists Daron Acemoglu and James Robinson argue that:

> Just as in the Soviet Union, the Chinese experience of growth under extractive political institutions is greatly facilitated because there is a lot of catching up to do...Of course, Chinese growth is considerably more diversified than Soviet growth; it doesn't rely on only armaments or heavy industry, and Chinese entrepreneurs are showing a lot of ingenuity. All the same, this growth will run out of steam unless extractive political institutions make way for inclusive institutions.[102]

---

[101] Haft, Jeremy R., *Unmade in China: The Hidden Truth about China's Economic Miracle* (Polity 2015).

[102] Acemoglu, Daron and James A. Robinson, *Why Nations Fail: The Origins of Power, Prosperity, and Poverty* (Crown Business 2012), p. 441.

Henry Paulson and Robert Rubin, two former US Treasury Secretaries, put the situation more diplomatically:

> China must de-emphasize government investment in its own infrastructure, which currently plays an outsize role in the economy, and enable private investment in services and other emerging sectors. And it must de-emphasize exports in favor of domestic-led growth, especially household consumption. These shifts can be advanced by opening the economy further to private-sector competition...[103]

India's economic development trend is more promising over the next several years. By some measures, India's growth rate during the first part of 2015 was 7.5 percent, surpassing China's, and the World Bank predicts a growth rate of over 8 percent by 2017. This reflects business-oriented reforms, the sharp drop in world petroleum prices, and an emphasis on infrastructure investments.[104]

Currently, industry is the dominant sector of the Chinese economy, whereas services are by far the dominant sector of the Indian economy.[105] In the coming years, some scholars anticipate a rapid development of manufacturing in India and a

---

[103] Paulson, Henry M. and Robert E. Rubin, "The Blame Trap: Why the US and China Need to Act on Each Other's Economic Critiques." *The Atlantic* June 2015, p. 28.

[104] The Indian Express, April 14, 2015, http://indianexpress.com/article/india/india-others/indias-gdp-growth-rate-to-reach-8-percent-by-2017-world-bank.

[105] See Anil K. Gupta, Girija Pande, Haiyan Wang, The Silk Road Rediscovered (Jossey Bass 2014), p. 30.

greater focus on services in China.[106] In addition, some predict that China and India will greatly increase their respective investments in each other's economies.[107]

### Prediction 3: New Products, Technologies, and Services Increase Trade

New products, technologies, and services are continuously replacing ones that are less efficient or less appealing to consumers. Economists sometimes call this "creative destruction." Some examples of creative destruction in recent years include the replacement of cameras using chemically processed film with digital cameras (and then the replacement of many stand-alone digital cameras by multipurpose smartphone digital cameras); the substitution of wireless phones for landline telephone systems; the miniaturization of computers; the replacement of traditional movie and television entertainment distribution with streaming Internet services; the substitution of e-books for printed books; and the replacement of library-based research with Internet search engines.

In 2015–2016, some of the new products, technologies, and services that may have a significant impact on international trade include smart watches, mobile payment systems, genetically engineered drugs, 3-D printing, improved electric cars, and enhanced applications of robotics and artificial intelligence. Innovations expected in the next few years include improved 3-D imagery, nano-fabrication of new materials, car-to-car anticollision systems, blood tests to detect cancer, and improved desalination technologies.[108]

---

[106] Ibid, p. 31.
[107] Ibid, pp. 39–43.
[108] http://www.technologyreview.com/lists/technologies/2015.

One measure of innovation is the number of patent applications filed. According to WIPO, 2.6 million patent applications were filed in 2013; 81 percent were filed in 5 offices—China, the United States, Japan, Korea, and the European Patent Office.[109] While China leads the world in patent applications, this appears to have been driven primarily by the government's five-year plan targets and does not reflect actual implemented innovations. In addition, the tendency to patent incredibly broad processes and patent almost identical concepts tends to inflate the number of applications.

The Global Innovation Index (GII) 2014,[110] an annual report compiled by WIPO and two business schools, paints a somewhat different picture than patent applications. The GII ranks countries based upon factors such as expenditures on education as a percentage of GNI, GMAT test takers, expenditures on education, gross capital formation, royalty and license fee payments as a percent of total trade, creative goods exports of as percent of total trade, and similar factors. The top ten economies ranked, all high-income countries, are, in order, Switzerland, United Kingdom, Sweden, Finland, the Netherlands, United States, Singapore, Denmark, Luxembourg, and Hong Kong. Korea is ranked sixteenth, Japan is ranked twenty-first, China, an upper middle-income country, is ranked twenty-ninth, and India, a lower middle-income country, is ranked seventy-sixth.

The GII confirms that innovations tend to originate in high-income economies with democratic political systems and spread from those economies throughout the world. High-income, resource-dependent economies with authoritarian

---

[109] WIPO Facts and Figures 2014, p. 12.
[110] https://www.globalinnovationindex.org/userfiles/file/reportpdf/ GII-2014–v5.pdf.

political systems, such as Saudi Arabia (thirty-eighth), Bahrain (sixty-second), Kuwait (sixty-ninth), Oman (seventy-fifth), and Brunei Darussalam (eighty-eighth) do not fare as well in the GII.

Innovations tend to be developed and initially exploited in high-income economies. They then spread at differing rates over time throughout the world. As an example, when I was working in Nigeria in 2013 and 2014, early generation Blackberry smartphones were predominately used, although later-generation smartphones had already replaced them in high-income economies.

### Prediction 2: Supply Chains Become More Complex, Leading to New Opportunities for Small and Medium Enterprises

Today, reduced trade-transaction costs have led to complex supply chains, even for humble products such as cotton T-shirts.[111] Further reductions in trade-transaction costs in the future will lead to longer and more complex global supply chains for both goods and services. While new trade agreements, such as TPP and T-TIP (discussed above in prediction 5) will increase market access and reduce trade-transaction costs, the most important improvements for trade in goods will likely come from improved trade facilitation and reduced air transport costs.

A key trade facilitation measure now being implemented around the world is the adoption of national single-window (SW) IT systems for processing imports and exports. These SW systems electronically connect all national border agencies seamlessly, eliminating repetitive document requirements and

---

[111] Rivoli, Pietra, *The Travels of a T-Shirt in the Global Economy* (John Wiley & Sons 2015).

greatly reducing processing time for trade transactions. The United States is planning to operate a single window by the end of 2016.

Another factor leading to more globalized supply chains for goods will be reduced air transport costs, resulting from a return of petroleum prices to closer to their historic levels (crude oil averaged around $40 per bbl from 1946–2015 in 2015 US dollars) as a result of increased supplies, particularly in North America, the decision by Saudi Arabia not to curtail petroleum exports to increase prices, and the removal of economic sanctions on Iran.

An OECD study predicts that the sourcing of intermediate products and services from foreign countries will continue to grow over the next fifty years, and supply chains will become more complex.[112] Currently, imports of intermediate products represent more than 50 percent of trade in goods,[113] and the domestic factor input is decreasing in most economies. This trend will continue. According to the study, there is a lower content of foreign intermediate inputs for services than for manufactured goods. However, this varies depending on the type of service. Services such as tourism, IT, and business consulting typically have significant foreign intermediate inputs, whereas "nontradable" services such as retail trade or real-estate activities typically do not.

The increasing length and complexity of global value chains has led to a reevaluation of the production process for goods in terms of specialized tasks and business functions rather than the creation of specific products. Suppliers may produce

---

[112] OECD. "Global Trade and Specialization Patterns Over the Next 50 Years." *OECD Economic Policy Paper.* July 2014.
[113] Ibid, p. 13.

intermediate products or services for a specific industry but typically participate at different stages of the process or with respect to different functions.

Significantly, small businesses will have a much greater opportunity to participate in international business transactions because of the increasing specialization and outsourcing of intermediate inputs. For example, Apple spent over $3 billion with around 7,000 small business suppliers in 2013.[114] Boeing actively solicits small and diverse suppliers,[115] as does Wal-Mart, BMW AG, Novartis, and many other major multinational firms making a wide range of products. It is likely that the outsourcing of intermediate inputs to small businesses will continue to grow rapidly in the future.

### Prediction 1: Cross-Border E-Commerce Expands Rapidly

The rapid expansion of cross-border e-commerce will likely be the most important development in international trade in the next decade. This will be particularly significant for small businesses engaged in trade transactions. It will open up new suppliers and customers for them around the world, both as participants in business-to-business supply chains and as participants in business-to-consumer transactions.

Electronic commerce, or e-commerce, also sometimes known as digital trade, means the advertising, production, and sale of products and services using the Internet. Cross-border e-commerce, abbreviated as CBEC, involves conducting international business using e-commerce platforms. However, the payment and/or delivery of the goods or services can be

---

[114] http://techcrunch.com/2014/07/11/
apple-spent-over-3b-with-7000–u-s-small-businesses-in-2013.
[115] http://www.boeingsuppliers.com/esd/getstart.html.

offline (e.g., invoicing and payment by a separate business system, delivery of goods by express courier or mail).

CBEC can consist of business-to-business transactions (B2B), business-to-consumer transactions (B2C), consumer-to-consumer transactions (C2C), and business-to-government transactions (B2G). However, B2B and B2C transactions are commercially the most significant.

Two developments demonstrate the rapidly growing significance of CBEC.[116] The first is the rise of Internet companies, such as Google, eBay, and Facebook, offering unique web services internationally. The second is the increasing participation of small- and medium-sized enterprises (SMEs) in international trade transactions facilitated by the Internet.

Internet firms offer a variety of products and services, including e-mail (for example, Google's Gmail and Yahoo!'s Yahoo! Mail), popular search engines, cloud applications for businesses, maps, mobile applications, payment systems such as PayPal, video sharing such as YouTube, streaming videos and music, online market places for B2C business (for example, eBay and Amazon), and e-books and other publications (for example, Amazon and Barnes and Noble). Most revenue for firms such as Google and Facebook comes from advertising, whereas firms such as eBay and Amazon, which provide online marketplaces for a variety of products and services, charge fees for their services.

Major Internet firms have opened offices in foreign markets to develop their business in those markets. The establishment of data centers in foreign markets allows Internet companies

---

[116] See US International Trade Commission. "Digital Trade in the US and Global Economies, Part 2." August 2014.

to provide faster and more reliable access to their websites. Their products and services are tailored for foreign markets. By and large, Internet enterprises located in the United States have taken the lead in developing international business, and a large percentage of their users are international.

| Internet Firms Based in the United States—Percent Foreign Users | | | |
|---|---|---|---|
| **Company** | **Period** | **Monthly Active Users (millions)** | **Percent Foreign Users** |
| Google | 3rd quarter calendar 2013 | 1,200 | 84 percent |
| Facebook | 3rd quarter calendar 2013 | 1,172 | 83 percent |
| Twitter | First half calendar 2013 | 218 | 77 percent |
| Yahoo! | 3rd quarter calendar 2013 | 800 | 75 percent |
| LinkedIn | 3rd quarter calendar 2013 | 259 | 66 percent |

Source: "Digital Trade in the US and Global Economies, Part 2," *USITC* August 2014, p. 193.

For economic and political reasons, China and Russia have restricted the services of foreign Internet firms and encouraged the development of their own national Internet providers. Web businesses in China include Alibaba, Tencent, Baidu, and Sohu. Web businesses in Russia include Yandex and Mail.Ru.

Small and medium enterprises have greatly increased their participation in international trade transactions through use of the Internet. The Internet is used to connect with customers and suppliers, provide information about products and services, take and place orders, and facilitate the delivery of products and services. Many transactions take place on company websites, but for small businesses, the development of large online Internet platforms, such as eBay, Alibaba, and Amazon, add credibility and reliability to business transactions conducted on the Internet. Use of the Internet to collect product information and purchase inputs from suppliers throughout the world reduces production costs and increases their competitiveness in domestic and foreign markets.

*Measuring CBEC*

Measuring CBEC is difficult, and accurate estimates do not currently exist apart from well-designed surveys. Measures can include orders received or placed by businesses and orders placed by individual consumers, but these measures may not capture the value of transactions or discriminate between domestic and international transactions. A Forrester Consulting survey published in December 2014 reported global e-commerce (including both CBEC and national) at over $1 trillion per year, expected to nearly double in four years.[117] This may be a conservative estimate. A recent survey of CBEC in China estimated B2B and B2C transactions in 2013 at approximately $500 billion, an increase of 31 percent from 2012.[118] According to this survey, B2B accounted for about 94 percent of all CBEC in 2013, but B2C is steadily increasing

---

[117] Forrester Consulting. "Seizing the Cross-Border Opportunity: How Small and Medium-Size Online Businesses Can Go Global." December 2014.
[118] iResearch Consulting Group, *2014 China Cross-Border E-Commerce Report*, p. 17, http://www.iresearchchina.com/samplereports/6149.html.

and is projected to exceed 10 percent of China's total CBEC by 2016.[119]

The Forrester Consulting survey of B2C CBEC in 2014 concluded that tangible goods dominate online purchases. Clothing and apparel are the most popular items purchased online. However, consumers in the Asia-Pacific region are more likely to purchase food products. The principle online shopping sites are located in the United States, China, and the United Kingdom. Europeans tend to order online within the European Union. Discovery of products is primarily through online exploration. CBEC users prefer to use large online market places, such as eBay, Alibaba, and Amazon, rather than the websites of small enterprises. The main concerns of consumers are shipping costs, delivery time, import duties and taxes, and the condition of the product upon delivery (or failure to deliver at all).

B2B e-commerce will continue to represent a much larger share of CBEC than increases in B2C. Historically, B2B CBEC consisted primarily of expensive and cumbersome EDI systems operated by major multinational firms for marketing, product orders, and aftermarket support. These are being replaced by cloud systems and online platforms, like Alibaba, that facilitate B2B transactions. However, B2B CBEC transactions conducted through online platforms are much more complex than B2C transactions. Marketing is more complicated because customers must understand in detail how products work and interact with other products and systems. Moreover, logistics arrangements for physical products are more complex because larger products may not be amenable to delivery by express couriers or the postal service and may incur delays resulting from customs inspections and the imposition of duties and

---

[119] Ibid.

taxes. In addition, payment arrangements may be more complicated for high-value products as payment may entail trade finance and may be conditioned on physical inspection of the goods and other factors

*Adjusting to a CBEC world*

The CBEC train has left the station, and it is gathering speed. But the track that it is traveling on must be carefully maintained and improved in order to prevent delays or even derailments. Trade-policy officials, government regulators, academics, and the business community as a whole must address the new economic reality of CBEC and work together to maximize its benefits.

> ### Online Shoppers in China in 2014
>
> * 15.3 percent of China's online shoppers engaged in CBEC.
>
> * Impediments to online shopping CBEC were unawareness of CBEC options and lack of foreign-language skills.
>
> * CBEC shoppers preferred to purchase from foreign shopping channels of domestic e-commerce sites (65.1 percent) and global online marketplaces (61 percent). Foreign e-commerce sites accounted for 45.3 percent.
>
> * Assured product quality, lower price, and brand preference were the top three reasons to purchase goods from e-commerce sites based in foreign countries.
>
> * Source: iResearch, 2015 China Cross-Border Shoppers Report

A first priority should be to develop accurate measures of B2B and B2C CBEC. Current measures are inexact and are not suitable for the development of CBEC business strategies and government policies. Concurrent with the development of accurate CBEC measurements, government policy makers should take steps to foster the growth of CBEC. Current impediments include localization requirements, market access limitations, data privacy and protection requirements, IPR infringement, uncertain legal liabilities, censorship, and border administration measures. These impediments must be addressed successfully in order to realize the maximum growth of CBEC.

## Reasons Consumers Used CBEC

- The item was not available in my country—75 percent of respondents
- The item was cheaper than in my country—74 percent of respondents
- Total cost (including shipping, duties, and taxes) is cheaper than in my country—74 percent of respondents
- Brand is not available in my country—67 percent of respondents
- Uniqueness of item—67 percent of respondents
- Preference for a particular merchant outside my country—40 percent of respondents

Source: Forrester Consulting

## Localization Requirements

Localization requirements refer to regulations and restrictions imposed on CBEC by national governments. They can include laws requiring use of local servers and local storage of data; local content requirements for digital products; and a local presence for processing electronic payments. Based upon a survey by the USITC,[120] a majority of US firms engaged in CBEC believe that localization requirements are a significant barrier to CBEC transactions.

## Market Access Limitations

Market access limitations in connection with CBEC refer to restrictions imposed because of the nationality of a business. For example, foreign firms are generally not able to obtain ISP licenses in China unless they

---

[120] "US Trade in the Digital and Global Economies, Part 2," pp. 81–86.

partner with a Chinese firm. Governing rules may also be opaque for foreign firms, leading to difficulty with regulatory authorities.

## Data Privacy and Protection Requirements

Data privacy and protection laws vary from nation to nation, and this can be a significant obstacle for firms engaged in CBEC, leading to unpredictability and extra expenses. EU data-protection requirements are considered to be the most difficult in the world to comply with.[121] Moving data out of the European Union is forbidden unless the receiving country is deemed to have adequate protection.

### IPR infringement

Intellectual property rights infringement is viewed by businesses as a serious impediment to engaging in CBEC. Abuses may include misuse of a firm's branded assets; unauthorized downloading or streaming of motion pictures, music, and publications; appropriation of trade secrets; and violation of patent rights. Major Internet websites, such

***Claimed Censorship of Internet Content in China***

Internet sites are blocked by IP address.

URL and search engine results are blocked and filtered.

Some virtual private networks are blocked.

Censorship rules are opaque.

Censorship discriminates against foreign firms.

Popular international websites, such as The New York Times, Bloomberg, Facebook, Twitter, Google, Hulu, YouTube, and LinkedIn, have been blocked.

The "Great Firewall" is used to slow down and degrade some foreign Internet services.

Source: "US Trade in the Digital and Global Economies, Part 2," USITC 2014.

---

[121] Ibid, p. 90.

as Alibaba, Amazon, eBay, and Facebook, have developed on-line procedures for policing IPR possible infringements.

## Uncertain Legal Liabilities

The clarity and uniformity of legal liabilities related to CBEC is important. As one example, e-commerce businesses in the United States are able to rely on the fair-use exception in US copyright law to make copies of documents for indexing purposes and subsequent access by search software, but this copyright exception is less clear in some other countries.

## Censorship

Censorship of Internet content has been reported as a significant problem in China. Respondents to the USITC survey also reported censorship in Russia, Saudi Arabia, and a number of other countries.[122]

## Border Administration Measures

B2B transactions normally involve relatively sophisticated business partners trading goods and services of significant commercial value. Customs and other border agencies review B2B goods transactions and assess appropriate duties and taxes in the same manner as they administer their responsibilities for trade in general. However, customs and other border administration measures can create special problems for consumers participating in B2C and C2C transactions.

B2C transactions and C2C transactions of goods typically involve small shipments handled by postal services or express couriers. Importers frequently claim tax exemptions based

---

[122] Ibid, p. 98.

upon the low value of the shipment. This can raise problems of tax avoidance and smuggling, particularly for developing countries that are heavily reliant on border revenue collections and do not have adequate systems to police these imports. On the other hand, if importing countries set a very low value on imports that are excluded from tax assessments, cumbersome border requirements can adversely affect very small CBEC transactions, making them uneconomic. Regional economic organizations, such as APEC, and national customs administrations are now exploring technologies and procedures to address this problem.

In addition to tax avoidance, border agencies are concerned about policing the smuggling of contraband, such as illegal narcotics, weapons and explosives, and counterfeit goods, contained in small packages resulting from B2C and C2C transactions. Close cooperation with postal authorities and express couriers and the deployment of scanning and other technologies are being developed to minimize these risks.

### Takeaways from Chapter 8

- International trade will continue to grow over the next ten years.

- Cross-border e-commerce is rapidly changing international trade and affecting local commerce. Businesses that do not adjust to this new world risk extinction.

# Chapter 9

# The Author's Journal

There are many truths of which the full meaning cannot be realized until personal experience has brought it home.

—John Stuart Mill

As I wrote *What You Need to Know to Go Global*, I added some of the experiences that I have had during my career that I thought would illustrate the points being made and were of anecdotal interest. However, I subsequently decided that these personal stories interrupted the flow of the book and would not be of interest to many readers. For those of you who may be interested, I have included them here, organized by chapter and topic. I hope you find them both entertaining and instructive.

## Introduction

As a university student, I did not study international business or international trade transactions, and I had no inkling then that I might be involved in any aspect of international business or international trade during my professional career. There was good reason for my indifference. I grew up in a middle-class family in America that spoke only English and never traveled internationally. The United States was a relatively insular economy in the 1960s compared to European and other developed economies, and careers in international business and international trade were simply not an option for most people. Even today, international trade is less important to the United States than to other major world economies (see the chart below), and international business and international trade topics are given only cursory attention in many business school curricula.

| Percent of Merchandise Trade to GDP 2014—Selected Economies | |
| --- | --- |
| United States | 23.3 percent |
| India | 41.8 percent |
| China | 45 percent |
| Belgium | 175.3 percent |
| Singapore | 262.9 percent |

Source: World Bank

Chapter 1  Why Is International Trade Important to the Future of Your Small Business?

## Opportunities for Small Businesses

I graduated from law school in 1969. Soon afterward, my first international trade work as a lawyer was to represent Swedish exporters of electrical generators and specialty steel products in antidumping proceedings brought by US manufacturers that were attempting to have additional duties imposed on those imports.

On my first business trip to Sweden more than forty years ago, I noticed almost all furniture in hotels, offices, and homes was Scandinavian modern, and the second- hand stores in Stockholm's old town, Gamla Stan, were jammed floor to ceiling with heavy, dark, nineteenth-century Victorian style furniture. I thought, *There are some interesting business opportunities here. Why not buy discarded nineteenth century furniture in Sweden at giveaway prices and ship it to the United States where antiques are highly sought after? Or buy Scandinavian modern furniture and sell it in the US to young couples looking for modern, inexpensive home furnishings?* As it turned out, someone else had the second idea. The IKEA furniture concept was just being developed at this time in Sweden, and in subsequent decades, IKEA grew from its small-business roots to a multinational enterprise with retail outlets throughout the world.

On a subsequent summer business trip to Sweden, I discovered that no one had ever heard of ice cream milkshakes. I proceeded to make milkshakes for my Swedish friends, who drank them with enthusiasm. American hamburgers were also generally unknown. Why not invest in a typical American diner or drive-in in Stockholm, featuring burgers and shakes? McDonald's soon seized this opportunity when it opened its first franchise in Stockholm in October 1973. Many years later when I was working in Russia, I discovered that American investors were operating a typical American diner in downtown Moscow. With its art deco design lit up at night with colorful neon lights, it looked like an alien spaceship next to the Stalinesque era buildings on Pushkin Square. The diner was very popular with both expats and Muscovites.

*****

While working recently in Armenia, previously a part of the Soviet Union, and Kosovo, a new nation that emerged from the former Yugoslavia, I observed that young professionals are generally fluent in English, and many are highly skilled IT specialists, software developers, and consultants. Salary levels, however, are only a small fraction of what would be paid to a comparably skilled person in the United States or Western Europe. Why not take advantage of this cadre of trained young professionals by selling their services to IT, software, and consulting firms in the US and other high-wage, developed countries? Or at a minimum, establish call centers in these countries to respond to consumer inquiries as has been done successfully in developing countries, such as India and the Philippines?

Shortly after the fall of the Berlin Wall and the dissolution of the Soviet Union, I was a director of a metals and minerals trading company based in New Jersey. Most of our business at the time was with South Africa and China. However, we realized that the political and economic changes taking place in Eastern Europe and Russia might result in new business opportunities for metals and minerals trading, and we were able to establish successful business relationships with ferroalloys firms in Hungary and Russia. More trading opportunities of this sort may occur in the future after significant political changes. For example, Myanmar (Burma) and Cuba now may be opening up to new business, and political changes in the future in countries like Venezuela, Iran, and North Korea may lead to similar opportunities.

More than twenty-years ago, I was US legal counsel for a Taiwanese businessman who set up an international hand tools manufacturing business. The tools were forged in Taiwan and then finished and assembled in Texas. It was important to do enough processing in the United States to make tools a US product (at the time, consumers of hand tools, frequently trade union members, strongly preferred products made in the United States) and enough manufacturing in Taiwan to keep manufacturing costs low. His business was highly successful and was emulated by other manufacturers of hand tools.

About the same time, I was legal counsel for a small Canadian trading firm that specialized in parallel-market merchandise— bona fide trademarked consumer goods that are sold at lower prices overseas than in the United States. My client would purchase trademarked products like batteries in Europe and sell them to discount chains in North America. The multinational manufacturers tried to stop parallel market trade through legal action but they were ultimately unsuccessful.

Another one of my clients at the time was a small business that imported nuts from around the world. A Seventh Day Adventist minister and his wife had founded the business. My client's business plan was to source and import nuts and dried fruits from producing countries around the world. Today, the business has grown to a large operation with offices and production facilities in several locations. They distribute to major grocery chains in North America.

Medical tourism is the travel of people to another country to obtain medical treatment. The United States has been a leading provider of medical tourism because of its advanced medical technology, highly trained professionals and leading medical institutions such as the Mayo Clinic and Johns Hopkins. However, as modern medical facilities, technology, and training have spread to more advanced developing economies such as Thailand, Dubai, and India, patients from developed countries have been referred to these new facilities because of cost considerations and the reduction of waiting times for elective surgery, such as hip replacements and plastic surgery. As an added incentive, traditional tourism to exotic locales like the Phuket beaches or the Taj Mahal is often combined with medical treatment.

Jordan has a well-regarded medical sector and attracts international patients for treatment from other Middle Eastern countries. Some years ago, I was asked to advise on how Jordan could expand medical tourism to compete with leading medical tourism destinations such as Thailand and India. It quickly became apparent that major problems in attracting medical tourists included the provision of follow-up treatment after a surgical procedure and adequate compensation in the event that the medical procedure was not properly performed. If these issues could be resolved, medical tourism could be greatly expanded. (In the United States, medical tourism is currently restricted because insurance companies and government health insurance programs generally do not reimburse medical expenses incurred in other countries.)

Dental services tourism also provides opportunities. While working in Pristina, Kosovo, one of my dental crowns fell out. What to do? I got a recommendation for a local dentist from a colleague and made an appointment. The facility was modern and well equipped, and the dentist, who spoke English, had been trained in Germany. The fee for fifteen minutes of service by the dentist and recementing the crown? No charge. Why not start a business to outsource major dental work, such as extensive crowns or dental implants, in similar inexpensive locations that are on the same technical level as in North America and Western Europe? (This is already happening. *Atlantic Magazine* reported that Americans are flocking to dental offices in Juarez, Mexico, and saving 65 percent to 70 percent of the cost of the procedures in the United States).

A few years ago, I worked as a consultant in Sao Tome e Principe, a very small island country off the west coast of Africa, formerly a Portuguese colony producing coffee and chocolate. Sao Tome is a beautiful volcanic island; its beaches and mountain vistas are spectacular, Portuguese colonial plantations are picturesque, and sports fishing is superb. However, Sao Tome's tourism potential is almost completely untapped. Scheduled air travel is infrequent, and only a few modern hotels exist and these are small. A modest investment in tourist facilities coupled with improved air transportation and an effective advertising campaign could result in a highly profitable tourist industry.

*****

Over the last two decades, I have worked as a consultant in Kazakhstan several times. The country is developing rapidly economically and is a major exporter of petroleum and petroleum products. The workforce is well educated and progressive. Kazakhstan's culture is generally secular, and its leadership is even considering changing the country's name because of a negative association with other "stans." American goods are highly sought after, and I have been asked to bring colleagues various consumer products from the United States. Recent Kazakh immigrants to the US have set up successful businesses exporting automobiles and consumer goods to Kazakhstan.

English is the world's business language today, and in most of the more than fifty countries where I have worked, a great demand exists for native English-speaking teachers. Japan actively recruits recent US college graduates as English teachers, as does China, Kazakhstan, and other countries with the financial resources to pay them. Even in poor countries that cannot afford to pay for English instruction, English teachers are in high demand for private lessons. This can provide an interesting and well-compensated business opportunity for recent college graduates and retirees who are interested in foreign travel. While traveling in China, I met a husband and wife, retired university professors, who had been recruited to teach English at a university in the south of China. Their compensation included free accommodations and a modest salary. They said they were enjoying the experience.

Personal connections made with foreign university students can also present business opportunities. While working as a consultant in Amman, Jordan, I interviewed Fadi Ghandour, the CEO of ARAMEX, a logistics and express courier company that Fadi had founded with an American partner. Fadi had been educated in the US and met his original US business partner while a student. At the time ARAMEX was founded in the early 1980s, there were no express courier companies based in the Middle East. ARAMEX started as a small business, initially partnered with a US-based courier firm. Over thirty years, it has grown to a large multinational, with thousands of employees in locations in the Middle East, Far East, and Africa.

*International Trade and Trade-Transaction Costs*
*Throughout History: The Inverse Relationship*
*Modern Times: Trade-Transaction Costs Rapidly Fall and Trade*
*Greatly Expands*
*1977–1980*

As a young political appointee to the US Treasury, I played a minor role in the negotiation of a GATT Agreement on Customs Valuation that established the methodology to be used by customs administrations when determining the value of goods for the application of duties and for statistical purposes. My view of the negotiations from the inside was instructive. At the time, the US and European Community (then ten members) dominated negotiations and frequently dictated negotiation results without much input from developing countries or, for that matter, from the private sector. I remember discussing the issue of valuation of R&D and engineering design work with my Treasury boss. We decided with no analysis that R&D and engineering work performed in the country of importation should not be added to a good's value because this would benefit US industry (then, as now, frequently products were developed and designed in the US and then manufactured elsewhere to reduce labor and other production costs). The negotiators without discussion then adopted our proposal and it became part of the Agreement on Customs Valuation that is followed by almost two hundred nations around the world today.

During the late 1970s and 1980s, I became personally involved with the development of free zones, an institution that significantly decreased trade-transaction costs for some goods and promoted investment in manufacturing for import and export. While I was a US Treasury official, I worked on changing regulations to encourage manufacturing in foreign trade zones in the United States, The plan was to promote the assembly of foreign manufactured automobiles and similar products in the United States and that plan was successful. Later, in private-law practice and as a consultant, I remained active in the development of zone programs in the US and around the world.

*The Rise of China in International Trade*

Some decades ago, I was legal counsel for a manufacturing firm that imported hand tool forgings from Taiwan and finished them at their plant in Texas. Their president, a very experienced American sales executive who was then about seventy years old, told me that if he was my age, he would go to China to do business, and he would be a multimillionaire within five years. Unfortunately, I didn't take his advice. But similar opportunities may exist in the future as new markets open up in countries like Burma and Cuba.

*Century's End: The "Asian Tigers," Peaceful Revolutions in the Soviet Union, and Eastern Europe and the "Washington Consensus"*

1991–1999

I was fortunate to have visited Hungary and Bulgaria on business a number of times shortly after the fall of communism. The two Eastern European countries seemed to be caught in a time warp circa about 1950: there was little street traffic, electric and other utilities were undependable, and restaurants and hotels were primitive. Only young people had any grasp of market-economy business; older professionals still thought in terms of government-planning goals.

My business colleagues and I were successful in developing a metals-and-minerals trading business through contacts in Hungary, but we failed with our efforts to develop wine exports to North America from Hungary and Bulgaria. My most vivid memory of the time was a business trip to Budapest in June 1991. My trip coincided with a national holiday to celebrate the withdrawal of Russian troops. My Hungarian colleague said that it was the most important event in Hungary in a long time. I asked, "Since your liberation from the Nazis?" He replied, "No, since the Turks left Hungary [in the seventeenth century]." Needless to say, other cultures have a much longer view of history than Americans.

My first international consulting assignment, in 1997, took me to Tbilisi in the Republic of Georgia to advise the Parliament about adopting trade remedy legislation. Georgia then was an economic basket case. Corruption was rampant, trade had collapsed, and government services had broken down. But a cadre of young Western educated professionals existed who would later change Georgia's economic narrative. Today, despite conflicts with Russia, it is one of the more successful post-Soviet economies. Subsequently, I undertook similar consulting assignments in Russia, Kazakhstan, Albania, Moldova, and other former communist countries as well as in developing economies in Africa, East Asia, and South America.

*2000–2015: New Technologies and International Agreements Accelerate the Decline of Trade-Transaction Costs*

The use of global value chains for service firms is not limited to big business. I have frequently done consulting work for a small firm specializing in economic and trade consulting that has principal offices in the United States, United Kingdom and India and project offices around the world. My recent consulting work for this firm included projects in Nigeria, Kazakhstan, Laos, Peru, and Myanmar.

### So Are You Convinced Yet?

If you're still not yet entirely convinced that international trade transactions will be important to your small business in the future, I'm not surprised. I've been involved with providing legal and consulting services regarding international trade transactions for most of my career, but until relatively recently, I still thought of myself as providing services solely to US-based clients, some of which happened to be under foreign ownership or control.

As a student, I had no interest in pursuing a career in international business or law. I graduated from law school in 1969 and went to work as a young lawyer for a New York-Washington, DC, law firm that specialized in representing airlines in regulatory proceedings. As it turned out, some of the firm's clients were international air carriers. Because of those international connections, the firm was hired to represent Swedish exporters of large power transformers and specialty steel products in antidumping investigations being conducted by the US government, and I was assigned to work on those cases. Despite several trips to Sweden to collect information for these cases, I still had no plans for a career focused on international trade.

My career path altered in 1980, when, after three years as a political appointee at US Treasury, I helped form a small law firm devoted to representing clients in international trade cases. At that time, our clients were mostly domestic producers that sought to exclude imports from US markets on grounds that they had been "dumped" or subsidized. The products involved were commodities easily traded in international commerce such as steel tubular and wire products. Soon importers also sought our legal services. However, although I was representing both domestic and foreign clients regarding international trade regulations, I still thought of myself as just a US lawyer providing legal services to domestic clients, some of which happened to be owned by foreign businesses.

My views started changing in the mid to late 1980s after an international inspection company based in Europe employed me. My job was to help the inspection company sell its services to developing country foreign governments. At about the same time, I also became a director of a small metals-and-minerals trading company and assisted them develop business relationships in countries such as Hungary and Russia. Now I was traveling to and working in other countries to facilitate international trade transactions. I was no longer exclusively an American lawyer representing US-based clients.

My transition became complete in the early 2000s, when I left most of my US-based law practice and devoted myself to working as an international consultant, advising foreign governments regarding customs administration, trade facilitation, and trade remedies. Now there was no doubt: I was involved in providing services internationally. My services were normally provided not in the United States but in the foreign countries concerned. I became something of a global vagabond, carrying out assignments in countries as diverse as Portugal, Switzerland, Belgium, Russia, Kazakhstan, Jordan, Morocco, South Africa, Nigeria, Chile, China, Mongolia, and Laos.

If you have been paying close attention to the story of accelerating globalization in chapter 1, you will see the parallels between my career and the dramatic increases in international trade over the last four decades. Forty years ago, it was easy for me to ignore the importance of international trade to my career. Today, that is not the case—almost all my professional work involves international trade.

Chapter 2   How Does Your Business Find and Maintain International Customers and Suppliers?

## Tool 1: Evaluate Your Product or Service for Going International

### Unique Products

One of my more interesting legal cases involved automatic activation devices for parachutes. These are used to automatically open a reserve parachute at a predetermined altitude if the main parachute fails to open because the jumper fails to activate it or for some other reason. I represented a small business that was importing the original product from Germany. At the time, no competing products were made in the United States. The legal issue I worked on involved the customs classification of the product, which determined the customs duty. (Customs classification is something the book discusses in chapter 6.) We argued to US Customs that the device should be duty free because there were no US businesses to protect. We supported this argument by pointing out that no duty was imposed by Germany on the device. Unfortunately, our arguments failed to persuade US Customs, which was reluctant to change its existing classification precedent.

The Persian carpet case mentioned in chapter 2 was another situation involving unique products. Although we were successful in obtaining permission to import the carpets, the case came to an unhappy end as far as I was concerned. I was paid for my legal services but also promised—but not in writing—to have an opportunity to purchase several carpets at actual acquisition cost for the business. Of course, I knew the acquisition cost for each carpet because those records allowed us to prove that the carpets had been exported from Iran to France prior to 1979. I had also done a lot of reading about carpet quality and craftsmanship, inspected high-quality carpets in museums, and was looking forward to buying some high-quality Persian carpets at prices I could afford. After the carpets from Paris arrived at the business's New York store, I rented a panel truck and drove to New York to pick out several carpets. When I arrived, the entire family was in the showroom engaged in a heated argument. It turned out that the argument was about me. Nothing had been put in writing, and I was told that I could not buy any carpets at cost.

### Tool 2: E-Commerce Levels the International Playing Field

My first real introduction to B2C e-commerce came in Moscow in September 2004. At the time, I was working for an international consulting firm, and we had just started an eighteen-month consulting project with the Russian Federation Customs Service. I decided that it would be useful to have a map of Russia over my desk. I assumed that we would jump in a car and go to a store in Moscow that sold maps. At least that is what I would have done in the United States at the time. My twenty-one-year-old Russian assistant looked at me with disgust and told me I was hopelessly out of date. She said the only reasonable thing to do would be to order the map on the Internet, and she proceeded to do this. About a week later, the map arrived. I unrolled it from the packaging tube and climbed onto my desk to put it on the wall. My assistant was again horrified. She declared emphatically that I could not put the map up on the wall: "We have people whose job it is to do that!" A few days later, two burly Russian men arrived and spent about twenty minutes positioning the map on the wall over my desk.

It turned out that Russia in 2004 was both advanced, embracing e-commerce before the United States, and backward, requiring specific workers to do specific tasks. Under communism, specialized stores selling to consumers were few and far between, so B2C e-commerce quickly developed. On the other hand, the traditions of employment stratification in Russia under Tsarism, and later communism, continued: Both regulations and custom specified that only certain workers could perform certain tasks.

When I first started traveling internationally for business in the early 1970s, international phone calls were very expensive. E-mail via the Internet did not exist and did not become widely available until the mid-1990s. I recall working in Mozambique in May 2001 and being reluctant to place an international phone call because the charge would exceed one hundred dollars for fifteen or twenty minutes. Today, all this has changed thanks to high-speed Internet and free voice and video over Internet services such as Skype. Now I am regularly able to communicate by voice and video with business colleagues half a world away at no cost as long as I have access to high-speed Internet.

### Tool 4: Make New Contacts

My wife owns and manages a small business that produces wearable art that she sells to high-end boutiques. She finds it invaluable to attend trade shows where suppliers of high-quality textile materials from Italy, the United Kingdom, Japan, and other countries show their latest fabrics. Many of my clients make it a point to regularly attend trade shows specific to their industry. Trade shows are an efficient way for them to display their goods and services to potential customers and also to meet suppliers.

### Tool 6: Visit Them

Earlier in my career, I represented a client in a court case on a trade issue without ever having met the key corporate officials in person. However, the business relationship was somewhat strained. I decided it was time to invest my time and money and meet the executive team at the corporate headquarters in Texas. It was fortunate that I did this. As it turned out, one of the executives confessed to having had a negative impression about me that I was able to dispel; the meeting went very well and led to a long-term business relationship.

### Tool 7: Handle Cultural Differences

It is particularly difficult to translate jokes into another language because humor depends so much on cultural context. I like to tell a story about the difficulty of translating humor to interpreters whom I work with. During the American occupation of Japan after WWII, an American general was addressing a large Japanese business group. The general always liked to start his speeches with a joke, and on this occasion, the joke he told was quite lengthy. When he finished, his interpreter said a few words and everyone laughed. After the speech concluded, the general pulled his interpreter to one side and angrily said, "You couldn't possibly have translated the joke. You only said a few words." His interpreter replied, "Yes. You are correct. Your joke was long and complicated, and they wouldn't have understood it. I said: 'The general has just told a funny story. Please laugh!'" The story may or may not be true, but it captures the difficulty of translating humor.

\*\*\*\*\*\*

From 2004 to 2006, I worked as a consultant in Moscow on a World-Bank-funded project designed to improve Russia's customs legislation. Although we were able to complete our consulting assignment successfully, the "Russian management style" discussed in chapter 2 continued to play out during the course of our work whenever our Russian counterparts were concerned about some aspect of our assignments. We would be called to a meeting with a senior official and threatened with contract termination, with much bluster, huffing, and puffing. I finally understood what was going on after watching a very funny Soviet-era movie called *Ivan the Terrible* in Russian or *Ivan Vasilievich: Back to the Future* in English. In the movie, two people from 1970s Russia, a thief and a petty Soviet bureaucrat, are transported back in time to the court of Ivan the Terrible, and Tsar Ivan the Terrible is transported to modern-day Russia. The same actor plays both the petty bureaucrat and the Tsar. The thief instructs the bureaucrat how to act like a Tsar: "Furrow your brow! Stamp your staff! Shout angrily and threaten them with execution! Otherwise they won't know you are the Tsar." This management style continues to be employed today by some in Russia and other regions influenced by Russian culture.

\*\*\*\*\*

I encountered another case of different perceptions of time in other cultures when I worked on a consulting project in Lusaka, Zambia, in 2002 for an international organization. The logistics project we were working on had been in process for years without much in the way of tangible results. I worked hard to put together an action plan to implement new procedures to solve the logistics problems, and we then had a stakeholders' meeting to discuss the various options and next steps. Much to my disappointment, nothing tangible happened after my work except that the international organization continued to sponsor more studies of the problem. There was apparently no urgency to implement a solution, even though an imperfect solution could have had a positive economic impact on logistics in eastern and southern Africa.

### Tool 8: Know How to Negotiate

### Deal with Culturally Driven Negotiation Tactics

Recently, when working in Yerevan, Armenia, I employed the "walkaway" tactic to buy a collection of colorful local volcanic rocks. A vendor at a stand adjacent to a historic island monastery was selling the rocks. After haggling for a few minutes, I started to walk away with my friends, who were also on the tour. After all, the tour bus was leaving. This prompted his "best" offer, which I quickly accepted.

### Build Relationships

When I was on a business trip in Istanbul, my wife e-mailed a photo of a necklace that a friend of hers owned and asked me to find something similar for her. I asked the concierge of the hotel where I was staying to check on jewelry shops, and I sent a copy of the photo to his smartphone. After checking, he referred me to a well-known shop. The shop sent one of their employees to my hotel to pick me up and take me to the shop. There, they served me coffee and pastries and went out of their way to establish a personal relationship. Eventually, they brought out the similar necklace, which, as it turned out, was not that expensive. However, they also showed me several beautiful, but much more expensive, necklaces and told me that if I bought one of the more expensive necklaces, they would include the necklace I was interested in buying at no charge. This negotiation all took place without my feeling any pressure to purchase. I ended up buying the necklace my wife wanted with a small discount from the original offering price. I achieved my objective, and the shop had made a sale and gained potential future customers, either from me and my family or people I would recommend.

Chapter 3: How Do You Get Paid?

**The Problems**

*The "Cheaters"*

Years ago, I worked closely with a European business executive who superficially seemed to be a charming, urbane person. He held a PhD in a physical science from a well-known Belgian university and had risen to chief executive of a multinational service firm. But after I got to know him, he always seemed to be gleeful about cutting corners and proposing shady deals. It was a game to him—making money by outwitting others. He urged me to aid and abet some of his questionable schemes, and I refused. When it came time for his business to pay my legal bill, it was no surprise to me that they reneged. Fortunately, I was able to obtain payment after a third party important to this person's business intervened on my behalf.

I ran into another "shady operator" more recently when I was working for a multinational consulting firm. My employer was a subcontractor to the general contractor, a small consulting firm that specialized in working in Central Asian countries. The general contractor's senior manager at the time was a Middle Eastern national who was very bright and knowledgeable about the local countries where we were working and spoke the local languages. However, my internal alarm went off when, at a staff holiday party that took place in one of the countries where we were working, the senior manager walked around the room handing out large sums of cash to certain people as "bonuses." I knew that large cash payments can be a sign of illegal activity and, at best, cash payments can lead to tax avoidance. Later, after my employer asked me to head up a project office in one of the regional countries for a project that was run by the general contractor, I found out that the senior manager had not registered the project office with the local government as was required to do business. Therefore, our presence in that country was illegal and put our local staff in jeopardy. I brought this to his attention in writing and was ignored. This concerned me enough that I found an excuse not to accept the position as manager of the project office.

Another client, an ordained minister, was anxious to get into the oil business in Nigeria. His church had a mission there, and through church and charitable activities, he had met senior Nigerian government officials who suggested that he and his church could make a lot of money trading oil. He had obtained financial backers for this from some of his church members. I was very skeptical about this proposed business from the start and counseled my client about the problems involved in doing business in Nigeria and potential liability under the US Foreign Corrupt Practices Act (kickbacks and bribes are unfortunately common practice in Nigeria). Subsequently, my client spent a lot of his time and investors' money traveling repeatedly to Nigeria and exploring various oil-trading opportunities without any success. I never doubted his personal integrity, but he seemed to be very naïve about the intentions and integrity of the people he was dealing with.

In another case, my law firm represented a group of people pursuing foreign claims through the United Nations and US Department of State. We set up payments to the claimants through our law firm to assure payment of our fees and this was provided for by our representation agreements. However, one of the claimants by fraud was able to have the State Department pay her claim directly and she then refused to pay our fee. We never collected it because the amount was not large enough to justify suing the client in California where she lived.

*The "Squeezers"*

Sometimes a businessman or woman is so proud of his or her ability to "squeeze" others that he or she boasts about the prowess in getting "a good deal." You should never ignore this warning; if his or her conduct is questionable toward others, there is no reason why this person won't treat you the same way. I've encountered this problem periodically during my career. A few of my experiences with characters of this type follow.

Shortly after the fall of the Soviet Union, I took on as a client a young "wheeler-dealer" who was interested in entering into distributor arrangements with consumer products producers in Eastern European countries. We traveled a number of times to Eastern Europe to explore possibilities but nothing ever developed, probably because he was never willing to make a significant financial commitment. He always paid my expenses, but I had deferred billing him for my services, at his request, until our business was completed. After I got to know him well on one of the international trips, he told me what he considered was a very amusing story about his wedding. He had booked a very expensive hotel in downtown Baltimore for the event. On the morning of the wedding, he visited hotel management and told them he was canceling because of unforeseen circumstances. The hotel, of course, had already set aside its facilities and prepared food. Following much argument, my client was able to negotiate a very substantial discount as a result of his ploy. After hearing this story, I quickly submitted an invoice for my services. True to form, he tried everything he could to avoid payment.

A certain percentage of people whom you do business with always want to renegotiate the price of goods or services after you think you have a deal with them and you have already provided them with goods or services. They think this is just "smart business." This tactic is common in cultures where, as part of business, everything is always negotiable. One of my clients—an international trading firm that purchased trademarked goods at lower prices in foreign markets and then resold them to wholesalers at higher prices in North America— always operated in this manner. Our personal relationship was good, but this client viewed my legal services no differently than the commodities they purchased and sold; my services were a commodity with a price that could always be negotiated down. If I didn't like this, then I was free not to do business with them in the future. Eventually, I exercised this option.

*Agreements That Break Down*

A more typical payment problem occurs when products or services have been contracted for and delivered in accordance with all contract terms, but the purchaser refuses to pay because of a subsequent problem. Sometimes this happens when goods or services have been delivered on "open account" (i.e., payment due a period of time after receipt) over a period of time without difficulties, but the purchaser then encounters financial problems. This happened to me when I was doing regular legal work for a well-known international conglomerate based in Pittsburgh. I had not been closely monitoring the firm's business situation; otherwise, I would have probably found out they were in financial difficulty and insisted on payment terms other than open account. Not monitoring a client's credit situation was a poor business practice on my part (and on the part of my law firm) because it is relatively easy to keep abreast of a business's credit situation through credit services and Internet articles. In addition, maintaining good, regular communication with a customer or client also may reveal problems. As it turned out, our invoice remained unpaid for many months despite my repeated inquiries. Ultimately, the firm filed for Chapter-11 bankruptcy, and we had the same status as other unsecured creditors. About a year later, we received a final payment that was only a fraction of our unpaid invoice.

Sometimes the failure to make good on an international agreement involves a changed international political situation. After the first Gulf War in 1991, I was retained by a group of US-citizen university professors who had their long-term employment contracts to teach at Kuwait University terminated because they were ethnic Palestinians. Prior to and during the Gulf War the Palestine Liberation Organization, led by Yasser Arafat, sided with Saddam Hussein. As a result, the Kuwaiti Education Ministry terminated with prejudice the contracts of all ethnic Palestinians teaching in Kuwait. We sued Kuwait University on behalf of the US-citizen professors in the United

States District Court for the District of Columbia for breach of contract and the University defended by asserting sovereign immunity (Under the legal doctrine of sovereign immunity, a government institution is immune from suit unless it gives its consent. However, if the state is involved in a commercial activity, it may be deemed to have given consent to be sued.) We won the jurisdictional issue on appeal, and the case was subsequently settled.

A more typical agreement failure occurs when the goods or services contracted for are not paid as specified. Some years ago, a Chinese exporter of goods retained our law firm to collect payments due and unpaid from various customers in the United States. These collection cases could be difficult. At times, the consumer was out of business or did not have the assets to pay. Additional complications involved different court rules and procedures applied in different state jurisdictions. Frequently, the expense of collecting the claims could exceed the amount of the debt. These payment problems could have been avoided, or at least minimized, if the Chinese exporter had been more cautious when entering into export agreements and, instead of selling on open account, applied the four methods to improve the probability of payment discussed in chapter 3.

### Step 4: Provide for an Effective Dispute-Resolution Process

Much of my career as a lawyer involved representing parties in international trade litigation. I represented foreign and domestic businesses in antidumping, countervailing duty, safeguards, and customs litigation before administrative agencies and courts. I also represented foreign and domestic parties in commercial disputes. My clients were mostly large businesses that could afford the expense and inconvenience of litigation. Even so, litigation is usually not a pleasant experience for a business, even when a litigant wins its case.

*****

Service of process on an international party can present difficulties even when that international party is physically in the country where the litigation is taking place. Some years ago, I worked with a Canadian consultant in Botswana whose former American citizen wife was seeking child support. His wife's attorneys somehow found out that he had traveled to the United States for a meeting and ended up chasing him unsuccessfully around Washington, DC, attempting to serve process.

Chapter 4: How Do You Protect Your Intellectual Property?

*Infringement of Intellectual Property Rights: An All-Too-Common Problem*

When I was recently working as a consultant in Nigeria, the National Agency for Food and Drug Administration and Control was having difficulty interdicting counterfeit pharmaceuticals because of widespread smuggling, corruption, and chaotic border enforcement. As a result, many consumers were injured, and, in some cases, died from using counterfeit drugs.

****

Some years ago, a business colleague of mine accompanied a customs broker to a meeting with a senior US customs official. The broker was wearing a fake Rolex watch and, during the meeting, conspicuously flashed it before the customs officer. The broker thought this was a great joke.

### Is It Parallel-Market Trade or Gray-Market Trade?

One of my most interesting international trade cases involved the importation by my client of genuine Duracell batteries manufactured Belgium at lower prices than Duracell sold them for in the United States. All aspects of the Belgian product—the physical composition, the packaging, and the labeling—were identical to the batteries produced and sold in the United States by Duracell; the only difference was that the prices charged in Europe were lower. My client, based in Canada, had a simple business plan: it purchased Duracell batteries in Belgium and resold them to discount stores in the United States, making a profit on this international arbitrage of goods. Low tariff rates and transport costs as well as improved logistics facilitate arbitrage in trademarked goods when multinationals attempt to maintain highly disparate pricing in different national markets. Those who believe the practice is merely good business usually call the practice parallel-market trade, whereas those whose economic interests are adversely affected typically call this practice gray-market trade.

In the event, Duracell USA's Management was outraged—their sales were being reduced at the expense of sales by Duracell Belgium, and Duracell's segmentation of its international markets was being threatened. Duracell USA took legal action under Section 337 of the Tariff Act of the United States to stop the battery imports, alleging trademark infringement, misappropriation of trade dress, and false representation of origin, seeking an order from the US International Trade Commission banning importation of the batteries. After a hearing and argument, an Administrative Law Judge (ALJ) agreed with Duracell USA. The ALJ's decision was then reviewed by the full Commission, which by a 3–2 vote, upheld the ALJ and issued a general exclusion order. The minority argued that the majority's decision was contrary to long-standing Treasury Department rules and that a proper remedy would have been additional labeling clearly indicating that the batteries originated in Belgium, not exclusion.

Under Section 337, the president can disapprove a Commission exclusion order if the president finds that it is contrary to the public interest. Following the Commission's decision, there was a flurry of lobbying directed at then president Ronald Reagan, with the Treasury Department arguing that for economic and trade policy reasons the exclusion order should be disapproved. After considering all arguments, the president disapproved the Commission's order, so Duracell's long legal battle ultimately ended in defeat.

Chapter 5: What You Need to Know about Logistics, Supply Chains, and Trade Facilitation

### 1. *Everything You Always Wanted to Know about International Trade Logistics*

Much of my work as an international consultant has involved providing advice to foreign customs administrations in developing countries regarding how they can make their operations more efficient.

Years ago when I began my career as a trade lawyer in the United States, there was little cooperation and trust between US Customs and the business community, which Customs called "the trade." Customs officers believed that many traders were "crooks" and scrutinized trade transactions with suspicion. Travelers' baggage was frequently examined for possible customs violations. Commercial shipments were also generally thoroughly examined. This required a lot of manpower (manpower is the correct term; there were few women employed as customs officers in that era), significantly slowing trade transactions, but it was ultimately not that successful in uncovering violations.

Traders, on the other hand, frequently voiced their opinion that customs officers were corrupt and were on the lookout for bribes. Traders were frustrated at the slow pace of customs administration and the inordinate delays to trade transactions, resulting in significant additional business costs and a climate encouraging corruption. Their view was reflected in perhaps apocryphal stories about customs officers in an unnamed African nation regularly reporting to their jobs every day, even though they hadn't received their government salaries in years. Czar Peter the Great supposedly rejected the suggestion of his advisers about paying officers of the newly formed Russian Customs with the comment: "Let the wolves feed themselves."

\*\*\*\*\*

## Trade Logistics Providers

### Customs Brokers

I have had several frustrating consulting assignments involving the professional standards for customs brokers. In Kosovo, customs brokers were not subject to licensing requirements, so anyone could "hang out a shingle" and claim to deliver customs-broker services. This was not a desirable situation, but we didn't help Kosovo to correct it because our project director was a libertarian who was opposed to any regulation, even self-regulation. In Nigeria, customs officers had been known to "moonlight" as customs brokers (or the husband or wife of a customs officer will be the broker). We obtained agreement to correct this by legislation. In Mongolia, the brokers and customs administration were anxious to develop regulations providing professional standards for brokers but others preferred to maintain the status quo.

## Express Couriers

Large-scale international express courier business is a relatively recent innovation. When I was a young lawyer in the early 1970s, one of my colleagues, also a young aviation lawyer, brought a prospective new client to our law firm called Federal Express (now FedEx). The company had been founded by Fred Smith to deliver mail and small packages to customers overnight, based on a spoke-and-hub system. This service was, at that time, subject to Civil Aeronautics Board (CAB) regulation and Federal Express was seeking CAB lawyers. However, the company was a startup and was losing money, and our law-firm management rejected Federal Express as too risky a client. My colleague subsequently left the law firm and went to work "in house" for Federal Express in Memphis. As the saying goes, the rest is history.

## Trade Advisers and Attorneys

I am an attorney, but much of my career has been as a trade adviser. Attorneys specializing in trade transactions can be trade advisers, but former customs officials, customs brokers, freight forwarders, and other professionals involved with trade transactions can also provide trade advisory services. For a consumer, the question is who has the particular expertise required. For example, for customs-operations issues, a broker or former customs officer may have more relevant knowledge than a lawyer. For shipping issues, a freight forwarder may the expert to consult.

## PSI Firms

During my career, several preshipment inspection (PSI) firms have employed me as outside counsel, and as an "in-house" employee. PSI firms can provide valuable services as third party verifiers of the quality, quantity, and price of goods shipped. They can also be used by some developing countries with poorly functioning customs administrations to verify customs information to reduce fraud and money laundering. However, unless PSI procedures are transparent, they can create delays and other barriers to trade.

## 2. Global Value Chains

### Free Zones

My introduction to free zones (in the United States, known as foreign-trade zones or FTZs) was when I worked for US Treasury in the late 1970s. At the time, FTZs were seldom used. However, when I was at the Treasury, we were able to push through changes to customs regulations to make manufacturing in FTZs more attractive. This was an era when imports, particularly automobiles from Japan and Germany, were increasing rapidly and the purpose was to attract the relocation of assembly of consumer products to the United States. The change in policy was successful and a number of major auto manufacturers subsequently located their assembly operations in the United States.

After leaving the Treasury, I represented the National Association of Foreign-Trade Zones at congressional hearings and also worked for a number of private zone operators. Later, I was retained by the World Bank as a zones consultant and advised on zones legislation in a number of countries including Cambodia, Ukraine, and Liberia.

### 3. The Importance of Trade Facilitation

### International Agreements Codifying Modern Customs Procedures

Much of my consulting career in recent years has involved the implementation of WCO Revised Kyoto Convention standards and best practices in developing countries. This has included work in Russia, Kazakhstan, Kyrgyzstan, Sao Tome e Principe, Nigeria, Kosovo, Chile, Peru, Laos, Jordan, China, and Mongolia. Modernization of border procedures in developing countries can, at times, be very difficult because of lack of infrastructure and resources and entrenched views.

Chapter 6: How Do You Navigate Government Regulations?

### 1. Regulations of Trade In Goods

#### a.  Import Regulations

Duties and other border taxes and fees are an important source of income for many developing countries, and their finance ministries frequently set revenue targets for customs collections. This puts considerable pressure on customs officers to meet these targets and can result in significant delays in processing imports and exports as they are examined to assure all duties and taxes due are collected. These delays and intensive border inspections without modern controls can also create an environment conducive to corruption. In one of the countries where I provided consulting services, the customs officers told a joke about finding an appropriate going-away gift for a director general who was retiring. Someone suggested a new European luxury car, but this was rejected as insufficient. Someone else suggested purchasing a condominium at a beach resort, but this was also rejected as insufficient. Another person said, "Why don't we make him chief customs inspector at the country's main port for a month?" Everyone thought that this was the best suggestion.

## Customs Classification of Goods and Tariff Rates

In the late 1970s when I worked for the US Treasury, the United States classified imports using its own tariff nomenclature, called the Tariff Schedules of the United States (TSUS), and European countries used a different nomenclature known as the Brussels Tariff Nomenclature or BTN. Negotiations began at the WCO in Brussels to develop a uniform, worldwide tariff nomenclature system. The main concern I recall on the part of some US policy officials was that the United States might be outvoted by the European Community countries (there were then ten EC members)—but it was never clear to me why that should matter. The technical aspects of the new nomenclature were left entirely to customs tariff specialists, and eventually the Harmonized System Nomenclature (HS) was developed and implemented in 1988.

## Customs Valuation of Goods

During the late 1970s, we were also negotiating what is now the WTO's Agreement on Customs Valuation (ACV). The big issue for US business was to eliminate what was known as "uplift," an increase in value above declared contract price frequently practiced by European countries by referring to "price lists" for automobiles and other commodities. When the ACV was concluded as part of the Tokyo Round GATT negotiations, transaction value was adopted as the primary basis of customs valuation and the use of price lists was prohibited.

It's amazing to reflect that less than forty years ago, there was no international uniformity regarding the methodology used for the classification and valuation of imports and exports. Today, most nations use the HS to classify goods and the ACV to determine value. These changes have resulted in a significant reduction in the time and cost for trade transactions.

## Origin of Goods

US law requires all goods or their containers to be marked with the country of origin. The failure to do so may result in forfeiture of the goods and penalties. One of my more interesting cases as a lawyer involved representing a manufacturer that imported steel forgings from Taiwan and finished them into hand tools in the United States. There was no country-of-origin labeling on the end product because in the manufacturer's view, sufficient processing had taken place to make it a product of the United States. US Customs disagreed and sought to prosecute the manufacturer for customs fraud. After the Justice Department declined to prosecute the criminal case, customs instituted a civil penalty action. However, customs failed to follow its own procedures, and the case was dismissed for violation of procedural due process.[123]

---

[123] Journal of Commerce, December 27, 1993, p. 1.

## Transit under Bond

One of my more unusual consulting assignments involved working in Lusaka, Zambia, in 2002 for COMESA, the Common Market for Eastern and Southern Africa—nineteen states stretching from Zimbabwe in the south to Egypt in the north. COMESA had adopted an agreement providing for transit of goods through COMESA states under customs bond. However, like so many international agreements in Africa, it had not been implemented. My assignment was to develop a plan for implementation. A logical approach was to adopt a system similar to the TIR system used in Europe and Asia since that had operated successfully for many years. This is what we proposed. However, neither the officials at COMESA, nor any of the other stakeholders, appeared anxious to move ahead with any new system, and our work ended up as a report gathering dust on a shelf.

Every day when I was in Lusaka working on the customs-bond project, I was driven from my hotel to COMESA headquarters. To make the drive, we had to transit a traffic circle. Almost every time when we reached the circle, a young man, apparently with a mental problem, was riding his motorbike around the circle, shouting with glee. This later became a metaphor in my mind for the project—much traveling around in a circle and many words, with nothing tangible accomplished.

### b. Trade Remedies: Safeguards, Antidumping, and Countervailing Duty Measures

I became a trade lawyer, representing parties in antidumping, countervailing duty, and safeguards cases, by accident. After graduating from law school, I went to work for a New York-Washington, DC, law firm that specialized in aviation law.

Many of their clients were foreign air carriers providing service to the United States. Through these connections, the firm was referred antidumping cases involving large power transformers and specialty steel products from Sweden, and the firm assigned me to work on these cases.

At the time, US Customs and the US Treasury were responsible for investigating the price discrimination aspect of antidumping cases and the US Tariff Commission (subsequently renamed the US International Trade Commission or USITC) was responsible for injury determinations. Treasury's policy at the time was to issue a dumping determination based upon averaging the prices of all exporters from a country subject to investigation. This meant that if there were two or more exporters in the country and only one of them was dumping, both would be subject to a dumping finding. Of course, this was unfair to the exporter that had not engaged in dumping.

As luck would have it, in my second case, our client was able to demonstrate that it was not dumping but another Swedish exporter was found to be dumping. By chance, I had gone to law school with a lead lawyer for the domestic industry petitioners. I pointed out to him that if Treasury continued to follow their "countrywide" antidumping finding policy, the average dumping rate would be quite low, but if our client was excluded, the rate would be much higher. We both then argued to the Treasury that they should adopt a new company specific dumping finding policy, which they did, using our case as precedent. This is still the rule today.

In a later trade case in the early 1980s, I represented a US producer of oil country tubular products in an antidumping action against imports from Japan. We were successful in obtaining high dumping margins, but the business situation changed rapidly because of an oil glut in the early 80s, and the US producer quickly lost interest in maintaining dumping duties.

About a decade later, I represented a US company that sought the imposition of antidumping duties on a type of lock washers. While the case was active, I traveled to the Republic of Georgia to explain WTO trade remedies to their administrative authorities and Parliament. It was a great experience—the Georgians were very appreciative, and I enjoyed the local culture. On my return, my office staff showed me an article that had appeared in *The Washington Post* about lawyers who were leaving law practice because they found the work boring and unsatisfying. Cited in the article as an example of the mind-numbing nature of legal work driving lawyers from law practice was the very lock washer antidumping case that I was working on! To this day, I don't know how the reporter came up with that example, but I had to agree that the example was correct.

## 2.    Trade In Services

I have had many professionally rewarding experiences providing international consulting services. One of my more interesting assignments, for the World Bank in 2007, involved preparing a delegation of government and business officials from Liberia to travel to China to inspect special economic zones. Liberia had just emerged from a devastating civil war and its infrastructure had been destroyed. However, the people I worked with were optimistic about the future and saw the establishment of a zones program as a way to revitalize Liberia's economy. I conducted several workshops to give local officials, including a tribal chief in full regalia, an overview of zones programs before their trip.

Perhaps the most appreciative people I worked with were business and government stakeholders in the new country of Kosovo. One of my consulting projects there involved developing a website that would provide guidance for businesses participating in international trade. Another project involved developing a customs financial guarantee system, working with local regulators and the insurance industry. In yet another project, I provided training regarding detecting money laundering. Almost everyone I worked with was anxious to learn and eager to help the new country get on its feet.

Trade in goods in Kosovo is very limited; most consumer products are imported from surrounding countries and from the European Union. On the other hand, Kosovo excels in trade in services with many highly trained professionals in IT and other fields who are fluent in English and other major European languages.

---

**Irish Pubs**

An Irish bar is a trade in services fixture in almost every large international city where I have worked. They seem to go hand in hand with the many Irish consultants working all over the world, providing traditional Irish food and beverages and a convenient place for expats to socialize. The Irish pub in Pristina, Kosovo, was Paddy O'Brien's. The Irish bar in Yangon, Myanmar, was Paddy O'Malley's.

---

A senior Cambodian government official whom I worked with on a World Bank funded project to develop special economic zone regulations was on the opposite end of the "appreciation scale." Nothing I could do pleased him, but fortunately, I applied the getting-paid principles discussed in chapter 2, and we were compensated in full for our consulting services.

When I was working on a consulting project in Moscow, Russia, in 2005, I had the opportunity to teach American business law at Pericles Law Center, a not-for-profit educational organization founded by Americans to help students in Russia obtain a "Western" legal education. The students were very bright, enthusiastic, and I may have learned more from them then they did from me. The dean of the school, an energetic American woman, insisted on a formal graduation ceremony for LLM recipients. She had a local tailor make an academic gown for me so that I could join other faculty at graduation.

Moscow was not an easy place to work. In 2004–2006 when I lived there, anti-American sentiments and bias against "foreigners" were strong. The "babushka" who monitored the coming and going of people in my apartment house engaged me in conversations about how progressive Russia was compared to America. I was occasionally stopped in the subway for a documents check—perhaps a pretext for a bribe. People were generally guarded, and I suspected those few who were overly friendly of ulterior motives. And then there was the weather— cold and colder. In Moscow, I was told the story of an African student who was studying at Moscow University and wrote home to his family describing his life. He said, "Moscow has two winters—one is white and the other is green."

As I worked as a service provider in foreign countries, I also became a service consumer—I purchased hotel, restaurant, and transport services as well as also tourism services in my free time. I've enjoyed seeing most of the more than fifty countries that I've visited, but occasionally, my local tourism has hit a snag. I still remember my first visit to Beijing in 2004, when I had been invited to participate in a regional conference on trade facilitation. After the long international flight, I arrived at the hotel and dropped off in a deep sleep only to be awoken by a phone call from a colleague.

"Get up! We're going to the Great Wall now!" he said. I roused myself, grabbed my camera (this was before digital cameras and smartphones), and arrived at the Great Wall only to discover that I had forgotten to load my camera with film! Fortunately, I had time to repeat the visit a few days later with a loaded camera.

Chapter 7: Social Responsibility Is Good Business

The international consulting firms that I usually work for are carrying out assignments in developing nations designed to improve trade facilitation, trade policies, government operations, and social conditions in general. These assignments are normally funded by donor agencies such as the US Agency for International Development (USAID), the World Bank, the Department of International Development of the United Kingdom (DFID), the European Union, the Asian Development Bank, and others. Usually, services provided in these assignments incorporate social responsibility objectives, such as gender equality and workers' rights. However, the profit motive can at times conflict with social responsibility objectives. On occasion, I have seen consulting projects abruptly terminated and local consultants poorly treated and even discharged without any apparent consideration of the personal and social ramifications of the action. I have also sometimes seen gender-equality objectives ignored in developing countries that have a strong patriarchal tradition.

I recall a small but notable socially responsible outcome from a project I worked on in Abuja, Nigeria. Our office cleaner was a bright, energetic young man from the Hausa tribe in northern Nigeria. He was literate and a devout Muslim, but his secular education had stopped at the elementary-school level. He had a wife and children to support. It turned out that the international-consulting firm had a program that made time and funds available to further the education of local employees. This, combined with money raised by the expat staff, allowed him to go to school at night to obtain high-school equivalency, possibly leading to university studies and professional work in the future.

## Chapter 8: The Future of International Trade Transactions—Five Predictions

### Prediction 5: New Regional Trade Agreements Lower Trade-Transaction Costs, Resulting in Increased Trade

You should never underestimate the pushback from organized labor and environmental groups against proposed new regional trade agreements. I first encountered this when I was on a business trip to Toronto in 1988 and was confronted by angry demonstrators who were demonstrating against a proposed US-Canada free-trade agreement, a precursor to NAFTA. Society in general usually benefits economically from free-trade agreements but some interest groups, particularly workers who jobs may be lost and environmentalists concerned about global warming and damage to ecosystems, may lose out.

### Prediction 4: China and India Continue Rapid Growth, Stimulating Trade

As this book went to press in early 2016, China was in the midst of an economic slowdown and financial market crises. But based on the very able Chinese businesspeople and investors I have met over the years, I would never bet against the long-term prospects for China. I believe that China will continue to evolve as one of the leading world economies. I have had less personal experience with India, but based on the Indian businesspeople and academics that I have met, I am equally optimistic about India's long-term prospects.

**Prediction 3: New Products, Services, and Technologies Increase Trade**

My career as an international trade lawyer and consultant has changed drastically over the last four decades as a result of new products and technologies. When I was legal counsel for a Swedish steel firm involved in an antidumping proceeding in the early 1970s, handling the documents necessary for the case was very complicated. I had to travel to Sweden to supervise copying of original documents by large, cumbersome photocopying machines. Computations were prepared and tabulated manually using adding machines. Legal submissions were prepared on automatic typewriters and editing was by cut-and-paste method—paragraphs were cut out of one typed version and pasted into another, then photocopied. Legal research took place in massive law libraries with extensive manual indexing systems. I had at least one secretary and paralegal to assist me in my work. Computers, which took up entire rooms, were difficult to program and used only by the largest of organizations, and even then only for accounting and a few other business applications. International communications took place by mail and by expensive telephone connections. Facsimile machines for document transmissions had only been recently introduced and were not widely used. Express courier service was also new. When documents needed to be delivered on an urgent basis to another city, a secretary or paralegal was frequently dispatched to manually carry them to their recipient.

Today, as a result of rapid changes in technology, I can perform the same tasks using a laptop computer and small copier much more efficiently and without the aid of a library or clerical staff. Written and verbal communications, document transmission, and research take place via Internet. I am able to make video calls around the world using Skype without charge. "Hard copies" of documents can be delivered quickly by express courier services. My productivity has greatly increased, and my business costs have been substantially reduced.

## Prediction 2: Supply Chains Become More Complex, Leading to New Opportunities for Small and Medium Enterprises

Most of my recent international consulting work has involved aiding developing countries to improve trade facilitation. This has included assistance implementing modern laws and regulations relating to customs administration and other border procedures as well as the development of single-window IT systems to expedite the border clearance of goods. This work has been interesting but, at times, frustrating when local entrenched special interests block improvements. One notable example of this was in Nigeria, where the customs administration was still operating under colonial era legislation dating from 1958, and partly as a consequence trade facilitation was poor. As part of an USAID project, I helped develop a modern customs law, and it subsequently was enacted by Nigeria's legislature.

## Prediction 1: *Cross Border E-Commerce Expands Rapidly*

During much of 2014, I worked as a consultant for the World Bank in Astana, Kazakhstan. A young and energetic Kazakh lawyer, Ruslan, was assisting me. Ruslan spent a good bit of his personal time "surfing" the Internet for various consumer goods and services—parts for his motorcycle, vacation packages, airline tickets, new music and videos, unique gifts for his family, and many other consumer products and services. Kazakhstan is an upper-middle level economy bolstered by petroleum revenue, but many consumer goods are still not available in brick-and-mortar stores there. Cross-border e-commerce has changed this; now goods and services are available via the Internet from any supplier in the world that participates in e-commerce. Normally, the only restrictions for tangible goods are delivery costs, duties, and taxes.

Because of a political change, Myanmar (Burma) is now emerging from a period of relative isolation. While working in Myanmar in early 2016, I discovered that CBEC had already taken hold and that consumer goods were being ordered online by local purchasers from Alibaba for delivery by truck to the China-Myanmar border—a much faster and cheaper option than the traditional orders by mail and subsequent shipment in containers by sea.

### Takeaways from Chapter 9

- When planning and conducting your international business transactions, be guided by the experience of those who have gone before you.

# About the Author

*Stephen Creskoff, photo by Midd Hunt*

Stephen Creskoff is a lawyer and leading expert on international trade transactions, trade facilitation, and the legal foundation for international trade. Over his career, he has worked as a trade lawyer and senior trade consultant for many international businesses and the World Bank, USAID, and other donor agencies in more than fifty countries, including Sweden,

Canada, Mexico, the United Kingdom, Germany, Portugal, Belgium, Switzerland, Hungary, Bulgaria, Japan, China, Russia, Ukraine, Georgia, Kazakhstan, Krygyz Republic, Mongolia, South Africa, Nigeria, Liberia, Zambia, Sao Tome e Principe, Cambodia, Laos, Myanmar, the Philippines, Kosovo, Albania, Moldova, Macedonia, Armenia, Jordan, Morocco, Brazil, Peru and Chile. Before becoming an international trade consultant, he was a law-firm partner based in Washington, DC, practicing trade and customs law and also served as Special Assistant to the Undersecretary and Deputy to the Assistant Secretary (Regulatory Policy), US Treasury Department between 1977 and 1980.

Mr. Creskoff's recent publications include Creskoff, Stephen, and Robert Kielbas. "Improving Trade Facilitation in Developing Countries: The Role of Affordable Customs Guarantees." 8 *Global Trade and Customs Journal*, (2013): 348–358; Creskoff, Stephen, and Petrit Gashi. "Tariffs as an Instrument of Trade Policy: The Unique Case of Kosovo." 8 *Global Trade and Customs Journal*, (2013): 137–148; "From Aid to Trade: Delivering Results" *USAID*, (July 2011) (joint contributor); Creskoff, Stephen, and Peter Walkenhorst. "Implications of WTO Disciplines for Special Economic Zones in Developing Countries." *World Bank Policy Research Working Paper 4892*, (2009); Creskoff, Stephen. "The WTO Trade Facilitation Negotiations: It's Time to Agree on Basic Principles." 3 *Global Trade and Customs Journal*, (2008): 149–162; and Creskoff, Stephen. "Trade Facilitation: An Often Overlooked Engine of Trade Expansion." 3 *Global Trade and Customs Journal*, (2008): 1–16.

Mr. Creskoff was an adjunct professor at Johns Hopkins University (1995–2001) and American University (1997–2001), teaching courses in international business negotiations, business law, and corporate social responsibility. He also was an adjunct professor at Pericles School of Law, Moscow, Russia (2005), where he taught business law. He has lectured frequently in the United States and around the world on trade remedies, trade facilitation, free zone, and globalization issues.

Mr. Creskoff is a graduate of the University of Pennsylvania and holds graduate degrees from the University of Maryland (JD, with honors) and Georgetown University (LLM, international law).

Mr. Creskoff lives in the United States. He maintains a website at *www.creskofftrade.com* and can be contacted at *stephen@ creskofftrade.com*

# Acknowledgments

Many people have helped make this book possible, and I would like to acknowledge by name some of the more important contributors. Dr. Sarah Bryant, the department chair when I taught international business negotiations and business law at Johns Hopkins University's Business School, encouraged me to write this book and was kind enough to read and comment on my early draft chapters. Dr. Lynn Reaser, chief economist of the Fermian Business & Economic Institute, and her colleagues reviewed the final manuscript and offered a number of useful suggestions. Jeffrey Snyder, Esq., head of the international trade group at Crowell and Moring law firm, provided helpful suggestions regarding my chapter on government regulations.

Amy Swift, Esq., formerly an intellectual property attorney for Microsoft and currently an international IP consultant, reviewed and commented on my chapter on protecting intellectual property in international trade. My friends and colleagues, Walter Hekala and Douglas Cruickshank, provided valuable comments regarding my chapter on logistics, as did Rebecca Fenneman, Esq. of the Federal Maritime Commission and Ruth Snowden, executive director of the Canadian International Freight-Forwarders Association.

In addition, my business colleagues and friends, Greg Jendreas, president of Bergandi Machinery, and Steven Smith, president of Weld-Aid, provided valuable insights into their international business operations, as did Faye Crowe, president of Crowe & Co. And my friend, Bill Krist of the Wilson Center, recounted his experiences with writing and publishing his recent book, *Globalization and America's Trade Agreements*, and provided sound advice regarding my search for a publisher for my book.

Lastly, much appreciation and love go to my wife, Andrea Creskoff, who, for many years, encouraged me to write, and to my stepdaughter, Jennifer Donner, who read an early draft chapter and had many useful suggestions.

This book would not have been completed without encouragement and support from those named above and many others. Thank you!

—Stephen Creskoff, March 2016

# Glossary of Terms

3PL—A third-party logistics provider, a business that encompasses the activities of a variety of different types of logistics providers.

ACE—Automated Commercial Environment, a CBP IT system.

ACV—WTO Agreement on Customs Valuation.

advance ruling—A ruling obtained from a customs administration prior to importation regarding how imports will be treated.

AEO—Authorized economic operator, an organization complying with certain supply chain security and trade facilitation standards.

AES—Automated export system.

AGOA—African Growth and Opportunity Act, a US-duty preference program that permits the duty-free importation of certain goods originating in qualifying African countries.

ANSI—American National Standards Institute.

APEC—Asian-Pacific Economic Cooperation, consisting of twenty-one member nations.

ASEAN—Association of Southeast Asian Nations.

ATA carnet—A customs document used for the temporary admission of certain goods without the payment of duties and taxes.

arbitrage—The practice of taking advantage of a price difference between two or more markets.

B2B—Business to business e-commerce.

B2C—Business to consumer e-commerce.

B2G—Business to government e-commerce.

bbl—Barrel of oil, forty-two US gallons

BIEC—US Border Interagency Executive Council.

BIS—Bureau of Industry and Security, US Department of Commerce.

B/L—Bill of lading.

boycott—A refusal to deal with a person or organization for competitive or political purposes.

BRIC countries—Brazil, Russia, India, and China, four leading developing countries.

BSI—British Standards Institution.

BSR—Business Social Responsibility.

BTN—Brussels Tariff Nomenclature.

bycatch—Fish or other sea creatures caught accidentally by fishermen and then thrown back into the water dead or dying.

C2C—Electronic commerce between consumers.

CAFTA—Central American Free Trade Agreement.

CBEC—Cross-border electronic commerce.

CBP—Customs and Border Protection, an agency within the US Department of Homeland Security.

CCL—Commerce Control List.

CEN—European Committee for Standardization.

CET—Common external tariff.

CFR—Cost and freight, an Incoterm where the seller delivers the goods onboard the vessel and pays the costs and freight necessary to bring the goods to the named port of destination.

CIF—Cost, insurance, and freight, an Incoterm where the seller delivers the goods onboard the vessel and pays the costs, insurance, and freight necessary to bring the goods to the named port of destination.

CIP—Carriage and insurance paid to, an Incoterm where the seller delivers the goods to a carrier or another person nominated by the seller at an agreed place and the seller must contract and pay for the cost of carriage necessary to bring the goods to the place of destination.

CISG—United Nations Convention for the International Sale of Goods.

cloud (or "the cloud")—An Internet term referring to a network of servers that allows users to access various applications on the Internet without having to purchase and maintain their own hardware and software.

Codex Alimentarius—A collection of standards, guidelines, and codes of safety pertaining to food safety issued by the Codex Alimentarius Commission.

COMESA—Common Market for Eastern and Southern Africa.

comparative advantage—An economic theory that holds that because of different factor endowments all parties benefit from international trade transactions.

consideration—Something of value given by both parties to a contract that induces them to enter into a contract.

CPT—Carriage paid to, an Incoterm where the seller delivers the goods to the carrier or another person nominated by the seller at an agreed place and that seller must contract for and pay the cost of carriage necessary to bring the goods to the named place of destination.

creative destruction—The continuous process of product and process innovation where new products and processes replace ones that are less efficient or less appealing to consumers.

CRF—Clear report of findings, a report issued by a preshipment inspection (PSI) company.

cross-border e-commerce (CBEC)—International digital trade.

C-TPAT—Customs-Trade Partnership Against Terrorism, the US version of an AEO program.

customs bond—A financial guarantee that a trader will pay all duties and taxes due on imports, exports, and transit goods and comply with all other regulatory requirements.

customs broker—An agent that clear a shipper's goods through customs.

customs declaration—The basic customs document indicating the type of goods involved in a trade transaction, the quantity and quality, the price or value, and other information required to be reported.

DAP—Delivered at place, an Incoterm where the seller delivers when the goods are placed at the disposal of the buyer on the arriving means of transport at the named place of destination ready for unloading.

DAT—Delivered at terminal, an Incoterm where the seller delivers the goods, once unloaded from the arriving means of transport, at the disposal of the buyer at a named terminal at the named port or place of destination.

D/Cs—Documentary collections.

DDP—Delivered duty paid, an Incoterm where the seller delivers the goods when the goods are placed at the disposal of the buyer at the named place of destination cleared for import with all duties and taxes paid.

DDTC—Directorate of Defense Trade Controls, US Department of State.

DFID—Department of International Development, United Kingdom.

demurrage—The period during which the charterer remains in possession of a vessel after the period allotted to load and unload cargo at a port has expired.

DHS—US Department of Homeland Security.

digital trade—Trade in which the Internet and Internet-based technologies play a significant role in the ordering, producing, or delivering of services or products.

drawback—Refund of customs duties and taxes on exportation of goods.

dumping—Selling goods in export markets below "normal value," resulting in injury or threat of injury to competitors in the country of importation.

e-commerce—The production, adverting, sale, and distribution of products and services using the Internet.

EARs—Export Administration Regulations.

EC—European Community, a predecessor to the European Union.

ECCNs—Export control classification numbers.

ECOWAS—Economic Community of West African States.

EDI—Electronic data interchange.

EDK—Explosive detection kit.

EU—European Union.

export factor—A bank or financial firm that purchases invoices or accounts receivable from exporters at a discount and then assumes the risk of debt collection.

Ex-Im—Export-Import Bank of the United States.

EXW—Ex Works, an Incoterm where the seller delivers when it places the goods at the disposal of the buyer at the seller's premises or another named place.

FAS—Free alongside, an Incoterm where the seller delivers when the goods are delivered alongside the vessel nominated by the buyer at the named port of shipment.

FCA—Free carrier, an Incoterm where the seller delivers the goods to a carrier or another person nominated by the buyer at the seller's premises or another named place.

FCPA—US Foreign Corrupt Practices Act.

FDA—US Food and Drug Administration.

FDI—Foreign direct investment.

FinCen—Financial Crimes Enforcement Network, the US FIU.

FIU—Financial Intelligent Unit, a government organization used to combat money laundering and terrorism financing.

FMC—US Federal Maritime Commission.

FOB—Freight on board, an Incoterm where the seller delivers the goods onboard the vessel nominated by the buyer at the named port of shipment.

freight forwarder—A business responsible for organizing international shipments for their clients.

FTA—Free-trade agreement.

FTZ—Foreign-trade zone, the US version of free zones.

GATS—WTO's General Agreement on Trade In Services.

GATT—General Agreement on Tariffs and Trade, now a WTO agreement.

GDP—Gross domestic product, the monetary value of all goods and services produced within an economy.

GI—Geographical indication, an intellectual property right.

GII—Global Innovation Index.

global value chain—A value chain that extends over two or more nations or economies.

GMAT—Graduate Management Admission Test.

GNI—Gross national income.

GPA—WTO's Government Procurement Agreement.

GSP—Generalized System of Preferences, a duty preference program that permits the duty-free importation of certain goods from developing countries.

GST—Goods and services tax.

GVC—Global value chain.

HMF—Harbor maintenance fee.

HS—Harmonized System Nomenclature, an international system for classifying goods that are imported and exported.

HTSUS—The Harmonized Tariff Schedules of the United States, based on the HS.

IATA—International Air Transport Association, a trade association of the world's airlines.

IC-DISC—Interest Charge International Domestic Sales Corporation.

ICC—The International Chamber of Commerce, based in Paris, France, is the largest business organization in the world with hundreds of thousands of members in more than 180 countries.

ICE—Immigration and Customs Enforcement, an agency within the US Department of Homeland Security.

IMF—International Monetary Fund.

incoterms—Predefined three letter commercial terms published by the International Chamber of Commerce (ICC). Examples are ex-works (EXW) and freight on board (FOB).

intermodal shipment—The transportation of goods in an intermodal container using multiple modes of transport.

international trade—The exchange of goods and/or services for value across international boundaries. The charter normally pays the ship owner for this extra use of the vessel.

IP—Intellectual property.

IPO—Initial public offering of stock.

IPR—Intellectual property rights.

IRU—International Road Transport Union, the administrator of the TIR system.

ISO—International Organization for Standardization, an independent nongovernmental organization that develops voluntary standards.

ISP—Internet service provider.

IT—Information technology.

ITAR—International Traffic in Arms Regulations.

ITDS—International trade data system.

JIT—Just in time, referring to inventory management systems.

L/C—Letter of credit.

LDC—Least developed country, according to United Nations indicators of socio-economic development.

letter of credit (L/C)—A document from a bank guaranteeing that a seller will be paid as long as certain conditions are met.

LOLO—A shipping term meaning lift on lift off.

logistics—The management of the flow of goods and related services between the point of origin and the point of consumption in order to meet the business requirements of organizations.

LPI—Logistics performance index, a measure of the logistics performance of various economies.

MERCOSUR—A common market, comprising a number of South American states.

MFN—Most favored nation treatment (a benefit given to one trading partner must be given to all others).

money laundering—Transferring the proceeds of criminal activity into supposedly legitimate funds or assets.

MPF—Merchandise processing fee.

multilateral agreement—A term used when more than two countries or economies participate in a trade agreement.

NAFTA—North American Free Trade Agreement.

national treatment—After goods have been imported a nation cannot discriminate in favor of products produced locally.

NGO—Nongovernmental organization, typically a not-for-profit citizens' group devoted to a social goal.

NHTSA—National Highway Traffic Safety Administration, an agency responsible for highway safety within the US Department of Transportation.

NRC—Nuclear Regulatory Commission, US Department of Energy.

NTB—Nontariff barrier to trade.

NVOCC—A nonvessel operating common carrier.

OECD—Organization of Economic Cooperation and Development.

OEM—Original equipment manufacturer.

OFAC—Office of Foreign Assets Control, US Department of Treasury.

offshoring—Relocation of manufacturing or service firms from high-cost, developed economics to lower-cost, developing economies.

onshoring—Relocation of offshored manufacturing or services firms to a developed economy because of changed economic and regulatory factors.

PCT—Patent Cooperation Treaty.

plurilateral agreement—A WTO term that refers to an agreement among some but not all WTO members. An example is the WTO Agreement on Government Procurement.

PSI—Preshipment inspection refers to the inspection of goods for quantity, quality, and price by a third-party inspection agency.

RFID—Radio frequency identification system.

risk management—As applied to customs administration, a statistical prediction whether a particular trader or specific shipments are good compliance risks.

RMB—Renminbi, the official currency of the People's Republic of China.

RORO—A shipping term meaning roll on, roll off.

R&D—Research and development.

RTA—Regional trade agreement.

SACU—Southern African Customs Union.

SAFE—WCO's SAFE Framework of Standards, an international agreement designed to improve supply-chain security.

SBA—Small Business Administration.

SCORE program—A nonprofit business association comprised of volunteer business counselors.

SDN—OFAC's Specially Designated Nationals List.

SDRs—Special drawing rights, an international reserve asset created by the International Monetary Fund, a potential claim on the currencies of IMF members.

SEZ—Special economic zone or free zone, an area outside the customs territory of a nation or economy, usually duty and tax free.

single window (SW)—An administrative system, usually electronic, that permits parties involved in trade transactions to submit documents and information at a single point to satisfy all regulatory requirements.

small business—Privately owned for profit enterprises that are considered to be "small" based on their number of employees, assets, and annual sales as well as the fact that they are not dominant in their field.

SME—Small- and medium-sized enterprises.

SOE—State-owned enterprise.

subsidy—A financial contribution by a government or any public body conferring a benefit to the recipient.

supply chains—Interbusiness systems involved in moving products or services from suppliers to consumers.

SW—Single window.

TBT—Technical barriers to trade, behind the border trade-transaction costs.

TEU—Twenty-foot equivalent, a measure of container capacity.

TFA—WTO's Agreement on Trade Facilitation.

TIB—Temporary importation bond.

TIC—Trade Information Center.

TIR transit—TIR stands for *Transports Internationaux Routiers* (International Road Transport), an international system of customs control for the carriage of goods by truck through multiple countries.

tradable services—Services that are traded internationally.

trade facilitation—How the procedures relating to the movement of goods across national borders can be improved. Trade facilitation is measured by the time and cost involved in moving goods and by stakeholder surveys.

trade-transaction costs—Those additional costs incurred when businesses engage in international trade transactions.

T-TIP—Transatlantic Trade and Investment Partnership, a proposed trade and investment agreement between the United States and the European Union.

TTP—Trans-Pacific Partnership, a trade and investment agreement between twelve Pacific-Rim countries.

TRIPS—WTO's Trade-Related Intellectual Property Rights Agreement.

TSUS—Tariff Schedules of the United States, the predecessor of the HTSUS.

UNCITRAL—United Nations Commission for International Trade Law.

USAID—US Agency for International Development.

USFCS—US Foreign and Commercial Service, an agency of the US Department of Commerce's International Trade Administration.

USITC—US International Trade Commission.

USML—US Munitions List.

USPTO—US Patent and Trademark Office.

value chain—A supply chain from the perspective of value added to products and services at each step of the production and distribution process. Value chains can be a firm level value chain, focusing on the activities of a single enterprise, or more typically an industry level value chain, including all the various processes involved in producing goods or services in a particular industry.

VAT—Value added tax, a tax added on the value added to a product, material, or service.

WCF—World Chambers Federation.

Wassenaar Agreement—A multilateral export control regime designed to restrict trade in armaments and dual-use items.

WCO—World Customs Organization.

WIPO—World Intellectual Property Organization.

WTO—World Trade Organization.

# Bibliography

Acemoglu, Daron, and James A. Robinson. *Why Nations Fail: The Origins of Power, Prosperity, and Poverty.* New York: Crown Publishers, 2012.

Asakura, Hironori. *World History of the Customs and Tariffs.* Brussels: World Customs Organization, 2003.

Borchert, I., G. Gootiiz, and A. Mattoo. "Policy Barriers to International Trade in Services." Policy Research Working Paper 6109, *World Bank*, June 2012.

Center for Economic Policy Research. "Reducing Transatlantic Barriers to Trade and Investment, Final Project Report." March 2013.

Clark, Gregory. *A Farewell to Alms: A Brief Economic History of the World.* New Jersey: Princeton University Press, 2007.

Collier, Paul. *The Bottom Billion: Why the Poorest Countries Are Failing and What Can Be Done About It.* New York: Oxford University Press, 2007.

Chan, Alexandra. "Investigative Report on the Working Conditions of UNIQULO's China Suppliers." *Students and Scholars Against Corporate Misbehavior,* January 2015.

Copeland, Lennie, and Lewis Griggs. *Going International.* Random House, 1985.

Economics and Statistics Administration and US Patent and Trademark Office. "Intellectual Property and the US Economy: Industries in Focus." March 2012.

Ferguson, Ian F., William H. Cooper, Remy Jurenas, and Brock R. Williams. "The Trans-Pacific Partnership (TPP) Negotiations and Issues for Congress." *Congressional Research Service*, March 20, 2015.

Fisher, Roger, and Scott Brown. *Getting Together: Building Relationships as we Negotiate.* Penguin, 1989.

Fisher, Roger, and William Ury. *Getting to Yes: Negotiating Agreement Without Giving In.* New York: Penguin Books, 2nd ed. 1991.

Forrester Consulting. "Seizing the Cross-Border Opportunity: How Small and Medium-Size Online Businesses Can Go Global." December 2014.

Friedman, Thomas L. *The World Is Flat: A Brief History of the Twenty-First Century.* New York: Farrar, Straus, and Giroux, 2005.

Fukayama, Francis. *The End of History and the Last Man.* Avon, 1992.

Global Intellectual Property Center. "Intellectual Property Protection and Enforcement Manual." *Global Intellectual Property Center.* 2009.

Goldsweig, Shelly B., and David M. Battram. *Negotiating and Structuring International Commercial Transactions.* American Bar Association, 1991.

Gupta, Anil K., Girija Pande, and Haiyan Wang. *The Silk Road Rediscovered: How Indian and Chinese Companies Are Becoming Globally Stronger by Winning in Each Other's Markets.* San Francisco: John Wiley & Sons, 2014.

Haft, Jeremy R. *Unmade in China: The Hidden Truth About China's Economic Miracle.* Cambridge, United Kingdom: Polity Press, 2015.

Harwell, Drew. "IPO delivers $300 million—in values." *The Washington Post.* April 17, 2015.

Hofstede, Geert. *Culture's Consequences: comparing values, behaviors, institutions, and organizations across nations.* Sage, 2nd ed. 2001.

Ilias, Shayerah, and Ian F. Fergusson. "Intellectual Property Rights and International Trade." *Congressional Research Service,* February 17, 2011.

Jensen, J. Bradford. "Overlooked Opportunity: Tradable Business Services, Developing Asia and Growth." *Asian Development Bank.* January 2013.

KPMG. "Effective Channel Management is Critical in Combating the Grey Market and Increasing Technology Companies' Bottom Line." 2008.

Krist, William. *Globalization and America's Trade Agreements.* Baltimore: Johns Hopkins University Press, 2013.

Mangan, John, Chandra Lalwani, Tim Butcher, and Roya Javadpour. *Global Logistics and Supply Chain Management.* United Kingdom: John Wiley & Sons. Ltd. 2nd ed., 2012.

Morrison, Wayne. "China's Economic Rise: History, Trends, Challenges, and Implications for the United States." *Congressional Research Service*, October 2014.

OECD. "Interconnected Economies: Benefiting from Global Value Chains." *OECD*, 2013.

OECD. "Global Trade and Specialization Patterns Over the Next 50 Years." *OECD Economic Policy Paper*, 2014.

Paulson, Henry M., and Robert E. Rubin. "The Blame Trap: Why the US and China Need to Act on Each Other's Economic Critiques." *The Atlantic*, June 2015.

Reinhardt, Forest, Robert Stavins, and Richard Vietor. "Corporate Social Responsibility Through an Economic Lens." *NBER*, May 2008.

Ripley, Amanda. "How to Graduate from Starbucks." *The Atlantic*, May 2015.

Rivoli, Pietra. *The Travels of a T-Shirt in the Global Economy: An Economist Examines the Markets, Power, and Politics of World Trade.* Hoboken, New Jersey: John Wiley & Sons, 2nd ed., 2015.

Rodrik, Dani. *The Globalization Paradox: Democracy and the Future of the World Economy.* New York: W. W. Norton & Company, 2011.

Sanati, Cyrus. "Our Favorite 8 Gadgets from the Consumer Electronics Show." *Fortune*, January 9, 2015.

Shackleton, Robert. "Total Factor Productivity Growth in Historical Perspective." *Congressional Budget Office*, March 2013.

Shapiro, Ronald M., and Mark A. Jankowski. *The Power of Nice: How to Negotiate So Everyone Wins—Especially You!* New York: John Wiley & Sons, Inc., 1998.

Tavares, Miguel Sousa. *Equator.* Bloomsbury, 2008.

Transparency International. "Exporting Corruption: Progress Report 2014: Assessing Enforcement of the OECD Convention on Combating Foreign Bribery."

US Commercial Service. "A Basic Guide to Exporting." 11th ed., 2015.

US Customs and Border Protection. "C-TPAT Program Benefits Reference Guide." January 2014.

US Department of Commerce. "75th Report of the Foreign-Trade Zones Board to the Congress of the United States." 2013.

US International Trade Commission. "Digital Trade in the US and Global Economies, Part 2." August 2014.

Usunier, Jean-Claude. *Marketing Across Cultures.* Prentice Hall, 1996.

VanGrasstek, Craig. "The Political Economy of Services in Regional Trade Agreements." *OECD*, 2011.

World Customs Organization. "Compendium of Authorized Economic Operator Programs." 2014.

Weiss, Kenneth D. *Building an Import/Export Business.* New Jersey: John Wiley & Sons, Inc., 4th ed., 2008.

World Bank. "Implementing trade single windows in Singapore, Colombia and Azerbaijan." 2014.

World Bank. "Special Economic Zones: Performance, Lessons Learned and Implications for Zone Development." 2008.

WTO. "Trade Policy Review: European Union." July 2015.

WTO. "Trade Policy Review of the United States of America." December 2014.

# Index

## A

Advance ruling 198, 215, 218, 222, 224, 225, 297, 391

African Growth and Opportunity Act 221, 391

Agreement on Customs Valuation 218, 348, 372, 391

American National Standards Institute 53, 391

Anticompetitive 279, 282, 288, 290, 292, 297

Antidumping xxiv, 23, 117, 212, 241, 242, 245, 248, 249, 250, 251, 253, 254, 255, 297, 341, 351, 364, 374, 375, 376, 381

Antitrust 183, 255, 291, 292, 294

Arbitrage 46, 47, 167, 168, 366, 392

Asia 8, 11, 12, 14, 19, 25, 26, 57, 74, 76, 78, 79, 86, 200, 209, 238, 275, 321, 334, 350, 374, 409

Asian-Pacific Economic Cooperation 391

Association of Southeast Asian Nations 281, 392

ATA carnet 114, 178, 231, 238, 239, 392

Authorized Economic Operator 176, 266, 269, 272, 391, 411

Automated Commercial Environment 209, 262, 391

Automated Export System 262, 391

## B

B2B 55, 56, 57, 102, 331, 333, 334, 335, 338, 392

B2C 55, 56, 57, 102, 174, 180, 331, 333, 334, 335, 338, 339, 354, 355, 392

B2G 331, 392

Bilateral trade agreement 280

Customs warehouse  180, 181, 191

# D

DAP  119, 120, 127, 395

DAT  127, 395

DDP  115, 119, 395

Demurrage  4, 199, 396

Digital trade  323, 330, 331, 332,
   394, 396, 411

Distribution  34, 38, 44, 47, 54, 55,
   71, 97, 133, 134, 159, 166,
   167, 168, 169, 171, 172, 173,
   181, 187, 188, 190, 192, 232,
   234, 322, 326, 396, 405

Documentary collections  122,
   126, 395

Drawback  230, 231, 240, 241, 258,
   297, 396

Dumping  20, 248, 249, 250, 251,
   252, 255, 375, 376, 396

Duties  xx, xxiii, xxiv, 3, 7, 78, 117,
   119, 177, 178, 180, 181, 189,
   193, 196, 204, 205, 206, 208,
   210, 211, 212, 213, 215, 216,
   217, 218, 219, 220, 222, 224,
   226, 227, 228, 231, 232, 233,
   234, 236, 237, 238, 240, 241,
   245, 248, 251, 252, 255, 256,
   257, 258, 259, 276, 290, 294,

297, 334, 335, 336, 338, 342,
348, 371, 372, 376, 383, 392,
395, 396

# E

E-commerce  55, 56, 57, 313, 319,
   330, 333, 334, 335, 338, 339,
   354, 355, 383, 392, 394, 396

Economic Community of West
   African States  396

European Community  348,
   372, 396

European Union  8, 23, 29, 31, 33,
   34, 40, 41, 42, 53, 147, 152,
   177, 217, 218, 236, 248, 249,
   253, 272, 280, 286, 291, 320,
   321, 322, 323, 324, 334, 337,
   377, 379, 396, 397, 405, 412

Export Administration  263, 396

Export control classification
   numbers  262, 263, 396

Export controls  260, 261, 262,
   263, 264, 265, 266, 276, 297,
   396, 406

Export declaration  125, 177, 256,
   261, 262

Export factor  397

Export-Import Bank  67, 397

Printed in the United States
By Bookmasters